# Mons, Anzac & Kut

# Mons, Anzac & Kut
## A British Intelligence Officer in Three Theatres of the First World War
## 1914-18

Aubrey Herbert

LEONAUR

*Mons, Anzac & Kut: a British Intelligence Officer in Three Theatres
of the First World War, 1914-18*
by Aubrey Herbert

Leonaur is an imprint of Oakpast Ltd

Material original to this edition and
presentation of text in this form
copyright © 2010 Oakpast Ltd

ISBN: 978-0-85706-365-6 (hardcover)
ISBN: 978-0-85706-366-3 (softcover)

http://www.leonaur.com

**Publisher's Notes**

The views expressed in this book are not necessarily
those of the publisher.

# Contents

This book is dedicated to

Lord Robert Cecil
and
The League of Nations

# Preface

Journals, in the eyes of their author, usually require an introduction of some kind, which, often, may be conveniently forgotten. The reader is invited to turn to this one if, after persevering through the pages of the diary, he wishes to learn the reason of the abrupt changes and chances of war that befell the writer. They are explained by the fact that his eyesight did not allow him to pass the necessary medical tests. He was able, through some slight skill, to evade these obstacles in the first stage of the war; later, when England had settled down to routine, they defeated him, as far as the Western Front was concerned. He was fortunately compensated for this disadvantage by a certain knowledge of the East, that sent him in various capacities to different fronts, often at critical times. It was as an interpreter that the writer went to France. After a brief imprisonment, it was as an intelligence officer that he went to Egypt, the Dardanelles and Mesopotamia. The first diary was dictated in hospital from memory and rough notes made on the retreat from Mons. For the writing of the second diary, idle hours were provided in the Dardanelles between times of furious action. The third diary, which deals with the fall of Kut, was written on the Fly boats of the River Tigris. When dots occur in the journal, they have their usual significance. The author was thinking his private thoughts, or, perhaps, criticizing some high authority, or concealing what, for the moment, at any rate, is better not revealed. In the retreat from Mons, only Christian or nicknames have generally been used. In the case of the other two expeditions names have been used freely, though where it was considered advisable, they have occasionally been disguised or initials substituted for them. This diary claims to be no more than a record of great and small events, a chronicle of events within certain limited horizons—a retreat, a siege and an attack. Writing was often hurried and difficult, and the diary was sometimes neglected for a period. If inaccuracies occur, the writer offers sincere apologies.

# Mons

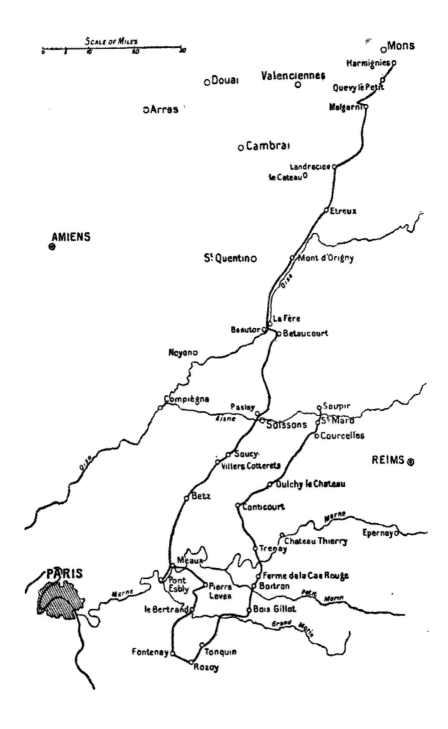

SCALE OF MILES

Mons
Harmignies
Quevy le Petit
Malgarni

Douai
Valenciennes
Arras
Cambrai

Landrecies
le Cateau

Etreux

AMIENS

St Quentin
Mont d'Origny

Oise

La Fère
Beautor
Betaucourt

Noyono

Compiègne
Paslay
Soupir
St Mard

Aisne
Soissons
Courcelles

Oise

Soucy
Villers Cotterets

REIMS

Oulchy le Chateau

Betz
Conticourt

Marne

Epernay

Chateau Thierry

Trenay

Meaux

Pont Esbly
Pierra Levea

Ferme de la Cae Rouge
Boitron

Petit Morin

PARIS
Marne

le Bertrand
Bois Gillot

Grand Morin

Fontenay
Tonquin

Rozoy

# Mons
AUGUST 12TH—SEPTEMBER 13TH, 1914

On Wednesday, August 12th, 1914, my regiment left Wellington Barracks at seven in the morning. I fell into step in the ranks as they went out of the gateway, where I said goodbye to my brother, who left that day. It was very quiet in the streets, as the papers had said nothing about the movement of troops. On the march the wives and relations of men said goodbye to them at intervals, and some of our people came to see us off at the station, but we missed them.

We entrained for Southampton—Tom, Robin, Valentine and I got into the same carriage. We left Southampton without much delay. I was afraid of a hitch, but got on to the ship without any trouble. On board everybody was very cheerful. Most people thought that the first big engagement would have begun and very likely have ended before we arrived. Some were disappointed and some cheered by this thought. The men sang without ceasing and nobody thought of a sea attack.

The next day (the 13th) we arrived very early at Le Havre in a blazing sun. As we came in, the French soldiers tumbled out of their barracks and came to cheer us. Our men had never seen foreign uniforms before, and roared with laughter at their colours. Stephen Burton of the Coldstream Guards rebuked his men. He said:

"These French troops are our Allies; they are going to fight with us against the Germans." Whereupon one man said:

"Poor chaps, they deserve to be encouraged," and took off his cap and waved it, and shouted *"Vive l'Empereur!"* He was a bit behind the times. I believe if the Germans beat us and invaded England they would still be laughed at in the villages as ridiculous foreigners.

We were met by a colonel of the French Reserves, a weak and in-

13

effective man, two Boy Scouts, and a semi-idiotic interpreter. We shed this man as soon as we were given our own two excellent interpreters. We had no wood to cook the men's dinners, and I was sent off with Jumbo and a hundred men to see what I could find. A French corporal came reluctantly with us. We marched a mile, when we found an English quartermaster at a depot, who let us requisition a heap of great faggots, which we carried back.

After breakfast I was sent with Hickie to arrange for billeting the men. Hickie rode a bicycle and lent me his horse, which was the most awful brute I have ever mounted in any country. It walked ordinarily like a crab; when it was frightened it walked backwards, and it was generally frightened. It would go with the troops, but not alone, and neither whip nor reins played any part in guiding the beast. Hickie couldn't ride it. Some French soldiers threw stones at it and hit me. Finally we got a crawling cab, then a motor, and went off about eleven kilometres to the Café des Fleurs, where the camp was to be. It was a piping hot day. We got a house for the colonel and Desmond belonging to Monsieur Saville, who said he was a friend of Mr. Yoxall, M.P. He had a very jolly arbour, where we dined. In the afternoon the troops came marching up the steep hill in great heat. Hickie and I found a man rather drunk, with a very hospitable Frenchman. The Frenchman said:

"We have clean sheets and a well-aired bed, coffee, wine or beer for him, if he desires them."

There was no question about the man's desiring them. Hickie almost wept, and said:

"How can you keep an army together if they are going to be treated like this?"

The sun had been delightful in the morning at Le Havre, but was cruel on the troops, especially on the reservists, coming up the long hill.

The French had been very hospitable. They had given the men, where they had been able to do so free of observation, wine, coffee, and beer. The result was distressing. About twenty of the men collapsed at the top of the hill in a ditch, some of them unconscious, seeming almost dying, like fish out of water. The French behaved very well, especially the women, and stopped giving them spirits. I got hold of cars and carried the men off to their various camps. Jack, Tom, and I slept all right in a tent on the ground. The next day I was sent down by the colonel with the drum-major, to buy beer for the regiment at

1/1d a gallon, which seemed cheap. I met Stephen while I was buying things. He told me we were off that night, that we were to start at 10, but that we should not be entrained till 4.30. I lunched with Churchill, who very kindly tried to help me get a horse. Long sent me back in his motor. At the camp, the colonel complained that the beer had not come, and that the drum-major and the men had been lost. I commandeered a private motor and went back at a tremendous rate into the town, all but killing the drum-major at a corner. We had a capital dinner. M. Saville gave us excellent wine, and the colonel told me to make him a speech. We then lay down before the march.

The next camp captured a spy, but nobody paid any attention. About 10.30 we moved off. It was a warm night with faint moonlight. Coming into the town the effect was operatic. As we marched or were halted all the windows opened and the people put their heads out to try and talk to us. At about half-past eleven it began to rain, but the me whistled the Marseillaise and "It's a long way to Tipperary." The people came out of the houses, trying to catch the hands of the men and walking along beside them. We were halted in front of the station, and waited endlessly in the rain. We then had an almost unspeakable march over cobbles, past interminable canals, over innumerable bridges, through what seemed to be the conglomeration of all the slums of all the world, to light that always promised us rest but never came. It poured without ceasing. At last we arrived at the station, and when we saw the train pandemonium followed. Everybody jumped into carriages and tried to keep other people out, so as to have more room. We were all soaked to the skin, and nobody bothered about anyone else. After that we got out and packed the men in. Tom, Charles, Jack, Hickie, and I got into one carriage. Lieutenants who tried to follow were hurled out. It was very cold. Tom had a little brandy, which did us some good. At about 5 a.m. We moved off. The next day we arrived at Amiens.

*Saturday, the 15th,* we arrived at Amiens to see a great stir and bustle. We had not had much to eat. We found several officers of the Coldstream Guards in their shirt-sleeves, who had got left trying to get food. I got masses later on at a wayside station, and a stream of people to carry it, and returned with rousing cheers from the men. At every station we were met by enormous crowds that cheered and would have kissed our hands if we had let them. They made speeches and piled wreaths of flowers upon the colonel, who was at first very shy, but driven to make a speech, liked it, and became almost garrulous. At Arras we had the greatest ovation of all. An old man in the crowd gave me a postcard, which I directed to a relation at home and asked him to post. This he did, adding a long letter of his own, to say that I was well and in good spirits. This letter and my postcard got past the censor.

Late that night we came to a place called Wassigny, where, after a lot of standing about, we went up to a farmhouse. Hickie and I lay down on the floor in a sort of an office at about half-past two, with orders to be off at five. The colonel slept outside, half on and half off a bench. He never seemed to need sleep.

We left the next morning, Sunday, the 16th, at five, for Vadencourt. I was wearing Cretan boots, and my feet already began to trouble me.

At Vadencourt we met the *maire* and his colleague, Monsieur Lesur. He took us first of all to the most beautiful place for a camp, a splendid field by a river for bathing, wooded with poplars, but no sooner had we got there than we were told the Coldstreamers had the right to it.

In Vadencourt everybody helped us. The people threw open their houses, their barns and their orchards. They could not do enough; but it was a long business and we had not finished until 1 o'clock, by which time we were pretty tired. Then the troops turned up, and we had to get them into billets. After that we lunched with the colonel. The French cottages were extraordinarily clean, never an insect, but plenty of mice rioting about at night. There were many signs of religion in all these cottages. Most of the rooms were filled with crucifixes and pictures of the Saints. The priests seemed to have a great deal of influence. Vadencourt was very religious, and the morning we went off they had a special service for the men, which was impressive. All the people seemed saintly, except the *maire*, who was very much of this world.

The men had fraternized with the people and, to the irritation of the colonel, wore flowers in their hair and caps. There was no drunkenness—in fact the men complained that there was nothing strong enough to make a man drunk. Generally there was not much to do, though one day the men helped with the harvest. The people couldn't have been kinder. It was, as one of the men said, a great "over taxation." Every day there was a paper published in amazing English. In one paper we found a picture of Alex Thynne, with contemptuous and angry references to a speech he had made against English tourists going to France; he wanted them to go instead to Bath, in his constituency, and so to please both him and his constituents.

It was a quiet life. There was little soldiering, and that, as someone said, was more like manoeuvres in the millennium than anything else. Everywhere corn was offered for our horses and wine for ourselves, but there was a great fear underlying the quiet. We were constantly asked whether the Germans would ever get to Vadencourt, and always said we were quite sure they would not. We used to mess at the inn close to my house. Of French troops we say practically nothing, except our two interpreters, Charlot, who talked very good English, and Bernard, a butcher from Havre, a most excellent fellow, who was more English than the English, though he could only talk a few words of the language. There was also another interpreter, head master of a girls' school in Paris. He said to me: *"Vous trouverez toutes espèces d'infames parmi les interprets, même des M.P.s"*

One day Hugo said that it would be interesting, before going into battle, to have our fortunes told. I told him he could not get a fortune-teller at Vadencourt. "Not at all, there is one in the village; I saw it written over her shop, *'Sage Femme'"* . . . I was very comfortable in my house, which was just out of bounds, but not enough to matter.

Monsieur Louis Prevot came in one day, with a beautiful mare, brown to bay, Moonshine II, by Troubadour out of Middlemas. He said that she could jump two metres. Her disadvantages were that she jumped these two meters at the wrong time and in the wrong place, that she hated being saddled and kicked when she was groomed: while Monsieur Prevot was showing me how to prevent her kicking she kicked right through the barn door. I bought her for £40. I think Prevot thought that the French Authorities were going to take his stables and that I was his only chance. When she settled down to troops she became a beautiful mount.

That day I went with Hickie through Etreux to Boué, foraging. I drove with a boy called Vanston behind a regular man-killer. It was far worse than anything that happened at Mons. Vanston talked all the time of the virtue of Irish women, of the great advantage of having medals and the delight old men found in looking at them, of the higher courage of the unmarried men and his keen anxiety to get into battle, and of the goodness of God. Hickie was upset because he thought that the man-killing horse was going to destroy the Maltese cart, which was, apparently, harder to replace than Vanston or me.

The night before we left the colonel gave us a lecture. As an additional preparation for the march we were also inoculated against typhoid which made some people light-headed.

We left Vadencourt on August 19th, Hickie and Hubert both ill, travelling on a transport cart. I rode ahead, through pretty and uneventful country. At Oisy, Hickie was very ill, and I got him some brandy. We were to camp beyond Oisy. When we got to the appointed place the *maire* was ill and half dotty. S. And I laboured like mad to find houses, but at last, when our work was finished we found that they had already been given to the Coldstreamers. Some of the people were excellent. One old fellow of seventy wept and wished that his house was a big as a barn, that he might put up the soldiers in it. A rough peasant boy took me round and stayed with us all the afternoon and refused to take a penny. But some of them were not so kind. In the end, billets were not found for a number of officers and men, who slept quite comfortably in the new-mown hay. We passed a big monastery where two Germans, disguised as priests, had been taken and shot the week before. I slept in a house belonging to three widows, all like stage creatures. They had one of the finest cupboards I have ever seen.

The next morning (August 20th) we marched off to Maroilles—a big dull town, and again some of the people were not over-pleased to see us. Here we had an excellent dinner. I slept at a chemist's. Hickie was sent back from Maroilles to Amiens with rheumatic fever. We got up at 4 o'clock the next morning (August 21st), and had a pretty long march to Longueville by Malplaquet.

As we crossed the frontier the men wanted to cheer, but they were ordered to be quiet, "so as not to let the Germans hear them." This order gave an unpleasant impression of the proximity of the Germans.

The men began to fall out a great deal on the road. The heat was very great. Many of the reservists were soft, and the feet found them out. Their rough clothes rubbed them. Tom carried rifles all day, and I carried rifles and kit on my horse, while the men held on to the stirrups.

By this time the *maires* of France seemed to be growing faint under the strain of billeting. We never saw the *maire* of Longueville. The country made a wonderful picture that I shall never forget. We marched past fields of rich, tall grass, most splendid pasture, and by acres and acres of ripe corn which was either uncut or, if cut, uncarried.

There was any amount of food for our horses, but one felt reluctant at first at feeding them in the standing corn. I went ahead when I could to forage for the mess, and because Moonshine danced continuously and produced confusion.

We lived chiefly on hard-boiled eggs, chocolate and beer, but we did better than most other companies, because generally, as Valentine said, the officers' vocabulary was limited to "omelette" and "*bière*."

Longueville is a very long town, with fine houses, and we did capitally there, but the men were tired. No. 3 dined luxuriously at a farm. Hugo and I billeted at two houses close to each other. At 6 o'clock I went to get some rest, when my servant told me that the order had come to stand to arms at once, as the Germans were close upon us.

I went outside and heard one cannon boom very faintly in the distance. Women were wringing their hands and crying in the streets, and the battalion was order to stand to arms. Then, after a time, we were ordered to march at ten, and went back to quarters. At this time we began to curse the Germans for disturbing the peace of Europe.

The women of the village brought us milk, bread, everything they could for the march. While we were dining the order came to make ready for a German attack. We went out at once. Bernard took me up and down various roads, and we put iron and wire and everything we could lay hold of, across them, making a flimsy defence. When we returned we heard that we were to march at 2 a.m., and at 11 those who could lay down to sleep. The woman in my house was very kind in getting bread and milk. At 2 o'clock we began marching. The horses were all over the place. Moonshine nearly kicked a man behind her heels, and Tom just missed being killed by the ammunition horse in front. It was very dark.

We marched to a place called Senlis. Dawn came, and then an enemy aeroplane appeared over us, which everybody at once shot at. Moonshine broke up two companies in the most casual way. The aeroplane went on. In Belgium the people were very good to us, during the week-end that we spent there. They were honest and pathetic. There were no signs of panic, but there was a ghastly silence in the towns.

Beyond Senlis we were halted on a plain near a big town which we did not then know was Mons. We were drawn up and told that the Germans were close to us and that we had to drive them back. Valentine and I lay down under the shelter of a haystack, as it was raining. It was a mournful day in its early hours. At about 10 a.m. I was sent for by the colonel, who had been looking for me, he said, for some time. He told me to ride after S. To Quevy-le-Grand. I rode fast, and caught up S. We stabled our horses and went round the town. Soames, a staff officer, told us we could have both sides of the road—as we understood, the pompous main road. Unfortunately he meant both sides of an insignificant road we had not even noticed. We took one of the biggest and most beautiful farms I have ever seen for headquarters, and proposed to put seven or eight officers in it. We, then, as usual, found that this house and all the rest had been given to the Coldstreamers, and we went to hunt for other billets. I thought I heard cannon, faint and dim. As we went on with our work the noise grew louder and louder. There was a big battle going on within four or five miles. Then in came the battalion from Senlis (which was burnt twenty-four hours later) at about twelve, and got into billets, while, at last, we had luncheon. Valentine and I were eating an omelette and talking Shakespeare, when suddenly we saw the battalion go past. We both got cursed because we had not been able to prophesy that the battalion would start within twenty minutes. We marched on till about half-past three, through rising and falling land, under a very hot sun. We were getting nearer to the battle. The sky was filled with smoke-wreaths from shells. "We are going slap-bang at them," said Hubert.

At 3.30 we found ourselves on a hill, by a big building which looked like a monastery. The road was crowded with troops and frightened peasants. Below the road lay the green valley with the river winding through it, and on the crest of the wooded hills beyond were the Germans.

We left our horses and marched down to the valley. As we passed the village of Harveng I inconsiderately tried to get a drink of water from a house. The men naturally followed, but we were all ordered on, and I had nothing to drink until 7 o'clock the next morning. The men or some of them, got a little water that night.

From behind us by the monastery the shells rose in jerks, three at a time. The Germans answered from the belt of threes above the cliffs. Our feelings were more violently moved against German as the disturber of Europe. I went into the first fight prepared only for peace, as I had left my revolver and sword on my horse. Tom said: "For goodness sake don't get away from our company; those woods will be full of Germans with bayonets tonight." we never doubted that we should drive them back. The colonel called the officers together and told us that the trees above the chalk cliffs were our objective. We then lay down in some *lucerne* and waited and talked. The order to move came about 5.30, I suppose. We went down through the fields rather footsore and came to a number of wire fences which kept in cattle. These fences we were ordered to cut. My agricultural instinct revolted at this destruction. We marched on through a dark wood to the foot of the cliffs and skirting them, came to the open fields, on the flank of the wood, sloping steeply upwards. Here we found our first wounded man, though I believe as we moved through the wood an officer had been reported missing.

The first stretch was easy. Some rifle bullets hummed and buzzed round and over us, but nothing to matter. We almost began to vote war a dull thing. We took up our position under a natural earthwork. We had been there a couple of minutes when a really terrific fire opened. We were told afterwards that we were not the target—that it was an accident that they happened to have stumbled on the exact range. But even if we had known this at the time, it would not have made much difference. It was as if a scythe of bullets passed directly over our heads about a foot above the earthworks. It came in gusts, whistling and sighing. The men behaved very well. A good many of them were praying and crossing themselves. A man next to me said: "It's hell fire we're going into." it seemed inevitable that any man who went over the bank must be cut neatly in two. Valentine was sent to find out if Bernard was ready on the far left. Then, in a lull, Tom gave the word and we scrambled over and dashed on to the next bank. Bullets were singing round us like a swarm of bees, but we had only a short way to go, and got, all or us, I think, safely to the next shelter, where we lay and gasped and thought hard.

Our next rush was worse, for we had a long way to go through turnips. The prospect was extremely unattractive; we thought that the fire came from the line of trees which we were ordered to take, and that we should have to stand the almost impossible fire from which the first bank had sheltered us. This was not the case, as the German trenches, we heard afterwards, were about 300 yards behind the trees, but their rifle fire and their shells cut across. We had not gone more than about 100 yards, at a rush and uphill, when a shell burst over my head. I jumped to the conclusion that I was killed and fell flat. I was ashamed of myself before I reached the ground, but looking round, found that everybody else had done the same.

The turnips seemed to offer a sort of cover, and I thought of the feelings of the partridges, a covey of which rose as we sank. Tom gave us a minute in which to get our wind—we lay gasping in the heat, while the shrapnel splashed about—and then told us to charge, but ordered the men not to fire until they got the word. As we rose, with a number of partridges, the shooting began again, violently, but without much effect. I think we had six or seven men hit. We raced to the trees. Valentine was so passionately anxious to get there hat he discarded his

21

haversack, scabbard and mackintosh, and for days afterwards walked about with his naked sword as a walking-stick.

When we reached the trees in a condition of tremendous sweat we found an avenue and a road with a ditch on either side. We were told that our trenches were a few yards over the father hedge, faced by the German trenches, about 250 yards off. There was fierce rifle and machine gun fire. Night fell; the wounded were carried back on stretchers; we sat very uncomfortably in a ditch. I was angry with Tom for the only time on the march, as he was meticulous about making us take cover in this beastly ditch when outside there was a bank of grass like a sofa, which to all intents and purposes was safe from fire. We were extremely thirsty, but there was nothing to drink and no prospect of getting water. After some time we moved down the road upon which we lay, getting what sleep we could. In the earlier part of the night there were fierce duels of rifle fire and machine guns between the two trenches. It sounded as if the Germans were charging. Our men in the road never got a chance of letting off their guns. Most of us dosed coldly and uncomfortably on the hard road. I woke up about 2 a.m., dreaming that a mule was kicking the splashboard of a Maltese wagon to pieces, and then realized that it was the German rifle fire beyond the hedge, hitting the road. I walked up the road for a few yards and heard two men talking, on of whom was, I suppose, Hubert, and the other must have been C. Hubert said: "Have I your leave, sir, to retire?"

"Yes, you have; everybody else had gone; it is clear that we are outflanked on the left, and it is suicide to stay." the battalion was then ordered to retire; No. 3 Company, doing rearguard, was ordered back to the fields which we had already crossed.

I said to Tom: "I hear upon the best authority that his is suicide."

Tom said: "Of course it is; we shall get an awful slating."

We moved back. There was a faint light and a spasmodic rifle fire from the Germans as we went back to the fields we had crossed. We could not make out why they did not open on us with shrapnel, as they had the range. We lay down on the new-cut hay, which smelt delicious. It seemed almost certain that we should be wiped out when dawn came, but most of us went fast asleep. I did. At 4 o'clock we were hurried off. We went down into the blinding darkness of the wood by the road we had gone the evening before. We went through the wood, past the monastery, up into the village. There we waited. The road was blocked, the villages were huddled, moaning, in the streets.

The men were very pleased to have been under fire, and compared notes as to how they felt. Everyone was pleased. But they felt that more of this sort of thing would be uncivilized, and it ought to be stopped by somebody now. In the dawn we crossed a high down, where we expected to be shelled, but nothing happened. We were very tired and footsore.

At 7 o'clock we got to Quevy-le-Petit and had a long drink, the first for seventeen hours. The smell of powder and the heat had made us very thirsty. Two companies were set to dig trenches. We were held in reserve, and all the hot morning we shelled the Germans from Quevy-le-Petit, while their guns answered our fire without much effect. One shell was a trouble. The remainder of the—Regiment (men without officers), who had had a bad time at Mons, had a shell burst over them and rushed through our ranks, taking some of our men with them. This was put right at once.

We were told that a tremendous German attack was to take place in the morning; we disliked the idea, as, even to an amateur like myself, it was obvious that there was hardly any means of defence. To stay was to be destroyed, as the colonel said casually, causing *"une impression bien pènible."*

We wrote farewell letters which were never sent. I kept mine in my pocket, as I thought it would do for a future occasion. They began to shell us heavily while we helped ourselves from neighbouring gardens. We did this with as much consideration as possible, and Valentine and I went off to cook some potatoes in an outhouse by a lane.

The peasants were flying, and offered us all their superfluous goods. They were very kind. Then an order to retire came, and in hot haste we left our potatoes. We retired at about 1 o'clock in the afternoon and marched to Longueville, or rather to a camp near it called Bavai. We reached this camp at about 10.30 at night. Moonshine behaved like the war-horse in the *Bible*. She had hysterics which were intolerable; smelling the battle a long way off. She must have done this the night before, when it was much nearer and I had left her with Ryan, for when I found her again see had only one stirrup. A sergeant-major captured her and picketed her for the night.

The orchard in which we camped blazed with torchlight and camp-fires and was extremely cheerful. Every now and then a rifle went off by accident, and this was always greeted with tremendous cheers.

I was very tired, and threw myself down to sleep under a tree, when up came the colonel, and said: "Come along, have some rum before you go to bed."

I went and drank it, and with all the others lay down thoroughly warm and contented in the long, wet grass, and slept soundly Foreign Office three hours. Next morning we were woken about 3 o'clock, but did not march off till 6 o'clock.

From Bavai we marched to Landrecies. Hubert rode ahead with me to do the billeting. We pastured our horses in the luxuriant grass and got milk at the farms. We did not see much sign of panic amongst the people, but coming to a big railway station we saw that all the engines of the heavy ammunition wagons had been turned round. Hubert saw and swore. In the morning we occupied a farm where I tried to buy a strap to replace my lost stirrup. We lay about under haystacks and talked to the farmer and his son. After about an hour it was reported that two hundred Germans were coming down the road, and Eric went off after them, with machine guns.

The retreat had begun in real earnest. This whole retreat was curiously normal. Everybody got very sick of it, and all day long one was hearing officers and men saying how they wanted to turn and fight. I used to feel that myself, though when one was told to do so and realized that we were unchaperoned by the French and face by about two million Germans, it did something to cool one's pugnacity, and one received the subsequent order to retire in a temperate spirit. Men occasionally fell out from bad feet, but the regiment marched quite splendidly. There was never any sign of flurry or panic anywhere. I think that most people, when they realized what had happened, accepted things rather impersonally. They thought that as far as our army in France was concerned, disaster, in the face of the enormous numbers that we had to fight, was inevitable, but that this disaster was not vital as long as the navy was safe.

My dates are not quite accurate here, as I cannot account for one day. It was Sunday, August 23rd, that we had the fight at Mons; I remember several men said: "Our people are now going to Evening Service at home." as we marched out; and it was Tuesday, September 1st, that we had the fight in which I and the others were taken prisoners.

Hubert and I arrived at Landrecies about 1 o'clock. Going in, we met S., a Staff officer, who told us where we could quarter the men. We went to a big house belonging to a man called Berlaimont, which Hubert wanted to have as headquarters. Berlaimont was offensive and did not wish to give his house. We went on to the *maire*, who gave us permission to take it. After lunch we went on billeting, finding some

24

very fine houses. We had a mixed reception. Berlaimont gave in ungraciously, and wrote up rather offensive orders as to what was not to be done: *"Ne pas cracher dans les corridors."* In other houses, too, they made difficulties.

I said: "After all, we are better than the Germans." they soon had the chance of judging.

The troops came in to be billeted. At 6 o'clock fire suddenly broke out in the town, and the cry was raised that the Germans were upon us. I ran back and got my sword and revolver at headquarters, and going out, found a body of unattached troops training a Maxim on the *estaminet* that was my lodgings. I prevented them firing. Troops took up positions all over the town. The inhabitants poured out pell-mell. It was like a flight in the Balkans. They carried their all away in wheelbarrows, carts, perambulators, and even umbrellas. I met and ran into M. Berlaimont, very pale and fat, trotting away from the town; he said to me with quivering cheeks: "What is it?"

I said: "It is the Prussians, M. Berlaimont. And they will probably spit in your corridors."

We had some dinner in a very hospitable house. At 8 o'clock there was some very fierce fighting; the Coldstreamers had been ordered outside the town. The Germans came up, talking French, and called out to Monk, a Coldstream officer: *"No tirez paz; nous sommes des amis,"* and *"Vive les Anglais!"*

A German knocked Monk under a transport wagon. Then our men grasped what was happening; they charged the Germans and the Germans charged them, three times, I believe. They brought up machine guns. Afterwards one of our medical officers said that we lost 150 men, killing 800 to 1000 Germans. It was there that Archer Clive was killed.

Just before dinner I met an officer of the regiment. I asked him if he had a billet. He told me he could not get one, and I said he could have mine and that I would find another. However, I found that my kit had already been put into the *estaminet*, and took him up to the market-place to find a lodging. We first went to an empty café, where all the liquor was left out, with no master or servants. We left money for what beer we drank. I then found a room in a tradesman's house. After dinner I went down to the main barricade with Jack. Wagons, including one of our own that carried our kit, had been dragged across the road and defences were put up like lightening. We loopholed the houses and some houses were pulled down. It was an extraordinarily picturesque scene. The town was pitch-black except where the torches glowed on the faces and on the bayonets of the men, or where shells flashed and burst. I thought of the taking of Italian towns in the seventeenth century. The Germans shelled us very heavily. It did not seem as if there was much chance of getting away, but no one was despondent. At about 1 a.m. There was a lull in the firing, and I went back to lie down in my room. There I fell asleep, and the shelling of the town did not wake me, though the house next to me was hit. About 2.30, in my sleep I heard my name, and found Desmond calling me loudly in the street outside. He said: "We have lost two young officers, L. And W. Come out and find them at once. The Germans are coming into the town, and we shall have to clear out instantly."

I said to him: "I don't know either L. or W. By sight, and if I did it is far too dark to see them."

"Well," he said, "you must do your best."

I went out and walked about the town, which was still being shelled, but I was far more afraid of being run over in the darkness than of being hit. Troops were pouring out in great confusion—foot, artillery, transport mixed—and there were great holes in the road made by the German shells. I met Eric, who said: "Come along with me to Guise;" also the driver of a great transport wagon, who said he had no orders, and begged me to come with him: he felt lonely without an officer.

It was quite clear to me that it was impossible to find these two officers. I met Desmond by headquarters and told him so; he said: "Very well, fall in and come along."

The regiment passed at that moment. Hubert and Tom told me to fall in, but I would not leave Moonshine, though there did not seem to be much more chance of finding her than W. and L. My groom and servant had both disappeared. The houses were all locked and deserted. I battered on a door with my revolver. Two old ladies timidly came out with a light. They pointed to a house where I could find a man, but at that moment a Frenchman came up, whom I commandeered. I went off to headquarters to see if a sergeant was left.

There was nobody there. The dinner left looked like Belshazzar's feast. I had a good swig of beer from a jug. My saddle and sword had gone. I went out with the Frenchman and saw that the troops were nearly out of the town. I determined to stay, if necessary, and hide until I could find my horse, but the Frenchman turned up trumps and we found her. We were terrified of her heels in the dark. I thanked the old ladies and apologized for having threatened them with my revolver.

There was no question of riding Moonshine bareback. I went back to get a saddle below headquarters, but the Germans were there, so the Frenchman swore. It was too dark to see, but they weren't our men. I took her back to where the medical officer was billeted. He had been waiting with a dying man and was about to leave the town. I asked him to let one of his men lead her, and went forward to see if I could get a saddle. In this I failed. As I got out of the town dawn was breaking. For some obscure reason one of our gunners fired a shell.

Everybody said: "I suppose that is to tell them where we are."

We all thought that the German artillery fire must catch us going out of the town. For the second time they let us off. By that time we had grasped the fact that they could outmarch us, but we did not know that they had come on motorcars, and ascribed their greater pace to what we believed to be the fact—that we were entirely unsupported by the French. My regiment were a good long way ahead. I joined an officer who was leading a detachment, and he was anxious that I should stay with him. As I walked along, pretty footsore, an unshaven man came up and asked me if I liked this sort of thing better than politics. I didn't say much, as I heard the soldiers discussing politicians in the dark at Landrecies, cursing all politicians every time a shell fell, and saying: "Ah, that's another one we owe to them. Why aren't they here?"

He offered me a horse. He was the colonel of the Irish Horse, Burns-Lindow. I took the horse gratefully, which had a slight wound on its shoulder and was as slow as an ox, poor beast. This drove me almost mad after Moonshine, and, meeting another officer, I fell into conversation with him. I asked if he saw anything wrong in my taking the saddle off this horse and putting it on to Moonshine when I found her. He said it was certainly irregular, and I then recognized who he was. I got away from him as soon as possible and, finding another officer of the Irish Horse, persuaded him to help me to take off the saddle and put it on to Moonshine, whom I had regained fairly chastened. I found the colonel, and we rode on to Etreux. Here we brought down an aeroplane after it had dropped a bomb on us. The officers tried to prevent the men shooting, but the noise made their commands useless. The C.O. Was very angry. He said: "I will teach you to behave like a lot of . . .s. Off you go and dig trenches."

One of the men said as we marched off: "If that was a friendly aeroplane, what did it want to drop that bomb on us for?"

He was quite right. It had done this, and the shell had fallen about thirty yards away. Our fire prevented us hearing it. Stephen came down in a Balaclava helmet and said that officers were the best shots at aeroplanes because pheasants had taught them to swing in firing.

At Etreux we were ordered to dig trenches, which we did. After this I slept under a hedge, where Bernard the Frenchman, gave me some rum, which was very welcome, as it was raining. At about 9 o'clock I felt Hubert, very angry, thumping me, as he thought I was a private who had taken his haversack to lie on.

The next morning everybody was in tremendous spirits. They had slept very well in the trenches and those outside had been housed in nests of straw. The officers were called up and spoken to by the colonel. He read out a message from Joffre to say that the British army had saved France. He told us that the retreat had been inevitable and had given the French time to take up adequate defensive positions. The impression I think most of us had was that we had been used as a bait. Then we were once more ordered to retire.

As I rode along in the morning going to La Fère an aeroplane passed fairly close over us; everybody fired at it at once; thousands of rounds must have been fired, and I found it useful in teaching Moonshine to stand fire. She took her first lesson well, though she broke up the formation of half a company. We often saw aeroplanes, and they were nearly always shot at, whether they belonged to friend of foe.

That day we marched to Origny, where we camped below a hill with a steep cliff to it. I went into the town and bought eggs, brandy, etc. There was every kind of rumour about: that we were completely surrounded by the Germans; that there were millions of them in front and behind; also that there had been a great French defeat at Charleroi.

We were all very jolly. At night the artillery poured past with the sound of a great cataract. We lay down on the hill-side, and every man going to get straw to cover him walked over Tom's face, who swore himself almost faint with rage. All our kit had been lost at Landrecies, and many of us had not great-coats.

We started at dawn; but had to wait to let other troops pass us. I was sent back to look for communicating files of the regiment that had been lost. I found them with difficulty and brought them on. The Germans were too near to us. That day we marched through great avenues of tall poplars and through a pleasant smiling country to La Fère. The regiment forgot its tiredness in a hunt after a strange horse which strayed into our camp and which Eric finally captured for transport. Both Desmond and he tried hard to take my saddle from me; for the saddle which I had first put upon Moonshine was Hickie's harness. Then Hickie was invalided, and I lost his saddle at Landrecies and then got the saddle from B.L., colonel of the Irish Horse. I beat them in argument, but thought they were quite capable of taking the saddle in spite of that.

We stopped some time to smoke and rest. The men were drawn up on a torrid cornfield. Valentine was overdone. He volunteered, like the man in the *Bible*, to get water. Finding that he would have to wait in a long queue, he returned without the water. Tom's anger beat all records. A deputation from another regiment came and asked him to repeat what he had said. They were surprised to find that it was his brother-in-law who had provoked these comments.

I saw John Manners and George Cecil, and gave them cigarettes. Near a great factory of some kind we marched past Sir Douglas Haig. I hurried past him.

La Fère was an old fortified city. We were told we were to have a rest and the next day's march was to be a very short one. We camped near Berteaucourt. It was very hot. I hobbled up to the village to get provisions, and found a French girl, the daughter of a farmer, who talked fair English. Near the village I spoke to a number of people. I told one peasant I thought it was a mistake that everybody should fly from their houses if they did not mean to clear out altogether, and that it was an invitation to the Germans to loot and burn. He said: "*Monsieur*, I quite agree with you. *Moi, je vais agir en patriote quand ils viendront. Je vais tout bonnement descendre dans ma cave.*"

The next day (the 29th) we camped above the village of Pasly. On the road I got boracic cream for my horse's cracked heel. We passed through a big town, Coucy, crowded with curious, frightened, silent people. It had a very fine castle. I bought some cigarette-holders, with cinema pictures inside, for the colonel. People pressed chocolate and all they could into my hands, taking payment unwillingly. Moonshine lost a shoe, but I managed to get her shod there. Reluctantly at Pasly I lent her to Robin, who went off to post his men in the village. The moment he had gone the O.C. Sent for me and told me we had got outside the area of our maps, and asked if I could get him a map. I started off at once to walk to Soissons. When he discovered where I was going he said it was out of the question; so I walked down to Pasly either to get a map there or to take the *maire*'s carriage and drive to Soissons. In Pasly there was a tenth-rate *maire* and a schoolmaster.

They provided me with an ancient map, the date of which was 1870. It did not even mark the monument of the schoolmasters whom the Germans and light-heartedly shot on their last visit to the village.

I found a half-wit, and paid him to carry up some wine, bread and eggs.

We camped above a quarry and talked of what was going to happen. There seemed only two alternatives. One was that we should get into Paris and take first-class tickets home to England, and the other that we should stay and get wiped out. For we still saw no French troops; we still believed ourselves to be 100,000 against a force of anything from one to two millions.

Eric had met a Lancer who had been full of German atrocities. I met him and talked to him afterwards. His stories sounded improbable. Eric had also seen an extraordinary thing happen that morning. He had seen an aeroplane which we were bombarding. It was flying in the blue sky when it was struck. It was there, and then it was not. It just disappeared.

*August 31st.* We got up fairly early, and I rode with Eric past caves in which there were houses and quarries down the steep hill-side to the plain of Soissons. It was a beautiful morning, very peaceful, and the air was scented. There was bright sunlight over the marching soldiers and the fields of green, tall grass. The C.O. Told me that our camping ground was at Coeuvre. I asked leave to ride into Soissons and see if I could not get clean shirts and handkerchiefs to replace what we had lost at Landrecies.

Soissons was like a sunlit town of the dead. Four out of five houses were shut. Most of the well-to-do people had gone. It was silent streets and blind houses. The clattering which Moonshine made on the cobbles was almost creepy. I stopped first of all at a saddler's shop and tried to get a proper bridle. The saddler was a rough democratic Frenchman, not a bad fellow, the sort of man who made the Republic. He took me to a boot shop which was my first need, where the people were very kind, and I bought a capital pair of boots for twelve *francs.* I went into the "Lion d'Or." they refused me a stall for Moonshine on the ground that the landlord and all his family were going. I insisted and bought her some fodder, also some food for myself. They drove had bargains.

Out of doors I met some English officers having breakfast. They had only just arrived. I left a man called Gustave to look after Moonshine and went out to spend a most laborious morning of shopping. After going to many different shops I found a bazaar like a mortuary, with two old women and a boy. They said to me: "Take whatever you want and pay as much or as little as pleases you. If the Germans come we shall set fire to this place."

They pressed every kind of souvenir on me, but it was extraordinary, with plenty lying round, how difficult it was to get what one needed. I was buying mostly for other people. It was like being turned loose in Selfridge's—boots, scissors, pocket-knives, electric torches, watches, bags, vests, etc. I also bought an alpenstock, as I had lost my sword and thought it might be useful as a light bayonet.

I then went and had a bath, the first proper one since England. The heat was very great. I felt dirty and wanted to shave my beard, as the men said every day that I became more like King Edward. I then intended to go to the Cathedral, but found the few English soldiers in the town moving out hurriedly. They said the Germans were coming in an hour. So I gave up the Cathedral and went and had lunch in a jolly little inn. There was some very excitable Frenchmen, one of whom asked me if I would sell him a lucky sixpence for a *franc* which he could wear round his neck. I suppose he was really pathetic; at the moment he only irritated me. He said: *"J'ai confiance—même s'ils vont à Paris j'aurais confiance.* But," he said, "where is the French army?"

They were all saying that by this time.

I went back to my boot shop. All the women there were crying. They insisted upon giving me some wine. At the hotel I found the hotel-keeper and his family going off, squeaking with anger at the ostler, Gustave, who was helping me to carry all I had bought in two great bags. The weight was very oppressive in the heat, and I was afraid of making Moonshine's tender foot worse on the hard road. Before I had got outside the town I had to get off and readjust everything, with the help of some very kind French people. While I was doing this, Westminster, with Hugh Dawnay, drove up in his beautiful car. I suggested his taking my things on to Coeuvre. He said, unfortunately he had other orders, and wanted to know where to lunch. I told him where I had lunched, but said that he would probably have to share his lunch with the Germans if he went into the town, as they must now be close behind us.

Riding on, I met some French troops, evacuating the town and with them a man of my regiment, who had hurt his knee. He could not walk, so I put him under the charge of a French sergeant. While I

31

was talking to him two other men of my regiment came up. They had fallen out on the previous day and had had nothing to eat since yesterday's breakfast. I took them into a French house, where the people were very hospitable; gave them food at once and insisted on giving them champagne, which they said was *déchampagnisé*. The men ate like wolves. One of them was a splendidly built fellow, called Sheridan.

Then we marched slowly on in the heat, for about two hours, when Sheridan said: "What is it is happening yonder, sir?" pointing to the horizon about a mile away. Soon rifle fire broke out, and Sheridan said: "There are Uhlans coming down the road."

There was a wood on our left, and we made preparations to get into this; the other man had fallen behind. They were both very done, but Sheridan was like a different man at the prospect of a fight. Out people, however, or rather the French, drove the German cavalry back at this moment, and we went on quietly. I was glad to be able to turn to the left, as the fighting on our right was pretty hot and I was weighed down with all the extra things I carried.

I fell into conversation with a medical officer, and asked him if he knew where Coeuvre was. Then an R.A.M.C. colonel came up and looked at my kit very suspiciously. He asked me who the general in command of the Division was. I said I had forgotten his name; I could not keep my head filled with these details. He said to me: "You don't seem to know who you are."

I said to him: "I know who I am; I don't know who you are, I don't want to. I hope to God I shall never see you again. Go to hell and stay there."

This made him angry, and he said: "Your regiment is ahead on the left, but the Germans are in front of you, if you wish to rejoin them," pointing in the direction from which I had come.

All this time I had been waiting for Sheridan and other numerous stragglers behind me, and at this point I turned round and rode off to see what had happened, thoroughly irritated with the R.A.M.C. colonel. This apparently convinced him that I really was a German, as the engagement in the rear was going on fairly close, and he came after me with a Major of the K.R.R., who was unhappy.

He said: "Will you come with me to my colonel?"

I said: "I will go with you anywhere to get away from this fussy little man, but if you think that a German spy would come on a racehorse, dressed like the White Knight, with an alpenstock, you are greatly mistaken."

He promised to have my stragglers looked after, and then I rode up to his regiment with him, when Blank came up and shook hands. We had not met since Eton. He cleared my character. After that I went on as fast as I could. I picked up some more of my regiment, including a sergeant who had sprained his ankle. I told him to ride, but found a motor and put him in that.

Soon we were stopped by a sentry in a wood, as it was growing dark. He said that his officer had told him to stop all on the road and send for him. Then came General Monro, who was also stopped. He was with a sad man. He forced his way through, and I asked permission to take on the men of my regiment. He told me that I should find my regiment at Soucy, and gave me the permission I wanted. In a few moments I met the officer who had had us stopped. He said the Germans were very close to us. We could hear firing near by.

I reached my regiment as night was falling. They were delighted with my arrest. We spent our last night very comfortably, though there was heavy dew. Tom, who had been frightfully overdone, always carrying rifles, was recovering, and everyone was cheerful and very keen to have a fight. Until now only Hickie had been invalided. The rum at night after a long march made a wonderful difference. The men got in very tired, footsore, cold and hungry, and had to sleep on the wet ground. A tot of rum sent them to sleep, and sent them to sleep feeling warm. Teetotalism on the march is an excellent thing, better still to drink nothing, but that nip at night made the difference between health and sickness, comfort and misery.

*September 1st.* The next morning we got up at 2 o'clock. The army was passing all round us already. It was like the sound of deep, slow rivers. For the first and last time we took a wrong turning, only for a couple of hundred yards. This was the only mistake I saw at all in the long march. After two hours we halted, and S. And I sat under a dripping tree and talked about the West Country. At the beginning S. said to me: "I shall be very disappointed if I go home without seeing a fight, but the worst of it is you can't make an omelette without breaking eggs, and I don't want to see my friends killed."

I said to him: "You are going to get your omelette all right now."

Some constituents passed me. They said: "This be terrible dangerous. Do'ee come along with we."

Moonshine would eat nothing, and worried me. I had become very fond of her.

33

At about 6 o'clock we halted on what I knew to be a tragic plain. In my mind I associate this plain with turnips, though I am not sure that any grew there. There was stubble, high and wet *lucerne*, and a mournful field where corn had been cut but not carried. We sat about on the wet, muddy ground for breakfast, while a thin, dismal rain fell.

The C.O. called us round and gave us our orders. He said: "We are required to hold this wood until 2 o'clock in the afternoon. We may have to fight a rearguard action until a later hour if there is a block in the road. We are to retire upon Rond de la Reine."

After this we breakfasted on hot cocoa; it tasted of Vaseline or paraffin, but it was warm.

It was apparent that if the First Division took long over their luncheon we should be wiped out. By this time everyone had got their second wind, their feet were hard and they were cheerful. Jumbo said he could go on walking for ever. I talked to Alex and agreed that we had seen a great deal of fun together. He had said, while we were crossing the Channel, that it was long odds, not, of course, against some of us coming back, but against any particular one of us seeing it through. This was not visibly true; we believed that we were three divisions against twenty-one or even twenty-eight German divisions. I wrote two letters, one of them a eulogy of Moonshine. I went to Desmond, asking him to post them. He said crossly: "You seem to think that Adjutants can work miracles. Charles asks for letters under fire, you want to post them on the battlefield. It is quite useless to write letters now."

He then borrowed some of my paper and wrote a letter. I have the picture in my mind of Desmond constantly sitting, in very tidy breeches, writing and calling for sergeants. We had little sleep. He never seemed to sleep at all. He was woken all the time and was always cheerful. We had nothing to do for a bit, and I read scraps about cemeteries from Shakespeare, to irritate the others. They remained cheerful. Then we moved off to the wood. Nobody had any illusions about the immediate future. One man said to me: "I may live to see many battles; I think I shall, for I am very keen on my profession, but I shall never forget this plain or this morning."

It must have been about 7.30 when we went into the wood. No. 4 held the extreme right; they were protected by a wall, which they loopholed, and a wire fence outside. No. 3 was next on a road that ran through the heart of the wood to Rond de la Reine. I did not see Tom; I thought I was sure to see him some time in the morning.

Stubbs was behind No. 3, down in the village (I forget the name). The C.O. said to me: "I want you to gallop for me today, so stick to me."

I lost him at once in the wood behind No. 4, but rode right down to a deserted farm and, swinging to my right, found him at the cross-roads.

I had seen a good deal of him the last days. He had a very attractive personality, and it was a delight to hear him talk about anything. I asked him what chance he thought we had of getting more than half of us away. He said he thought a fairly good chance. Then he said to me: "How is your rest-cure getting on now? There is very little that looks like manoeuvres in the millennium about this, is there?"

I had told him some time before that I looked upon this expedition as a rest-cure, as in some ways it was. We talked about Ireland and Home Rule, riding outside the wood. The grey, damp mist had gone and the day was beautiful.

He sent me first to Hubert, Second-in-Command, with the order that in the retreat every officer was to retire down the main road, with the exception of Stubbs, who was to retire as he liked. I imagine that he was afraid that men would be lost in the wood. By this time the firing had begun, some way off, but our men could see the Germans coming over the rising land. The C.O. ordered me to find Colonel Pereira of the Coldstream Guards and tell him that, as soon as our own troops, now fighting the Germans in front of him, would fall back through his lines, after this he was to fall back himself.

I went off at a hand gallop, and had got halfway there, with the wood on my left and open land on my right, when the Germans began shooting at about three-quarters of a mile. Our men were firing at them from the wood, and I felt annoyed at being between two fires and the only thing visible to amuse our men and the Germans. I turned into the wood, and, galloping down a sandy way, found the road filled with refugees with haunted faces. We had seen crowds of refugees for days, but I felt sorrier for these. I suppose it was that the Germans were so very near them. I gave my message to Pereira, who advised me to go back through the wood, but I knew the other way and thought I should soon be past the German fire. I had not, however, counted on their advancing so quickly. When I came to the edge of the wood they were firing furiously—shrapnel, machine gun and rifle fire. Our men had excellent cover, and were answering. I then tried to make my way through the wood, but it was abominably rough. There were ferns and brambles waist-high, and great ditches; the wood was very beautiful with its tall trees, but that, at the moment, was irrelevant. Moonshine stood like a goat on the stump of a tree that made an island among the ditches, and I turned back to take the way by the open fields. When I got outside the fire had grown very bad. I raced for an orchard that jutted out of the wood. Bullets hummed and buzzed. Coming to it, I found that there was wire round it. I then popped at full speed, like a rabbit, into the wood again, through a thicket, down an enormous ditch, up the other side, bang into some barbed wire, which cut my horse. It was like diving on horseback. I turned round and galloped delicately out again, riding full tilt round the orchard.

I found the colonel, who was standing under shelter at the crossroads to the left of the road, facing the enemy, that led through the heart of the wood. He mounted the bank and watched the Germans advancing. I sat under the bank with M. and Alex. The German shells began to fall close to us, knocking the trees about in the wood. There were some sergeants very excited and pleased at the idea of a fight.

They said: "Now has come the time for deeds, not words." They felt that they were the me of the moment.

We considered whether the Germans were likely to charge down the road along which I had come, but thought we could hold them effectively in check from our corner and that the fire from the wood would reach them.

It was, I suppose, now about 10.30. Desmond, the colonel and I rode back into the big, green wood. It was very peaceful. The sun was shining through the beech-trees, and for a bit the whole thing seemed unreal. The C.O. talked to the men, telling them to reserve their fire till the Germans were close on them.

"Then you will kill them and they won't get up again." That made them laugh.

The German advance began very rapidly. The Coldstreamers must have begun falling back about this time. The Germans came up in front and on our left flank. There was a tremendous fire. The leaves, branches, etc., rained upon one. One's face was constantly fanned by the wind from their bullets. This showed how bad their fire was. My regiment took cover very well, and after the first minute or two fired pretty carefully. Moonshine was startled to begin with by the fire, but afterwards remained very still and confidential. Desmond did not get off his horse; he told me to lead my horse back into the wood and then come back to the firing line. The colonel then told me to gallop up to the Brigadier to say that the retreat was being effectively carried out; that there were two squadrons advancing and he did not know what force of infantry. In this estimate he was very much out, as subsequent events proved. Eric, now at home wounded, said to me: "The Germans seemed hardly to have an advance guard; it was an army rolling over us."

When I found the Brigadier he wanted to know if the C.O. seemed happy about things. I said I thought on the whole he did. There were bullets everywhere and men falling, but the fire was still too high. One bullet in about half a million must have hit a man. I reported to the colonel. Our men had then begun to retire down the main road to Rond de la Reine. A galloper came up and, as far as I heard, said that we were to hang on and not retreat yet. This officer was, I think, killed immediately after giving his message. The colonel said that the Coldstreamers had already begun to retreat, that we couldn't hold on there, but must go back to the position we had left. We were ordered to resume the position which Hubert had been told to leave. The Germans were by this time about 250 yards away, firing on us with machine guns and rifles. The noise was perfectly awful. In a lull the C.O. Said to the men: "Do you hear that? Do you know what they are doing that for? They are doing that to frighten you."

I said to him: "If that's all, they might as well stop. As far as I am concerned, they have succeeded, two hours ago."

The men were ordered to charge, but the order was not heard in the noise, and after we had held this position for some minutes a command was given to retreat. Another galloper brought it, who also, I think, was shot. Guernsey, whom I met with his company, asked me to gallop back and tell Valentine he must retire his platoon; he had not received the order. I found Valentine and got off my horse and walked him some yards down the road, the Germans following. He, like everybody else, was very pleased at the calm way the men were behaving.

I mounted and galloped after the colonel, who said: "If only we could get at them with the bayonet, I believe one of our men is as good as three of theirs."

He started in the direction of the Brigadier. Men were now falling fast. I happened to see one man drop with a bayonet in his hand a few yards off, and reined in my horse to see if I could help him, but the C.O. called me and I followed him. The man whom I had seen was Hubert, though I did not know it at the time. The C.O. said: "It is impossible now to rescue wounded men; we have all we can do."

He had a charmed life. He raced from one place to another through the wood; cheering the men and chaffing them, and talking to me; smoking cigarette after cigarette. Under ordinary conditions one would have thought it mad to ride at the ridiculous pace we did over the very broken ground, but the bullets made everything else irrelevant. At about 1 o'clock we went up to the Brigadier at the corner of the road. The fighting there was pretty hot. One of the men told the colonel that Hubert was killed. The colonel said: "Are you sure?"

The man said: "Well, I can't swear."

I was sent back to see. The man said he was about 400 yards away, and as I galloped as hard as I could, G. called to me: "To the right and then to the left."

As I raced through the wood there was a cessation of the firing, though a number of shots came from both sides. They snapped very close. I found Hubert in the road we had been holding. I jumped off my horse and put my hand on his shoulder and spoke to him. He must have been killed at once, and looked absolutely peaceful. He cannot have suffered at all. I leant over to see if he had letters in his pocket, when I heard a whistle 25 or 30 yards behind me in the wood. I stood up and called: "If that is an Englishman, get outside the wood and up to the corner like hell; you will be shot if you try and join the rest through the wood. The Germans are between us."

I bent over to pick up Hubert's bayonet, when again a whistle came and the sound of low voices, talking German. I then thought the sooner I was away the better. As I swung into the saddle a shot came from just behind me, missing me. I rode back as fast as Moonshine could go. The lull in the firing had ceased, and the Germans were all round us. One could see them in the wood, and they were shooting quite close. The man who finally got me was about 15 or 20 yards away; his bullet must have passed through a tree or through Bron's greatcoat, because it came into my side broken up. It was like a tremendous punch. I galloped straight on to my regiment and told the colonel that Hubert was dead. He said: "I am sorry, and I am sorry that you are hit. I am going to charge."

He had told me earlier that he meant to if he got the chance.

I got off and asked them to take on my horse. Then I lay down on the ground and an R.A.M.C. man dressed me. The Red Cross men gave a loud whistle when they saw my wound, and said the bullet had gone through me. The fire was frightfully hot. The men who were helping me were crouching down, lying on the ground. While he was dressing me a horse—his, I suppose—was shot just behind us. I asked them to go, as they could do me no good and would only get killed or taken themselves. The doctor gave me some *morphia*, and I gave them my revolver. They put me on a stretcher, leaving another empty stretcher beside me. This was hit several times. Shots came from all directions, and the fire seemed to be lower than earlier in the day. The bullets were just above me and my stretcher. I lost consciousness for a bit; then I heard my regiment charging. There were loud cries and little spurts of spasmodic shooting; then everything was quiet and a deep peace fell upon the wood. It was very dreamlike.

It is really very difficult to reconstruct this fight. I think every man's attention was fixed like iron on doing his own job, otherwise they would all have noticed more. I carry in my mind a number of very vivid pictures—Desmond on his horse, Valentine and I discussing fatalism, the C.O. smoking cigarettes in the cinema holders I had bought for him a few days before.

As I lay on the stretcher a jarring thought came to me. I had in my pocket the flat-nosed bullets which the War Office had served out to us as revolver ammunition. They were not dum-dum bullets, but they would naturally not make as pleasant a wound as the sharp-nosed ones, and it occurred to me that those having them would be shot. I searched my pockets and flung mine away. I did not discover one which remained and was buried later on—but neither did the Germans. It was first hearing German voices close by that jogged my memory about these bullets, and the Germans were then so close that I felt some difficulty in throwing the bullets away. The same idea must have occurred to others, for later I heard the Germans speaking very angrily about the flat bullets they had picked up in the wood, and saying how they would deal with anyone in whose possession they were found.

The glades became resonant with loud, raucous German commands and occasional cries from wounded men. After about an hour and a half, I suppose, a German with a red beard, with the sun shining on his helmet and bayonet, came up looking like an angel of death. He walked round from behind, and put his serrated bayonet on the empty stretcher by me, so close that it all but touched me. The stretcher broke and his bayonet poked me. I enquired in broken but polite German what he proposed to do next; after reading the English papers and seeing the way he was handling his bayonet, it seemed to me that there was going to be another atrocity. He was extraordinarily kind and polite. He put something under my head; offered me wine, water, and cigarettes. He said: *"Wir sind kamaraden."*

Another soldier came up and said: "Why didn't you stay in England—you who made war upon the Boers?"

I said: "We obeyed orders, just as you do; as for the Boers, they were our enemies and are now our friends, and it is not your business to insult wounded men."

My first friend then cursed him heartily, and he moved on.

The Germans passed in crowds. They seemed like steel locusts. Every now and then I would hear: "Here is an officer who talks German," and the crowd would swerve in like a steel eddy. Then: *"Schnell Kinder!"* and they would be off.

They gave a tremendous impression of lightness and iron. After some hours, when my wound was beginning to hurt, some carriers came up to take me to a collecting place for the wounded. These men were rather rough. They dropped me and my stretcher once, but were cursed by an officer. They then carried me some distance, and took me off the stretcher, leaving me on the ground. The Germans continued to pass in an uninterrupted stream. One motor cyclist, but with a bayonet in his hand, was very unpleasant.

He said: "I would like to put this in your throat and turn it round and round," waving it down to my nose.

That sort of thing happened more than once or twice, but there were always more friends than enemies, though as night fell the chance of being left without friends increased. As it grew dark, I got rather cold. One of the Germans saw this, covered me with his coat, and said: "Wait a moment, I will bring you something else."

He went off, and, I suppose, stripped a dead Englishman and a dead German. The German jersey which he gave me had no holes in it; the Englishman's coat had two bayonet cuts.

The wounded began to cry dreadfully in the darkness. I found myself beside Robin, who was very badly wounded in the leg. The Germans gave me water when I asked for it, but every time I drank it made me sick. At, I suppose, 9.30 or 10 p.m. They took us off into an ambulance and carried us to a house that had been turned into a hospital. I was left outside, talking to a Dane, who was very anti-German, though he was serving with them as a Red Cross man. He cursed them loudly in German. He said it was monstrous that I hadn't been attended to, that the Germans had had a defeat, and would be beaten.

I said: "Yes, it's all true, but please stop talking, because they'll hear you and punish me."

Just before 12 o'clock they carried me into the hospital on to the operating table, and dressed my wound quickly.

Then I was helped out to an outhouse and lay beside Robin. It was full of English and German wounded. They gave us one drink of water and then shut and locked the door and left us for the night. One man cried and cried for water until he died. It was a horrible night. The straw was covered with blood, and there was never a moment when men were not groaning and calling for help. In the morning the man next to Robin went off his head and became animal with pain. I got the Germans to do what was possible for him. I asked the Germans to let me out, and they helped me outside into a chair, and I talked to an officer called Brandt. He sent a telegram to the German authorities to say that Robin and I were lightly wounded, and asking them to let our families know. He would not let me pay. I would have liked to have done it for everyone, but that wasn't possible.

They took us away in an ambulance at about 11 o'clock. It was a beautiful September day, very hot indeed. The heat in the covered ambulance was suffocating, and Robin must have suffered horribly. He asked me the German for "quick," and when I told him, urged the Germans on. There were great jolts and . . .

At Viviers I found Shields, who said to me: "Hello, you wounded, and you a volunteer, too?"—as if a volunteer ought to be immune form wounds.

We were carried upstairs and told that Valentine and Buddy, whom I had last met under the cedars, were in the same hospital. Valentine had the point of his elbow shot away just after I had left him. He raised his hand to brush a wasp off his neck, and only remembered pitching forward when a bullet struck his elbow. He woke up in a pool of blood. A German came up and took the flask of brandy that I had given him after my visit to Soissons. He gave Valentine a drink, and then, when Valentine had said he did not want any more, swigged the whole of the rest off. It was enough to make two men drunk, solidly, for hours. Later, five Germans came up to Valentine and ragged him. One of them kicked him, but an officer arrived, took all their names, promised Valentine they should be punished, and attached an orderly to him for the night. Buddy was badly wounded in the back and arm. He found his servant in the church at Viviers. Then we all met at the house in Viviers. The doctors gave Robin and me a strong dose of *morphia*. That afternoon a German doctor, whose name was Hillsparck, came in and woke me. He gave me a gold watch with a crest on it, and a silver watch and a purse of gold (£8 in it). He said that a colonel to whom the watch belonged had been buried close by in the village of Haraman, and asked me if I could say who he was. We heard that the colonel had been killed, and I imagined it must have been him, but we could not tell, as apparently every single man of the seventy odd who had charged with him had been killed. The doctor left this watch with me. In the hospital we believed that the general of the Division, Monro, and also our own Brigadier, General Scott Kerr, were wounded, and that the colonel and T. were killed.

Our experiences on the field were all the same. We were all well treated, though occasionally we were insulted. In hospital an old *ober-stadt* was in command of the doctors. He was very good to us. The English doctors were W., in command, S. next, Rankin and Shields. They were all good doctors. W., Rankin and Shields were excellent fellows. Rankin, who has been killed since, himself wounded, was dressing the wounded on the field and was recommended for the V.C. Shields has been killed in the same way, and I believe would have been recommended but that his C.O. was also killed. They were both the best sort of man you can find.

After a couple of days I moved into Buddy and Valentine's room. A little way down the street there was the *château*, full of wounded Germans. Our men were carried there to be operated upon.

W. and the other doctors who went to help discovered that there were 311 wounded Germans as against 92 of our own, so we didn't do badly.

Every morning the German sentries used to come in and talk to us. My German and Buddy's was very weak, but we managed to get along all right. Downstairs those who were lightly wounded sat outside in the chairs they took from the house, in the sunny garden. It was a fairly luxurious house, with paper marked "F.H." I thought it was a girls' school, for the only books we could find were the Berger de Valence and Jules Verne.

My side was painful the first few days. Then they cut me open and took out the bullet, which was all in bits. It was rather hard lines on the others to perform an operation in the room, but I felt much better for it. The food difficulty was rather acute. There was very little food, and what there was was badly cooked. We lived principally on things that S. called *chupatti*—thick, unleavened biscuits. The men began to give trouble. There was nobody in command of them. There was an ex-comedian who was particularly tiresome. We had to ask the Germans to punish one man for us. About the fourth day one of the orderlies escaped—Drummer McCoy. He passed for four days through the German lines, and on one occasion watched a whole army Corps go by from the boughs of a tree. Then he found the French, who passed him on to the English, where he went to the Staff and told them of us. That is how we were picked up so quickly on the 11th.

Here is a copy of my diary for September 9th:

The people are beginning to return, but not the priest, who is with the army. We want him for the regiment. Up till this time only six of the wounded have died. The Germans tell us every kind of story—the United States are declaring war on Japan, Italy on France, Denmark on England, etc. etc. Also that Paris has been given twelve hours to accept or reject the German terms, and if the French government is obdurate the town will be bombarded. We are told that we are to be taken as prisoners to Magdelburg. It is a week since I have had a cigarette.

*Thursday, September 10th,* we are all very anxious to get news home, but there is no chance. Last night S. Herbert died. I had a Testament, and Valentine and I found verses which W. Read over his grave. Valentine has bad pain. Three bones broken in his arm and the point of his elbow gone. Buddy is better, but hit cruel hard. Robin has a bad wound, and is very restless. They don't like giving us *morphia.* Luckily I have got my own medicine chest, which is a good thing for all of us, as I can give the others sleeping draughts. Last night a French cavalry patrol came within two miles of us. Early this morning there was rifle fire close by. It sounded in the wood that we suppose is Haraman. We think the Germans may evacuate this place at any time. The bandages have given out. Stores are not coming in. There is a big aeroplane depot quite close by, and the whole air is full of aeroplanes. It looks and feels as if there might be a big battle round here soon. They have shot an old man wandering about the aerodrome. But he was asking for it.

*9 a.m.* The aeroplanes are being shifted from the depot. Last night we heard that arms were issued to all the wounded Germans in hospital who could carry them. This morning the Germans are digging trenches hard. There are Red Crosses everywhere. The doctors want

43

us to go down to the cellars if we are shelled. The French women in the village say that the French are coming. The firing is increasing.

*9.15 a.m.* The German hospital across the way is ordered to be ready to move at once.

*10.25 a.m.* An order has come for all prisoners to parade at the church at 12 o'clock. The German lightly wounded are being sent on. We are very anxious as to whether they mean to take us, too. More of our wounded who have died are being buried.

*11.10 a.m.* A German doctor has come. He said: "They are going and taking all (of our) prisoners, 18 (of our) lightly wounded, and leaving 25 (of their) badly wounded." French wounded are now coming in. We have no more bandages at all. A German sentry with whom I had talked has just come in. I asked him some days ago to buy some handkerchiefs. He said: "I have not been able to buy you any handkerchiefs, or to get the cigarettes you wanted, but here is one of my own handkerchiefs, which I have washed. We have got to go."

*8 p.m.* The last order is that the previous orders are countermanded and the Germans are to stay on ten days.

*Friday, September 11th.* Our English prisoners were marched off this morning. We are full of speculation as to what has really happened. Valentine, Buddy, and I are well.

*10.10 a.m.* There are many machine guns about four miles away.

*10.30 a.m.* There is a heavy rifle fire within a mile. It is very trying lying here in bed. We have nothing to read except *The Rajah's Heir* which V. sent to me and which has become known as the treasure-house of fun. It is a sort of mixture of Hymns Ancient and Modern and the Fairchild Family.

2 p.m. There is a Maxim within a few hundred yards of the house. Rifle volleys outside in the garden. A rising wind and rain threatening.

*3 p.m..* Heavy rain. The French are visible, advancing.

*3.10 p.m.* The French are here. They came in in fine style, like conquerors; one man first, riding, his hand on his hip. The German sentries who had been posted to protect us wounded walked down and surrendered their bayonets. The German doctors came to us for help. I offered to go, but W. Went. The French infantry and cavalry came streaming through. Our wounded went out into the pouring rain to cheer them. They got water from our men whose hands they kissed. The German guns are on the skyline. The Germans are in full retreat, and said to be cut off by the English.

*5 p.m.* A heavy bombardment of the German guns began from here. I have come upstairs to a long low garret with skylights, in order to leave Valentine and Buddy more room. Through the skylight one can see every flash of the French and German guns. The doctors all come up here to watch with their field glasses through my skylights.

*Saturday, September 12th.* Yesterday, when W. went down, he found the German doctors receiving cavalier treatment from the French. He explained to the French that they had treated us with the greatest kindness; after that the French treated with courtesy the old ober-stadt. Shields carved a great wooden tombstone for the thirteen men who had died up to date. It is a month today since I left England.

This afternoon Colonel Thompson, English staff officer attached to General Manoury, who had been attached to the Serbian army through the last war, came in. McCoy, who had escaped, had found him and told him about us at Viviers. He said he would take me into Villers Cotterets after he had done some other business. We talked a lot about the Balkans, but I finally went back and lay down in my garret and shall not get up again today.

*Sunday, September 13th.* I went off with Thompson this morning. We passed through the wood where we had had the fight, and a long grave of 120 men was shown to me by McCoy.

# Anzac

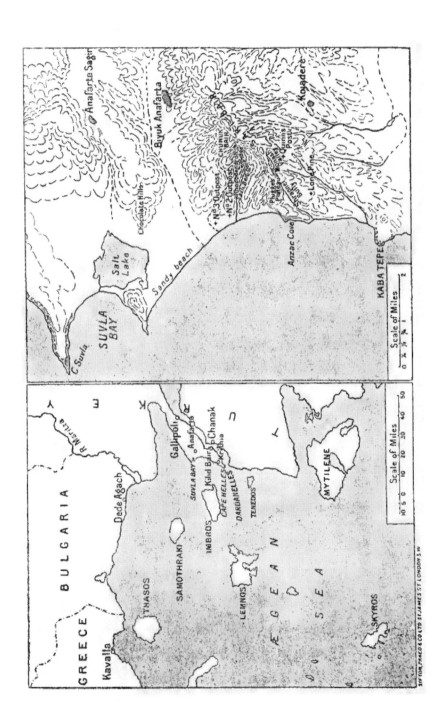

GREECE

BULGARIA

Kavalla

Dede Agach

THASOS

SAMOTHRAKI

IMBROS

LEMNOS

Gallipoli

Suvla B.

Anafarta

Kilid Bahr

CAPE HELLES

DARDANELLES

Chanak

Krithia

TENEDOS

MYTILENE

SKYROS

R. MARITZA

AEGEAN SEA

Scale of Miles
10 5 0    10   20   30   40   50

SIFTON, PRAED & CO LTD ST JAMES ST LONDON S W

SUVLA BAY

C. Suvla

Salt Lake

Sandy beach

Chocolate Hills

Anafarta Sagir

Byuk Anafarta

Anafarta

N° 3 Outpost
N° 2 Outpost
Chunuk
BAIR
Nek
Rhododendron
Spur

Chailak
Pope's Hill
Quinn's Post
Plateau 400
Lone Pine

Anzac Cove

Koyadere

KABA TEPE

Scale of Miles
0  ¼  ½  ¾  1            2

# Anzac, 1915

When I was passed fit for active service, after some time in hospital, I left England for Egypt with five other officers. Four of these had strange histories. One is, perhaps, the most romantic figure of the war, another now governs a great Province, while two, after many adventures, were prisoners of war in Turkey, for different but dreary periods.

I was sent to the East because it had been my fortune to have travelled widely, and I had a fairly fluent smattering of several Eastern languages. On arriving at Gilbraltar about December 14th, 1914, we heard the first news of submarines. One of these was reported to have passed through into the Mediterranean a few days previously.

When I reached Egypt just before Christmas, superficially everything was calm. This calm did not last very long. I was given intelligence work to do, under Colonel Clayton, who had played a very great part in achieving our success in the East. Reports constantly came in from Minia, Zagazig and Tanta of Turkish and German intrigues. General Sir J. Maxwell commanded the Forces in Egypt. Prince Hussein had just been proclaimed *sultan*, and Egypt had been declared to be under British protection. Rushdy Pasha was prime minister and triumvirate of Sir Milne Cheetham at the Residency, Sir R. Graham as Adviser to the Ministry of the Interior, and Lord Edward Cecil as Adviser to the Ministry of Finance, directed the government. It was difficult to believe that the Egyptian, who then had all the advantages, really meant mischief. Most people, I think, agreed with Lord Cromer, and believed that his policy of making taxes light and easy for the Egyptian had succeeded, but the East is never logical, as we all know, and the natural consequence constantly does not follow the parental cause. Mecca rose to join us after Kut had fallen; the rebellion in Egypt only took place when the English had achieved a complete victory over Turkey, and held Palestine and Syria. I quote the following incident as an illustration of the difficulty of sometimes following this mentality:

A Syrian reported to me that a great Egyptian family, whom I will call the Ashakas, had conspired to bring 15,000 rifles into the country and to engineer a rising. The rifles were to be imported from the Greek islands and from Greece, by means of Greek sponge-fishers. One of these, who had the pleasant and appropriate name of Son-of-the-Dagger, met me in a café in an obscure side street in Cairo. There he revealed the conspiracy, explaining that only the landing-place for the arms had still to be decided upon. He and his companions were to receive a commission on every rifle landed, and he wanted to know what the British government would be ready to pay for his betrayal of his patrons.

On reporting this to the proper authorities, I was told that they were aware of the existence of this plot. The next day frantic messages from the Greek came, and I met him, disturbed in his mind. He said that the Ashakas had become suspicious of him and the other Greeks, and that he feared for his life. He asked to be arrested immediately after the seizure of the arms and thrown into prison with the Egyptians, and then to be flogged before them, in order to convince them that he was acting honourably by them. He was very anxious to be paid for both pieces of treachery, by the Egyptians and by us. On making my report to the authorities I learned that the Ashakas had betrayed the Greeks by denouncing them as traitors.

The whole affair had been a result of Levantine nerves. The Ashakas in the past had been strong Nationalists. When the war between the Turks and ourselves broke out, in spite of the fact that it seemed possible, and indeed likely, that Egypt might again become a Turkish province, their politics changed, and they hastily became Anglophile, but their past record haunted them. They feared the British government almost as much as the Turks, and yearned to prove themselves loyal.

After much thought it appeared to them that the simplest way of achieving this would be to supply valuable military information to the British. That, however, was an article which they did not possess, and they therefore hit upon the idea of getting up a bogus conspiracy in order to be able to denounce it. This seemed the simplest way to safeguard themselves, and they hurriedly adopted the plan. The instruments that they chose were subtle Greeks, who were more proficient in the art of intrigue than the Ashakas, and had an even more degraded morality. It took only a few days for the Ashakas to realized the infidelity of the Greeks, and to inform against them still more hurriedly, but meanwhile the Greeks had spoken first. In the end, when the hair of the Ashakas had turned grey, they made a clean breast of the whole affair to the British authorities, and were, I believe, forgiven.

*"Happy is the country that has no history"* is a proverb which is often untrue, but Egypt was certainly happy, compared with the rest of the world, early in 1915. Then history moved rapidly towards us. The thunder of the guns in France was no longer something removed and irrelevant. The Turks massed across the desert, and prepared to attack the canal. Many of the English thought that we were living on a sleeping volcano, but there was general confidence, and no one doubted our power to cope with the situation. The Turks attacked skilfully and bravely, but the odds against them were too heavy. They were, however, able to shell H.M.S. *Harding* in the canal, and a few of their men swam across to Egypt. Complete serenity reigned in Cairo. I remember going to the opera that night. General Sir John Maxwell was listening, quite unruffled, to the performance. I heard a civilian say in a scandalized voice to him: "They have gone and broken the *Harding*. What next?"

To which Sir John answered: "Well, they'll have to mend it, I suppose."

Two ladies landed at Port Said and had their train shelled as it steamed slowly along the banks of the canal to Cairo. They wondered placidly if this was the normal state of things in Egypt.

These attacks added to the labours and quickened the energies of the intelligence in Egypt, but still there were only vague rumours to be heard. One of these foretold that there was to be a general rising of Islam on April 27th.

I remember long conversations with a specialist with regard to this possibility; he disbelieved in it, then or at any time, for, as he said very rightly, Islam had to contend with great difficulties from the point of view of communications—waterless deserts, impassable seas, mountain ranges, unbridged by our telegraph. My friend, who was remarkable, would not have an office like any other man in his position; he disconcerted friend and foe alike by changing his address every few days, and when one wished to see him, and after the unusual event of catching him, he would make an appointment such as: *"The third lamp-post in the Street of Mohammed Ali at dusk."* When he had gone beyond recall, one remembered that the Mohammed Ali Street was several miles long, and that he had not said at which end was the appointed lamp-post; so he was well qualified to speak of the disadvantages accruing from lack of communications.

Prisoners began coming in, but not much was to be obtained from them. They were mostly shattered and rather pathetic men. The first to arrive were some escaped Syrian schoolmasters, who had been conscripted by the Turks, and gave a very graphic account of a hot and harassing journey ahead of their comrades to Egypt, where their friends and relations lived. Then came a blind old gentleman of eighty, who fell into our front-line trench. It had been his habit, every two years, to visit his son in Egypt, and he had not realized that there was a war going on.

Amongst the Turkish prisoners of the first attack there was one old quartermaster seriously ill, whose manners and courage made him the friend of all his captors, but, like the rest, he told us nothing. There was probably more information amongst the prisoners who had been interned, if they had been willing to speak, but they were not. I met one of these to whom fate had been unusually cruel. He was an Albanian whose home had been in Montenegro. When the amiable Montenegrins seized the land of the Albanians, he had been beaten and cast out; thence he had gone to Turkey, but the Albanians had been the first to attack the Turks, and were, indeed, the main cause of the ruin of the Ottoman Empire, so in Turkey he was *bastinadoed* and thrown into prison. Somehow he managed to escape and arrived in Egypt. In Egypt he was arrested as a Turk, and again thrown into prison. In prison he was continually beaten by his fellow-prisoners, who were Turks, as an Albanian and an enemy of Islam.

There were no tangible proofs of a conspiracy; one used sometimes to get black looks in the bazaar, and scowls from the class of the Effendis. On the other hand, we were very strongly supported by men of the type of the late *sultan* Hussein and Adly Yeghen Pasha.

It would be difficult to meet a more attractive or courteous gentleman than the late *sultan*. He was of the advanced school of enlightened Islam; neither his literary tastes, his philosophy, nor his pleasure in European society allowed him to forget his own people for a moment. Adly Yeghen Pasha, then Minister of Education, is an exceptional and outstanding figure in Egypt, with a marked personality. The other Ministers mixed freely with European society, and there was no sign of anything but friendliness.

At the end of February I was sent on the battleship *Bacchante*, commanded by Captain Boyle, which lay for about a fortnight off Alexandretta, occasionally bombarding telegraphs, or wagons that were said to be loaded with artillery wheels. One morning we saw two carts crawling along, drawn by bullocks, carrying the alleged wheels of artillery northward from Alexandretta. In order to warn the two drivers shells were fired from the great battleship a hundred yards ahead of them. The men left their oxen, taking refuge in a neighbouring ditch, while the oxen went slowly forward alone, like automata. Our guns then fired upon the carts, which were about half a mile distant, and one of the oxen was immediately hit. On this one of the two Turks left the ditch, cut the wounded animal free, and continued to lead the two carts. Again our guns fired ahead of him to give him warning, but he went on steadfastly at about a mile an hour to what was certain death. In the end he was left lying by his dead oxen and his broken cart. We had given him every chance that we could, and if the admiration of a British ship for his courage could reward a dead Anatolian muleteer, that reward was his.

Life outside Alexandretta was uneventful. Occasionally a Turkish official came out to discuss various questions that arose. He used to sway and bow from the tiller of his boat while I swayed and bowed from the platform below the gangway of the cruiser. It is perhaps worth saying that when I expressed to him Captain Boyle's regret for the death of the Turkish muleteer it was an event that he would not condescend to notice.

We discovered one curious fact of natural history, that with a searchlight you can see the eyes of dogs or jackals at night more than half a mile away. A previous ship had reported that men came down to the shore with electric torches, and it was only after some days that we discovered that these will-o'-the-wisp appearances were in reality the eyes of dogs.

But though life was uneventful, it was very pleasant on the ship, and all were sorry when the cruise came to an end.

I remember the last night at dinner in the wardroom the name of a distinguished Admiral occurred in the conversation. He was a man who had a great reputation for capacity and also eccentricity, that came mainly from his habit of concentrated thinking. When he was deep in thought and his eyes caught any bright object, he would go up to it like a magpie and play with it. He would sometimes to up and fiddle with the button of a junior officer on the quarter-deck, looking at it very attentively, to the great discomfort of the junior officer, or even with that of a stranger to whom he had been introduced. The legend grew from this idiosyncrasy, that those may believe who wish to. It was said that one night at a dance he sat out for a long time with a girl in a black dress. His eye caught a white thread on her shoulder, and unconsciously while he talked he began pulling at it. The story goes on to say that when the girl went home she said to her mother: "I know I went out with a vest tonight, and now I wonder what has happened to it."

I remember at the same dinner Dr. Levick, who had been with Captain Scott in the Antarctic voyage, told a curious story of prophecy. He had been to a fortune-teller after the idea of going with Captain Scott had occurred to him, but before he had taken any steps. The fortune-teller gave a description of the melancholy place where he was to live for two years, of the unknown men who were to be his companions, and particularly one who had strangely flecked hair.

I returned to Cairo and office work with some reluctance. Friends of mine and I took a house, which somehow managed to run itself, in Gezireh. It was covered with Bougainvillea and flowers of every colour, and was a delight to see. Sometimes it lacked servants completely, and at other times there was a black horde. Gardeners sprang up as if by enchantment, and made things grow almost before one's eyes.

I quote from my diary of March 8th, 1915:

News today that King Constantine won't have Greece come in, and that Venizelos has resigned. At a guess, this means that either Greece of King Constantine is lost. If Constantine goes, Venizelos might shepherd his son through his minority.

*March 14th.* I left Luxor Tuesday night, after a wonderful time. My guide was a Senoussi—something-or-other Galleel. He had a tip of white turban hanging, which he said was a sign of his people. He was rather like one of the Arabs out of a Hichens book, and I expect about as genuine. A snake-charmer came with us. He gave me the freedom of the snakes as a man is given the freedom of a city, but as one scorpion and two snakes—one of them a so-to-speak *soi-disant* cobra—stung and bit him during the day, it's not likely to be of much help to me. He did some very mysterious things, and called snakes from every kind of place—one from a window in the wall, a five-foot long cobra, and a Coptic cook found its old skin in the next window.

In justice to the snake-charmer it ought to be said that he was only stung and bitten as a consequence of a quarrel with an archaeologist.

In Egypt every archaeologist looks upon the local magician or

snake-charmer as his competitor, and hates him. When the archaeologist is telling the tourist the history of Ramesis II the attention of the
tourist is distracted by a half-naked man doing the mango trick. My
archaeologist friend, irritated by the presence of the snake-charmer,
declared that his snakes were all doped and his scorpions were tame
town scorpions, green, and not yellow like the country scorpions. He
found a bucolic scorpion under a stone, of the proper colour, which
instantly stung the snake-charmer; he then insisted upon stirring up
his snakes with a stick, with the unfortunate results that have already
been mentioned.

The Egyptian has always seemed to me harder to understand than
his neighbours. It may be because there is less in him to understand.
The Greeks, Turks, and Arabs have all got very salient characteristic
qualities, but though the characteristics of the Egyptians are probably as strongly marked, they are less conspicuous to the foreigner's
eye; in other words, the Egyptian has less in common with the outer
world than any of the Asiatic, of even African, peoples who surround
him. Lane, in his Modern Egyptians, says that they refused to believe
that the ordinary traveller was not an agent for the government,
because they could not understand the desire for travel, and their
character had not changed since his day. Here is a story of Egyptian
guile and credulity:

An Egyptian was anxious to get some job profitable to himself
done, and he went to one of the kavasses (guards) at the Agency for
advice. The kavass professed himself able to help. He said: "The man
for you to go to is Mr.. Jones, that high English official. He will get
what you want done, but I warn you that Mr.. Jones is an expensive
man. Give me three hundred pounds, and I will see what can be
done." The three hundred pounds was duly paid, and for a long time
nothing happened. The petitioner grew impatient and importunate,
and was eventually satisfied for the moment by an invitation to lunch
with a Levantine who passed himself off as Mr. Jones. At luncheon
the Levantine, who was of German extraction, wore his hat, banged
his fist on the table, smoked a pipe, interrupted, and generally acted as
an Englishman abroad is supposed by some to behave. Then occurred
an interval of inaction; the petitioner again grew restive, and this time
complained to the authorities. Finally the transaction was discovered,
and the kavass was sent to gaol.

Events moved in Egypt. The Australian and New Zealand troops
poured in, and splendid men they were. But there was little love lost

between the Australians and the Egyptians, though the British troops and the natives fraternized occasionally. The native Egyptian was, it must be admitted, constantly very roughly treated, for the average Australian, while he was at first apt to resent superiority in others, felt little doubt about his own claim to it. The Australian and New Zealand Corps was commanded by General Birdwood, and the New Zealand and Australian Division by General Godley.

I joined the New Zealand Division as interpreter and intelligence officer, and we all made preparations to start early in April. I was anxious to buy a beautiful snow-white Arab, that had won most of the races at Cairo, from a friend of mine, but General Godley spoke simply but firmly. "You aren't the Duke of Marlborough," he said. "You can't have that white pony unless he's dyed, and even then it would wash off in any rainstorm. You may get yourself shot, but not me."

I agreed with the less reluctance because I had found that the pony pulled furiously and would certainly lead any advance or retreat by many miles. The day for our departure approached. The golden sunlight and tranquillity of Egypt was tragic in its contrast to what was coming.

Every intelligence officer was a Cassandra with an attentive audience. In every discussion there was, as far as I saw, unanimity between military, naval, and political officers, who all wished the landing to take place at Alexandretta, and deplored (not to use a stronger word) the project of the Dardanelles, which the Turks had been given ample time to fortify.

The heat increased and the English officers' wives, who had come to Egypt to be with their husbands, were given a taste of a ferocious *khamsin* that affected their complexions. In the spring of 1915 this wind came in waves and gusts of lurid heat. It was like a Nessus shirt, scorching the skin and making slow fire of one's blood. After the *khamsin*, which had the one advantage of killing insects with its heat, locusts came. They made a carpet on the ground and a shadow against the sun. Life was intolerable out of doors, and they followed one into the recesses of the house. A friend of mine said to me: "What on earth had they got to grumble about in Egypt in the time of the Pharaohs? They had one plague at a time then; we are having all the lot at once."

I quote from my diary:

Yesterday I saw Todd, who had been on the Annie Rickmers when she was torpedoed off Smyrna. The crew was Greek. There were five

Englishmen on board, and a good many wounded. The Greeks were all off at once, taking all the boats. They had no interpreter with them. He said the English in Smyrna were angry at being bombarded, and came aboard with Rahmy Bey, the *vali*, to complain. Rahmy was always Anglophile.

Early in April Sir Ian Hamilton came and went. He had a great review of the troops in the desert on a glorious day. It was a splendid sight, and one I should have enjoyed better if I had not been riding a mountainous roan horse that bolted through the glittering Staff.

Many old friends, Ock Asquith, Patrick Shaw-Stewart, Charles Lister and Rupert Brooke, had come out to Egypt in the Naval Division, and we lunched, dined, and went to the Pyramids by moonlight.

The first week in April we made our preparations for leaving, and I went to say goodbye to native friends. One of them was an old Albanian Abbot of the Bektashi sect, whose monastery was in the living rock in a huge cave behind the Mokattan Hills. He had a fine face and a venerable beard, and I spent much time talking to him, drinking his coffee, by a fountain in the cool garden outside his home. I was sorry to say goodbye to the delightful Zoo in Cairo, with the hawks calling unceasingly in the sunlight, and a hundred different birds. Another pleasure there was Said, an attractive and intellectual hippopotamus, who performed a number of tricks.

On April 10th I went to Alexandria to report aboard the German prize-ship *Lutzow*, and on the 12th we sailed. We discovered that night at dinner that the puritanical New Zealand government had ordained that this boat should be a dry one, but it made no difference to our mess, which was very pleasant. On April 13th we made a new discovery, that the boat was even drier than we expected, as there was not enough water, and the men had to shave in salt water. On April 15th we came into Lemnos Harbour, with a keen wind and a rustling deep blue sea, and white-crested waves, with cheer on cheer from French and English warships, from German prizes with British crews, from submarines, and even from anchored balloons.

The next day I went ashore with a couple of other officers to buy donkeys, who were to carry our kits. Mudros was not too bad a town, and was a very curious spectacle in those days. There were great black Senegalese troops with filed teeth who chased the children in play, though if the children had known what their home habits were the games would probably have ceased abruptly.

There were Greeks dressed in fantastic costume and British troops of all sorts. Many old friends from the East were there, among them Colonel Doughty Wylie, who in a few days was to win his V.C. and lose a life of great value to his country.

I met a friend, Bettelheim, nicknamed "Beetle," whose life had been one long adventure. When last I had seen him he had been an official in Turkey, and in a rising had been dragged from his carriage on Galata Bridge in Constantinople by the mob, with his companion, the Emir Arslan. Emir Arslan was torn to pieces, but "Beetle," with his marvellous luck, escaped.

Many of us lunched together under a vine, drinking excellent wine at a penny a glass. Everybody was extremely cheerful, and there was great elation in the island air. The talk was, of course, about the landing. A friend of mine said: "This is a terrible business; entire staffs will be wiped out."

He seemed to think that the staffs were the most important thing.

After lunch I went to see the mayor, to help me buy all that I wanted. He was rather shaky with regard to his own position, as Lemnos had not yet been recognized by us as Greek, and our recognition was contingent on the behaviour of the Greek government. He was a very good linguist, talking French, a little English, Italian, Greek, Turkish, and Arabic. I think it was he who quoted to me the story of the Khoja Nasr-ed-Din. Nasr-ed-Din was lent a saucepan by a friend; he returned it with another small saucepan, saying it had produced a child. Next year the friend offered a huge saucepan at the same date, which the friend considered the breeding-time of saucepans. Later on, when his friend applied for the return of the saucepan, Nasr-ed-Din said: "It is dead."

His friend expostulated: "How can a saucepan die?"

"Well," said Nasr-ed-Din, "if it can have a child, why can't it die?"

Lemnos itself, though then it was a pageant, is on the whole a dreary island. The land was green, as all lands are in the spring, but there was not the carpet of anemones that one finds in Crete, Cyprus, and other islands, nor was there even asphodel.

On Friday, April 16th, we heard that the *Manitou* had been torpedoed, and that a number of men had been drowned. This was not the case, though she had had three torpedoes fired at her.

At this time we believed that we were to make three simultaneous attacks, the New Zealanders taking the centre of the Peninsula. A rather melancholy call to arms was issued by General Birdwood, the pith of which was that for the first few days there would be no transport of any kind. This made it all the more necessary to obtain the donkeys, and with the help of the mayor of Mudros I bought six, and one little one for £1 as a mascot. It was a great deal of trouble getting them on board. The Greek whose boat I had commandeered was very unfriendly, and I had to requisition the services of some Senegalese troops.

*Diary. April 21st, 1915.* Mudros. Inner Bay. Monday, the 19th, I tried to dine on H.M.S. *Bacchante,* but failed to find her. Dined on the *Arcadia.* Came back with Commodore Keyes. . . . Met ——— (a journalist turned censor). He said that the Turks had thirty 15-inch howitzers on Gallipoli, also wire entanglements everywhere. The general impression is that we shall get a very bad knock, and that it may set the war back a year, besides producing an indefinite amount of trouble in the East.

*Tuesday, April 20th.* I went ashore to get porters, but the mayor was in a nervous state, and I failed. I tried to get back in a dinghy with a couple of Greeks, and we nearly got swamped. A gale got up. Finally made the *Imogen,* tied up by the *Hussar,* and at last reached my destination. Great gale in the night. I hope we don't suffer the fate of the Armada. It is said that our orders are to steam for the outer harbour at once.

It was curious to see the *Imogen,* once the Ambassador's yacht at Constantinople. In those days she was treated with reverent care. The Mediterranean had to be calmed by the finest weather before she travelled. Now she had to sink or swim with the rest. Her adventures did not end at Lemnos. Travellers may see her name written proudly on the harsh cliffs of Muscat in the Persian Gulf, and today she is probably at Kurna, the site of the Garden of Eden.

On Thursday, April 22nd, I was able to get two Greek porters, Kristo Keresteji (which being interpreted means Kristo the Timber-merchant) and Yanni, of the little island of Ayo Strati. Kristo was with me until I was invalided in the middle of October. He showed the greatest fidelity and courage after the first few days. The other man was a natural coward, and had to be sent away when an opportunity offered, after the landing.

*Diary. Friday April 23rd.* I have just seen the most wonderful procession of ships I shall ever see. In the afternoon we left for the outer harbour. The wind was blowing; there was foam upon the sea and the air of the island was sparkling. With the band playing and flags flying, we steamed past the rest of the fleet. Cheers went from one end of the harbour to the other. Spring and summer met. Everybody felt it more than anything that had gone before.

After we had passed the fleet, the pageant of the fleet passed us. First the *Queen Elizabeth*, immense, beautiful lines, long, like a snake, straight as an arrow. This time there was silence. It was grim and very beautiful. We would rather have had the music and the cheers. . . . This morning instructions were given to the officers and landing arrangements made. We leave at 1.30 tonight. The Australians are to land first. This they should do tonight. Then we land. . . . Naval guns will have to cover our advance, and the men are to warned that the naval fire is very accurate. They will need some reassuring if the fire is just over their heads. The 29th land at Helles, the French in Asia near Troy. This is curious, as they can't support us or we them. the Naval Division goes north and makes a demonstration. . . . The general opinion is that very many boats must be sunk from the shore. Having got ashore, we go on to a rendezvous. We have no native guides. . . . The politicians are very unpopular.

The sea was very quiet between Lemnos and Anzac on April 24th. There were one or two alterations in plans, but nothing very material. We expected to have to land in the afternoon, but this was changed, and we were ordered to land after the Australians, who were to attack at 4.30 a.m. Some proposed to get up to see the first attack at dawn. I thought that we should see plenty of the attack before we had done with it, and preferred to sleep.

*Diary. Sunday, April 25th.* I got up at 6.30. Thoms, who shared my cabin, had been up earlier. There was a continuous roll of thunder from the south. Opposite to us the land rose steeply in cliffs and hills covered with the usual Mediterranean vegetation. The crackle of rifles sounded and ceased in turns. . . . Orders were given to us to start at 8.30 a.m. . . . The tows were punctual. . . . We were ordered to take practically nothing but rations. I gave my sleeping-bag to Kyriakidis, the old Greek interpreter whom I had snatched from the *Arcadia*, and took my British warm and my Burberry. . . . The tow was unpleasantly open to look at; there was naturally no shelter of any kind. We all packed in, and were towed across the shining sea towards the land fight. . . . We could see some still figures lying on the beach to our left, one or two in front. Some bullets splashed round.

As we were all jumping into the sea to flounder ashore, I heard cries from the sergeant at the back of the tow. He said to me: "These two men refuse to go ashore." I turned and saw Kristo Keresteji and Yanni of Ayo Strati with mesmerized eyes looking at the plops the bullets made in the water, and with their minds evidently fixed on the Greek equivalent of "Home, Sweet Home." They were, however, pushed in, and we all scrambled on to that unholy land. The word was then, I thought rather unnecessarily, passed that we were under fire.

It was difficult to understand why the Turkish fire developed so late. If they had started shelling us during our landing as they shelled us later, our losses would have been very heavy. We frequently owed our salvation in the Peninsula to a Turkish weakness and a Turkish mistake. They were constantly slow to appreciate a position and take full advantage of it, and their shrapnel was generally fused too high. Hardly any man who landed escaped being thumped and bumped on different occasions by shrapnel, which would, of course, have killed or seriously wounded him if the burst had not been so high. I remember on the afternoon of the first landing a sailor was knocked down beside me, and I and another man carried him to what shelter there was. We found that, while the bullet had pierced his clothes, it had not even broken his skin. Said the sailor: "This is the third time that that's 'appened to me today. I'm beginning to think of my little grey 'ome in the West."

So were others.

We had landed on a spit of land which in those days we called Shrapnel Point, to the left of what afterwards became Corps headquarters, though later the other spit on the right usurped that name. I took cover under a bush with a New Zealand officer, Major Browne. This officer had risen from the ranks. He fought through the whole of the Gallipoli campaign, and in the end, to the sorrow of all who knew him, was killed as a Brigadier in France.

The shrapnel fire became too warm to be pleasant, and I said: "Major, a soldier's first duty is to save his life for his country." He said: "I quite agree, but I don't see how it's to be done." We were driven from Shrapnel Point to the north, round the cliff, but were almost immediately driven back again by the furious fire that met us.

*Diary.* We were being shot at from three sides. All that morning we kept moving. There were lines of men clinging like cockroaches under the cliffs or moving silently as the guns on the right or left enfiladed us. They only thing to be done was to dig in as soon as position, but a good many men were shot while they were doing this. General Godley landed about twelve, and went up Monash Gully with General Birdwood. We remained on the beach. . . . We had no artillery to keep the enemy's fire down.

We spent a chilly night, sometimes lying down, sometimes walking, as the rain began to fall after dark, and we had not too much food. My servant, Jack, who was a very old friend, and I made ourselves as comfortable as we could.

There was a great deal of inevitable confusion. We were very hard pressed; as every draft landed it was hurried off to that spot in the line where reinforcements were most needed. This naturally produced chaos amongst the units, and order was not re-established for some time. It was a terrible night for those in authority. I believe that, had it been possible, we should have re-embarked that night, but the sacrifices involved would have been too great. Preparations for the expedition had been totally inadequate. The chief R.A.M.C. officer had told me the ridiculously small number of casualties he had been ordered to make preparations for, and asked my opinion, which I gave him with some freedom. As it was, we had to put 600 men on the ship from which we had disembarked in the morning, to go back to hospital in Egypt, a four days' journey, under the charge of one officer, who was a veterinary surgeon.

*Diary. Monday, April 26th.* At 5 o'clock yesterday our artillery began to land. It's a very rough country; the Mediterranean *macchia* everywhere, and steep, winding valleys. We slept on a ledge a few feet above the beech. . . . Firing went on all night. In the morning it was very cold, and we were all soaked. The navy, it appeared, had landed us in the wrong place. This made the army extremely angry, though as things turned out it was the one bright spot. Had we landed anywhere else, we should have been wiped out.

I believe the actual place decided on for our landing was a mile further south, which was an open plain, and an ideal place for a hostile landing from the Turkish point of view.

Next morning I walked with General Godley and Tahu Rhodes,

his A.D.C., up the height to the plateau which was afterwards called Plugges Plateau. The gullies and ravines were very steep, and covered with undergrowth. We found General Walker, General Birdwood's Chief of Staff, on the ridge that bears his name. Bullets were whining about, through the undergrowth, but were not doing much harm, though the shelling on the beach was serious.

*Diary.* We believed that the Turks were using 16-inch shells from the Dardanelles, and we were now able to reply. The noise was deafening, and our firing knocked down our own dugouts. The generals all behaved as if the whole thing was a tea-party. Their different Staffs looked worried for their chiefs and themselves. Generals Godley and Walker were the most reckless, but General Birdwood also went out of his way to take risks. The sun was very hot, and our clothes dried while the shrapnel whistled over us into the sea.

At noon we heard the rumour that the 29th were fighting their way up from Helles, and everybody grew happy. We also heard that two Brigadiers had been wounded and one killed.

The Australians had brought with them two ideas, which were only eliminated by time, fighting, and their own good sense. The "eight hours' day" was almost a holy principle, and when they had violated it by holding on for two or three days heroically, they thought that they deserved a "spell." Their second principle was not to leave their pals. When a man was wounded his friends would insist upon bringing him down, instead of leaving him to the stretcher-bearers. When they had learned the practical side of war, both these dogmas were jettisoned. In Egypt the Australians had human weaknesses, and had shown them; in Gallipoli they were the best of companions. Naturally, with the New Zealand Division, I saw more of the New Zealanders, who had the virtues of the Australians and the British troops. They had all the dash and *élan* of the Australians and the discipline of the Englishmen.

*Diary. Tuesday, April 27th.* Last night, or rather this morning at about 1 o'clock, I was called up by C. He said: "We are sending up 40,000 rounds of ammunition to Colonel Pope." Greek donkey-boys, with an Indian escort, were to go up with this ammunition. I asked if any officer was going, and was answered "No:" that there was no officer to go. I said that I would go if I could get a guide, but that I did not talk Hindustani, and that the whole thing was risky, as we were just as likely without a guide to wander into the Turks as to find our own people; also that if we were attacked we should be without means of communicating, and that the Greeks would certainly bolt. At the Corps headquarters I found an absolutely gaga officer. He had an A.D.C. Who was on the spot, however, and produced a note from Colonel Pope which stated that he had all the ammunition he wanted. The officer, in spite of this, told me to carry on. I said it was nonsense without a guide, when Pope had his ammunition. He then told me to take the mules to one place and the ammunition to another. I said that I had better take them both back to my headquarters, from which I had come. He then tried to come with me, after saying that he would put me under arrest, but fell over two tent-ropes and was nearly kicked by a mule, and gave up in mute despair.

I may add that this officer was sent away shortly afterwards. The next night he was found with a revolver stalking one of the Staff officers, who was sleeping with a nightcap that looked like a turban, to shelter his head from the dew. My persecutor said that he thought he was a Turk.

*Diary.* Three of us slept crowded in one dug-out on Monday night. The cliff is becoming like a rookery, with ill-made nests. George Lloyd and Ian Smith have a charming view, only no room to lie down in. Everybody's dug-out is falling on his neighbour's head. I went round the corner of the cliff to find a clean place to wash in the sea, but was sniped, and had to come back quick. The Gallipoli Division of Turks, 18,000 strong, is supposed to be approaching, while we listened to a great artillery duel not far off. An Armenian who was captured yesterday reported the Gallipoli Division advancing on us. On Tuesday night things were better. I think most men were then of the opinion that we ought to be able to hold on, but we were clinging by our eyelids on to the ridge. The confusion of units and the great losses in officers increased the difficulty.

This was the third day of battle. My dugout was twice struck. A tug was sunk just in front of us. . . . The interpreters have all got three days' beards which are turning white from worry. The shells today did not do so much damage; they whirled over us in coveys, sometimes hitting the beach and flying off singing, sometimes splashing in the sea, but a lot of dead and wounded were carried by.

About this time the spy mania started, which is one of the inevitable concomitants of war. Spies were supposed to be everywhere. In the popular belief, that is "on the beach," there were enough spies to have made an opera. The first convincing proof of treachery which we had was the story of a Turkish girl who had painted her face green in order to look like a tree, and had shot several people at Helles from the boughs of an oak. Next came the story of the daily pigeon post from Anzac to the Turkish lone; but as a matter of fact, the pigeons were about their own business of nesting.

We had with us, too, a remarkable body of men who were more than suspect, and whose presence fed the wildest rumours. These were called Zionists, Zionites, and many other names. They were the Jewish exiles from Syria, who looked after the mules, and constituted the Mule Corps, under Colonel Patterson, of lion-hunting fame. They performed very fine service, and gave proof of the greatest courage. On several occasions I saw the mules blown to bits, and the men of the Mule Corps perfectly calm, among their charges. One night it did seem to me that at last we had got the genuine article. A panting Australian came to say that they had captured a German disguised as a member of the Mule Corps, but that he had unfortunately killed one man before being taken. When I examined this individual he gave his name as Fritz Sehmann, and the language in which we conversed most easily was German. He was able to justify himself himself in his explanation, which turned out to be true. He had been walking along the cliff at night with his mule, when the mule had been shot and fallen over the cliff with Fritz Sehmann. Together they had fallen upon an unfortunate soldier, who had been killed by the same burst.

It was work of some difficulty to explain to the Colonial troops that many of the prisoners that we took—as, for instance, Greeks and Armenians—were conscripts who hated their masters. On one occasion, speaking of a prisoner, I said to a soldier: "This man says he is a Greek, and that he hates the Turks."

"That's a likely story, that is," said the soldier; "better put a bayonet in the brute."

The trouble that we had with the native interpreters is even now a painful memory. If they were arrested once a day, they were arrested ten times. Those who had anything to do with them, if they were not suspected of being themselves infected by treachery, were believed to be in some way unpatriotic. It was almost as difficult to persuade the officers as the men that the fact that a man knew Turkish did not make him a Turk. There was one moment when the interpreters were flying over the hills like hares.

*Diary. Wednesday, April 28th.* I got up at 4 a.m. This morning, after a fine, quiet night, and examined a Greek deserter form the Turkish army. He said many would desert if they did not fear for their lives. The New Zealanders spare their prisoners.

Last night, while he was talking to me, Colonel C. was hit by a bit of shell on his hat. He stood quite still while a man might count three, wondering if he was hurt. He then stooped down and picked it up. At 8 p.m. last night there was furious shelling in the gully. Many men and mules hit. General Godley was in the Signalling Office, on the telephone, fairly under cover. I was outside with Pinwell, and got grazed, just avoiding the last burst. Their range is better. Before this they have been bursting the shrapnel too high. It was after 4 p.m. Their range improved so much. My dugout was shot through five minutes before I went there. So was Shaw's. . . . Colonel Chaytor was knocked down by shrapnel, but not hurt. The same happened to Colonel Manders. We heard that the Indian troops were to come tonight. Twenty-three out of twenty-seven Auckland officers killed and wounded.

*11 a.m.* All firing except from Helles has ceased. Things look better. The most the men can do is to hang on. General Godley has been very fine. The men know it.

*4.30 p.m.* Turks suddenly reported to have mounted huge howitzer on our left flank, two or three miles away. We rushed all the ammunition off the beach, men working like ants, complete silence and furious work. We were absolutely enfiladed, and they could have pounded us, mules and machinery, to pulp, or driven us into the gully and up the hill, cutting us off from our water and at the same time attacking us with shrapnel. The ships came up and fired on the new gun, and proved either that it was a dummy or had moved, or had been knocked out. It was a cold, wet night.

The material which General Birdwood and General Godley had to work upon was very fine. The Australians and the New Zealanders were born fighters and natural soldiers, and learnt quickly on active service what it would have taken months of training to have taught them. But like many another side-show, Anzac was casual in many ways, as the following excerpt from this diary will show:

*Diary. Thursday, April 29th.* Kaba Tepé. I was woken at 2.30 a.m., when the New Zealanders stood to arms. It was wet and cold, and a wind blew which felt as if it came through snowy gorges. The alarm had been given, and the Turks were supposed to be about to rush the beach from the left flank in force. Colonel Chaytor was sent to hold the point. He told me to collect stragglers and form them up. It was very dark, and the stragglers were very straggly. I found an Australian, Quinn, and told him to fetch his men along to the gun emplacement, beyond the graves, on the point where Chaytor was. Everyone lost everyone.

I found Colonel Chaytor with an Australian officer. He said to me: "Go out along the flank and find out where the Canterbury Battalion is, and how strong. On the extreme left there is a field ambulance. They must be told to lie down, so that the Turks will not shoot them." I said I would look after them. We started. I heard the Australian, after we had gone some hundred yards, ordering the Canterburys in support to retire. I said: "But are your orders to that effect? A support is there to support. The Canterburys will be routed or destroyed if you take this support away." He said: "Well, that's a bright idea." He went back, and I heard him say, in the darkness: "This officer thinks you had better stay where you are." I don't know if he was a colonel, or what he was, and he did not know what I was.

I found the field ambulance, a long way off, and went on to the outposts. The field ambulance were touchingly grateful for nothing, and I had some tea and yarned with them till morning, walking back after dawn along the beach by the graves. No one fired at me.

When I got back I heard the news of Doughty's death, which grieved me a great deal. . . . He seems to have saved the situation. The description of Helles is ghastly, of the men looking down into the red sea, and the dying drowned in a foot of water. That is what might have, and really ought to have happened to us.

One hears the praise of politicians in all men's mouths. . . .

A beautiful night, last night, and a fair amount of shrapnel. Every evening now they send over a limited number of howitzers from the great guns in the Dardanelles, aimed at our ships. That happens also in the early morning, as this morning. Tonight an aeroplane is to locate these guns, and when they let fly tomorrow we are to give them an immense broadside from all our ships.

At this time the weather had improved, but we were living in a good deal of discomfort. We were not yet properly supplied with stores, the water was brackish, occasionally one had to shave in salt water, and all one's ablutions had to be done on the beach, with the permission of the Turkish artillery.

The beach produced a profound impression on almost all of us, and has in some cases made the seaside distasteful for the rest of our lives. It was, when we first landed, I suppose, about 30 yards broad, and covered with shingle. Upon this narrow strip depended all our communications: landing and putting off, food and water, all came and went upon the beach—and the Turkish guns had got the exact range. Later, shelters were put up, but life was still precarious, and the openness of the beach gave men a greater feeling of insecurity than they had in the trenches.

*Diary.* Our hair and eyes and mouths are full of dust and sand, and our nostrils of the smell of dead mules.

There were also colonies of ants that kept in close touch with us, and our cigarettes gave out. Besides these trials, we had no news of the war or of the outer world.

*Diary.* Tahu and I repacked the provisions this morning. While we did so one man was shot on the right and another on the left. We have been expecting howitzers all the time, and speculating as to whether there would be any panic if they really get on to us. The Turks have got their indirect, or rather enfilading, fire on us, and hit our mules. One just hit a few yards away.... Imbros and Samothrace are clear and delicate between the blue sea and the hot sky. The riband of beach is crowded with transport, and Jews, Greeks, Armenians, New Zealanders, Australians, scallywag officers, and officers that still manage to keep a shadow of dandyism between their disreputable selves and immaculate past. And there's the perpetual ripple of the waves that is sometimes loud enough to be mistaken for the swish of shrapnel, which is also perpetual, splashing in the sea or rattling on the beach. There is very little noise on the beach in the way of talk and laughter. The men never expected to be up against this. When we left Lemnos we saw one boat with an arrow, and in the front of it "*To Constantinople and the Harem.*" Precious few of those poor fellows will ever see Constantinople, let alone the Harem.

*May 1st.* A beautiful dawn, but defiled by a real hymn of hate from the Turks. Last night the Torgut Reiss sent us some shells. This morning it was supposed to be the *Goeben* that was firing. I woke to hear the howitzers that everybody had been talking of here droning over us, and watched them lifting great columns of water where they hit the sea. Then there came the sigh and the snarl of shrapnel, but that to the other is like the rustle of a lady's fan to the rumble of a brewer's dray. This hymn of hate went on for an unusually long time this morning from the big stuff. A lot of men were hit all round, and it has been difficult to wash in the sea. All the loading, unloading, etc., is done at night. The picket-boats are fairly well protected. The middies are the most splendid boys. We are all very cramped and the mules add to the congestion. We shall have a plague of flies before we are done, if we don't have a worse plague than that. The New Zealanders are all right. . . .

Colonel White, Rickes, and Murphy, all hit at breakfast this morning, but not hurt. One of the Greek donkey-boys says he is a barber. This would be a great advantage if he wasn't so nervous and did not start so much whenever there is a burst.

There is a fleet of boats in front of us, and even more at Helles; the Turks must feel uncomfortable, but another landing, between us, would be pretty risky. They are fighting splendidly. Opinion are divided as to what would happen if we fought our way to Maidos. Many think we could be shelled out again by the *Goeben*. This expedition needed at least three times the number of men. The Indians have not come, and the Territorials cannot come for a long time.

General Godley wants to change headquarters for us. Colonel Artillery Johnston's battery is on our right, facing the Turks, and only a few yards away. The Turks spend a lot of time shooting at it, missing it, and hitting us. Another man killed just now. Shrapnel, heaps of it, is coming both ways on us. Nobody speaks on the beach. We have two tables on the top of the dugout. One is safe, and the other can be hit. The punctual people get the safe table.

B. has lunched. He says that Rupert Brooke died at Lemnos. I am very sorry; he was a good fellow, and a poet with a great future. B. was blown up by a shell yesterday. He has to go back tonight. While we lunched a man had his head blown off, 20 yards away. . . .

Orders have come that we are to entrench impregnably. We are practically besieged, for we can't re-embark without sacrificing our rearguard, and if the howitzers come up we shall be cut off from the beach and our water. A lot more men have been killed on the beach. . . .

*Sunday, May 2nd.* 6 a.m. Shrapnel all round as I washed. Beach opinion is if this siege lasts they must be able to get up their heavy guns. The Indians have gone to Helles, and the Naval Division is being taken away from us. New Turkish Divisions are coming against us. There are no chaplains here for burial or for anything else.

Waite took a dozen prisoners this morning—gendarmes, nice fellows. They hadn't much to tell us. One of them complained that he had been shot through a mistake after he had surrendered. There ought to be an interpreter on these occasions. . . .

It is a fiery hot day, without a ripple on the clear sea, and all still but for the thunder coming from Helles. I bathed and got clean. The beach looks like a mule fair of mutes, for it is very silent. We are to attack tonight at seven. We have now been here a week, and advanced a hundred yards farther than the first rush carried us. There is a great bombardment going on, a roaring ring of fire, and the Turks are being shelled and shelled. At night the battleships throw out two lines of searchlights, and behind them there gleam the fires of Samothrace and Imbros. Up and down the cliffs here, outside the dugouts, small fires burn. The rifle fire comes over the hill, echoing in the valleys and back from the ships. Sometimes it is difficult to tell whether it is the sound of ripples on the beach or firing.

*Monday, May 3rd.* I was called up at 3 a.m. To examine three prisoners. Our attack had failed, and we have many casualties, probably not less than 1000. The wounded have been crying on the beach horribly. A wounded Arab reported that our naval gun fire did much damage.

The complaint is old and bitter now. We insist that the Turks are Hottentots. We give them notice before we attack them. We tell them what we are going to do with their Capital. We attack them with an inadequate force of irregular troops, without adequate ammunition (we had one gun in our landing) in the most impregnable part of their Empire. We ask for trouble all lover the East by risking disaster here.

The *Goeben* is shelling the fleet, and (11.30) had just struck a transport. The sea is gay, and a fresh wind is blowing, and the beach is crowded, but there is not a voice upon it, except for an occasional order. . . .

The Turks are now expected to attack us. We suppose people realize what is happening here in London, though it isn't easy to see now troops and reinforcements can be sent us in time—that is, before the Turks have turned all this into a fortification. A good many men hit on the beach today. The mules cry like lost souls.

*Tuesday, May 4th.* The sea like a looking-glass, not a cloud in the sky, and Samothrace looking very clear and close. The moon is like a faint shadow of light in the clear sky over the smoke of the guns. Heavy fighting between us and Helles. A landing is being attempted. Pessimists say it is our men being taken off because their position is impossible. The boats coming back seem full of wounded. It may have been an attempt at a landing and entrenching, or simply a repetition of what we did the other day at Falcon Hill or Nebronesi, or whatever the place is.

The attack has failed this morning. Perfect peace here, except for rifles crackling on the hill. Ian Smith and I wandered off up a valley through smilax, thyme, heath and myrtle, to a high ridge. We went through the Indians and found a couple of very jolly officers, one of them since killed. There are a good many bodies unburied. Not many men hit. We helped to carry one wounded man back. The stretcher-bearers are splendid fellows, good to friend and enemy. At one place we saw a beastly muddy little pond with a man standing in it in trousers, shovelling out mud. But the water in the tin was clear and cool and very good....

General Godley and Tahu Rhodes got up to the Turkish trenches, quite close to them. The Turks attacked, threw hand-grenades, and our supports broke. The general rallied the men, but a good many were killed, amongst them the general's orderly, a gentleman ranker and a first-rate fellow.

*Wednesday, May 5th.* Kaba Tepé. The other day, when our attack below failed, the Turks allowed us to bring off our wounded. This was after that unfortunate landing.

Went on board the *Lützow* today, and got some of my things off. Coming back the tow-rope parted, and we thought that we should drift into captivity. It was rough and unpleasant.

Thursday, May 6th. Very cold night. The dead are unburied and the wounded crying for water between the trenches. Talked to General Birdwood about the possibility of an armistice for burying the dead and bringing in the wounded. He thinks that the Germans would not allow the Turks to accept.

Colonel Esson landed this morning. He brought the rumour that 8,000 Turks had been killed lower down on the Peninsula. We attacked Achi Baba at 10 a.m. There was an intermittent fire all night.

This morning I went up to the trenches with General Godley

by Walker's Ridge. The view was magnificent. The plain was covered with friendly olives. . . . General Birdwood and General Mercer, commanding the Naval Brigade, were also there. The trenches have become a perfect maze. As we went along the snipers followed us, seeing Onslow's helmet above the parapet, and stinging us with dirt. Many dead. I saw no wounded between the lines. On the beach the shrapnel has opened from a new direction. The Turks were supposed to be making light railways to bring up their howitzers and then rub us off this part of the Peninsula. This last shell that has just struck the beach has killed and wounded several men and a good many mules. . . .

*Friday, May 7th.* A bitter night and morning. . . . This morning a shell burst overhead, when I heard maniac peals of laughter and found the cook flying up, hit in the boot and his kitchen upset; he was laughing like a madman. It's a nuisance one has to sit in the shade in our dining-place and not in the sun. They have got our exact range, and are pounding in one shell after another. A shell has just burst over our heads, and hit a lighter and set her on fire.

The mules, most admirable animals, had now begun to give a good deal of trouble, alive and dead. There were hundreds of them on the beach and in the gullies. Alive, they bit precisely and kicked accurately; dead, they were towed out to sea, but returned to us faithfully on the beach, making bathing unpleasant and cleanliness difficult. The dead mule was not only offensive to the army; he became a source of supreme irritation to the navy, as he floated on his back, with his legs sticking stiffly up in the air. These legs were constantly mistaken for periscopes of submarines, causing excitement, exhaustive naval manoeuvres and sometimes recriminations.

My special duties now began to take an unusual form. Everyone was naturally anxious for Turkish troops to surrender, in order to get information, and also that we might have fewer men to fight. Those Turks who had been captured had said that the general belief was that we took no prisoners, but killed all who fell into our hands, ruthlessly. I said that I believed that this impression, which did us much harm, could be corrected. The problem was how to disabuse the Turks of this belief. I was ordered to make speeches to them from those of our trenches which were closest to theirs, to explain to them that they would be well treated and that our quarrel lay with the Germans, and not with them.

*Diary. Friday, May 7th.* At 1.30 I went up Monash Valley, which the men now call the "Valley of Death," passing a stream of haggard men, wounded and unwounded, coming down in the brilliant sunlight. I saw Colonel Monash at his headquarters, and General Godley with him, and received instructions. The shelling overhead was terrific, but did no damage, as the shells threw forward, but the smoke made a shadow between us and the sun. It was like the continuous crashing of a train going over the sleepers of a railway bridge.

Monash, whom I had last seen at the review in the desert, said: "We laugh at this shrapnel." He tried to speak on the telephone to say I was coming, but it was difficult, and the noise made it impossible. Finally I went up the slope to Quinn's Post, with an escort, running and taking cover, and panting up the very steep hill. It felt as if bullets rained, but the fact is that they came from three sides and have each got about five echoes. There's a *décolleté* place in the hill that they pass over. I got into the trench and found Quinn, tall and open-faced, swearing like a trooper, much respected by his men. The trenches in Quinn's Post were narrow and low, full of exhausted men sleeping. I crawled over them and through tiny holes. There was the smell of death every-where. I spoke in three places.

In conversations with the Turks across the trenches I generally said the same thing: that we took prisoners and treated them well; that the essential quarrel was between us and the Germans and not between England and the Turks; that the Turks had been our friends in the Crimea; and I ended by quoting the Turkish proverb: *Eski dost dushman olmaz* (An old friend cannot be an enemy). These speeches probably caused more excitement amongst our men than in the ranks of the Turks, though the Constantinople press declared that a low attempt to copy the *muezzin's* call to prayer had been made from our lines. There were many pictures drawn of the speech-maker and the shower of hand-grenades that answered his kindly words. It must be admitted that there was some reason for these caricatures. Upon this first occasion nothing very much happened—to me, at any rate. Our lines were very close to the Turkish lines, and I was able to speak clearly with and without a megaphone, and the Turks were good enough to show some interest and in that neighbourhood to keep quiet for a time. I got through my business quickly, and went back to the beach. It was then that the consequences of these blan-dishments developed, for the places from which I had spoken were made the object of a very heavy strafe, of which I had been the innocent cause, and for which others suffered. When I returned two days later to make another effort at exhortation, I heard a groan go up from the trench. "Oh, Lord, here he comes again. Now for the bally bombs." On the first occasion, when not much had happened, it had been: "Law, I'd like to be able to do that meself."

*Diary. Friday, May 7th.* On getting back here we had a very heavy fire, which broke up our dinner party, wounded Jack Anderson, stung Jack (my servant), hit me. Jack is sick. . . . Here are three unpleasant possibilities:

1. Any strong attack on the height. The navy could help then. We should be too mixed in the fighting.

2. The expected blessed big guns to lollop over howitzers.

3. Disease. The Turks have dysentery already.

There is an uncanny whistling overhead. It must come from the bullets and machine guns or Maxims a long way off. It sounds eldritch. T. very sick after seeing some wounded on the beach, and yet his nerves are very good. Eastwood told me that he was sure to get through. I told him not to say such things. He had three bullets through his tunic the other day. I went on the *Lutzow* to get the rest of my stuff off, and found Colonel Ryan ("Turkish Charlie")[1] full of awful descriptions of operations. Many wounded on the boat, all very quiet. . . Had a drink with a sailor, the gloomiest man that ever I met. He comes from Southampton, and thinks we cannot possibly win the war. It's become very cold.

Most of the diary of May 9th is too indiscreet for publication, but here are some incidents of the day:

Worsley[2] says it's very hard to get work done on the beach; in fact its almost impossible. It was sad that the gun which had been enfilading us was knocked out, but it is enfilading us now, and it looks as if we shall have a pretty heavy bill to pay today. The beach is holding its breath, and between the sound of the shrapnel and the hiss there is only the noise of the waves and a few low voices. . . . Harrison, who was slightly wounded a few days ago, was yesterday resting in his dugout when he was blown out or it by a shell. Today he was sent to the

---

1. Because he had been through the siege of Plevna and was covered with Turkish decorations.
2. Supply officer of the New Zealand Division.

*Lutzow*, and we watched him being shelled the whole way, his boat wriggling. It seems as if the shells know and love him. I am glad he won't be dining with us any more; a magnet like that is a bore, though he is a very good fellow. The land between us and the 29th is reported to be full of barbed wire entanglements.

*Monday, May 10th.* Raining and cold. Jack better.
Colonel Braithwaite woke me last night with the news of the sinking of the *Lusitania*. Last night we took three trenches, but lost them again this morning. S.B. came last night; I was glad to see him.

S.B. had been a great friend of mine in Egypt and brought me and others letter, of which we were badly in need, and stores, which were very welcome. We met upon the beach and decided to celebrate the occasion in the intelligence dugout, for my friend had actually got some soda and a bottle of whisky, two very rare luxuries on the beach.

*Diary.* We went into the intelligence dugout and sat there. Then a shell hit the top of the dugout. The next one buzzed a lot of bullets in through the door. The third ricocheted all over the place and one bullet grazed my head. I then said: "We'd better put up a blanket to save us from the ricochets." at the same time J. Was shot next door and Onslow's war diary was destroyed. A pot of jam was shot in General Cunliffe Owen's hand, which made him very angry. V., the beach-master, dashed into our intelligence dugout gasping while we held blankets in front of him. Two days ago a man was killed in his dugout next door, and another man again yesterday. Now two fuses had come straight through his roof and spun like a whipping-top on the floor, dancing a sort of *sarabande* before the hypnotized eyes of the sailors. . . .
Also S.B.'s whisky was destroyed in the luncheon basket. He broke into furious swearing in Arabic.

*Wednesday, May 12th.* Rain, mud, grease, temper all night, but we shall long for this coolness when it really gets hot. No bombardment this morning, but the Greek cook, Christopher of the Black Lamp, came and gave two hours' notice, with the rain and tears running down his face. I am not surprised at his giving notice, but why he should be meticulous about the time I can't think. Conversation about the shelling is getting very boring.
Had a picturesque walk through the dark last night, past Greeks,

Indians, Australians, across a rain-swept, wind-swept, bullet-swept hillside. Many of the colonels here are business men, who never in their wildest dreams contemplated being in such a position, and they have risen to the occasion finely. The generals have at last been prevailed upon not to walk about the beach in the daytime. . . . Two German and on Austrian submarines expected here. The transports have been ordered to Mudros.

*Thursday, May 13th.* Very calm morning, the echoes of rifle fire on the sea. I went with C. To take General Russell up from Reserve Gully to Walker's Ridge. It was a beautiful morning, with the sky flaming softly, not a cloud anywhere, and the sea perfectly still. The scrub was full of wildflowers; not even the dead mules could spoil it. Guns thundered far off. . . . After breakfast examined an intelligent Greek prisoner, Nikolas, the miller from Ali Keni. Then I was telephoned for by Colonel Monash in great haste, and went off up his valley with a megaphone as quickly as possible. In the valley the men were in a state of nerves along the road because of the snipers. The Turks had put up a white flag above their trenches opposite Quinn's Post. I think this was an artillery flag and that they hoped to avoid the fire of the fleet by all means. . . . The people at Helles aren't making tremendous headway, and it seems unlikely, except at tremendous cost, and probably not then, that they will. We are pretty well hung up except on our left; why not try there? The Turks are not yet entrenched or dug in there as in other places. . . . I had to bully Yanni of Ayo Strati till he sobbed on the cliff. I then threatened to dismiss him, after which he grew cheerful, for it was what he wanted. . . .

The Turks have again got white flags out. Have been ordered to go up at dawn.

*Friday, May 14th.* 4 a.m. Walked up the valley. The crickets were singing in the bushes at the opening of the valley and the place was cool with the faint light of coming dawn. Then a line of stretcher-bearers with the wounded, some quiet, some groaning. Then came the dawn and the smell of death that infects one's hands and clothes and haunts one.

They weren't over-pleased to see me at first, as after my speech the other day they had had an awful time from hand-grenades, and their faces fell when I appeared. I spoke from the same place. Then I went to another, and lastly to a trench that communicated with the Turkish trench. The Greek who had surrendered last night came down this trench and the Turks were said to be five to ten yards off. It was partly roofed, and there were some sandbags, between two and three feet high, that separated us from them. Leading into this was a big circular dugout, open to heaven. I got the men cleared out of this before speaking. In the small trench there were two men facing the Turks and lying on the ground with revolves pointed at the Turks. I moved one man back out of the way and lay on the other—there wasn't anything else to be done—and spoke for five minutes with some intervals. Once a couple of hand-grenades fell outside and the ground quivered, but that was all. I then got the guard changed. . . .

The loss of the *Goliath* is confirmed and the fleet has gone, leaving a considerable blank on the horizon and a depression on the sunlit beach. Four interpreters were arrested today and handed over to me.

I put them on to dig me a new dugout, round which a colony of interpreters is growing; Kyriakidis, who is a fine boy, aristocratic-looking, but very soft, who I want to send away as soon as possible; and others. My dugout is in the middle of wildflowers, with the sea splashing round. Since the ships have all gone we are, as a consequence, short of water. . . . The Turks have been shelling our barges hard for an hour. We are to make an attack tonight and destroy their trenches.

*Saturday, May 15th.* The attack has failed. There are many of our wounded outside our lines. Have been told to go out with a white flag. Was sent for by Skeen to see General Birdwood in half an hour. While Colonel Skeen and I were talking a shell hit one man in the lungs and knocked Colonel Knox on the back without hurting him. General Birdwood was hit yesterday in the head, but won't lie up, General Trottman the day before. While we talked water arrived. A message came from Colonel Chauvel to say there was only two wounded lying out. . . . In a few minutes telephone messages arrived from the doctor in the trenches that the two wounded had died. . . . I came back to headquarters, and heard General Bridges[3] asking the general if he might go up Monash Valley. In a few minutes we heard that he was shot in the thigh. The snipers are getting many of our men. If the Germans were running this show they would have had 200,000 men for it.

Last night Kyriakidis heard a nightingale. I notice that the cuckoo has changed his note, worried about the shrapnel. I don't blame the

---

3. Commanding Australian division.

bird. My new dugout is built. It has a corridor and a patio, and is sort of Louis Quinze. The food is good, but we are always hungry.

Went out with Colonel N. He is a very great man for his luxuries, and looks on cover as the first of these. He is very funny about shelling, and is huffy, like a man who has received an insult, if he gets hit by a spent bullet or covered with earth. They have got the range of our new headquarters beautifully—two shells before lunch, one on either side of the kitchen range. The men and the mess table covered with dust and stones. The fact is our ships have gone; they can now do pretty much as they like.

Most people here agree that the position is hopeless, unless we drive the Turks back on our left and get reinforcements from Helles, where they could quite well spare them.

*Sunday, May 16th.* A day fit for Trojan heroes to fight on. As a matter of fact, there is a good deal of Trojan friction. Went into the intelligence dugout, as five men were hit below it. They have just hit another interpreter, and are pounding away at us again. I was warned to go out with a flag of truce and a bugler this afternoon.

*Monday, May 17th.* I walked out to the left with S.B., and bathed in a warm, quiet sea. Many men bathing too, and occasionally shrapnel also. There was a scent of thyme, and also the other smell from the graves on the beach, which are very shallow. I got a touch of the sun, and had to lie down. When I got back I heard that Villiers Stuart had been killed this morning, instantaneously. He was a very good fellow, and very good to me.

*Tuesday, May 18th.* Last night Villiers Stuart was buried. The funeral was to have been at sunset, but at the time we were savagely shelled and had to wait. We formed up in as decent a kit as we could muster, and after the sun had set in a storm of red, while the young moon was rising, the procession started. We stumbled over boulders, and met stretcher-bearers with dead and wounded, we passed Indians driving mules, and shadowy Australians standing at attention, till we came to the graves by the sea. The prayers were very short and good, interrupted by the boom of our guns and the whining of Turkish bullets overhead. His salute was fired above his head from both the trenches. . . .

We shelled the village of Anafarta yesterday, which I don't much care about. A good many here want to destroy the minaret of the mosque. I can see no difference in principle between this and the destruction of Rheims Cathedral. Kyriakidis told me a Greek cure for sunstroke. You fill the ears of the afflicted one with salt water; it makes a noise like thunder in his head, but the sunstroke passes. Christo thereupon got me salt water in a jug without telling me, and several thirsty people tried to drink it....

A German submarine seen here.... A day of almost perfect peace; rifle fire ceased sometimes for several minutes together, but 8-inch shells were fired into the trenches.... Men are singing on the beach for the first time, and there is something cheerful in the air. The enfilading gun has been, as usual, reported to be knocked out, but gunners are great optimists. No news from Helles.... Turkish reinforcements just coming up. Attack expected at 3 a.m. We stand to arms here.

*Wednesday, May 19th.* Work under heavy shell fire. This grew worse about 6.30. Several heavy shells hit within a few yards of this dugout and the neighbouring ones, but did not burst. A little farther off they did explode, or striking the sea, raised tall columns and high fountains of white water. Colonel Chaytor badly wounded in the shoulder. A great loss to us. He talked very cheerfully. I have got leave to send away Ashjian.... This, after all, is a quarrel for those directly concerned. The Germans have brought up about twelve more field guns and four or five Jack Johnsons, and the shelling is very heavy. Saw a horrid sight: a barge full of wounded was being towed out to the hospital ship. Two great Jack Johnsons came, one just in front of them; then when they turned with a wriggle, one just behind them, sending up towers of water, and leaving two great white roses in the sea that turned muddy as the stuff from the bottom rose. They had shells round them again, and a miraculous escape. It's cruel hard on the nerves of wounded men, but of course that was bad luck, not wicked intentions, because the enemy couldn't see them.

If the Turks had attacked us fiercely on the top and shelled us as badly down here earlier, they might have had us out. Now we ought to be all right, and they can hardly go on using ammunition like this. Their losses are said to be very great. New Turkish reinforcements said to be at Helles. They have done what we ought to have done. Now they are throwing 11-inch at us. It's too bad.... I saw Colonel Skeen. He said to me: "You had better be ready to go out this afternoon. We have just shot a Turk with a white flag. That will give us an excuse for apologizing:" quite so: it will also give the Turk an excuse for retaliating. A Turkish officer just brought in says that the real attack is to be this afternoon, now at 1.30. I spent an hour in the hospital, interpreting for the Turkish wounded. The Australians are very good to them. On returning I found the general's dugout hit hard. Nothing to be done but to dig deeper in.

From the third week of May to the third week in June was the kernel of our time in Anzac. We had grown accustomed to think of the place as home, and of the conditions of our life as natural and permanent. The monotony of the details of shelling and the worry of the flies are of interest only to those who endured them, and have been eliminated, here and there, from this diary.

During this month we were not greatly troubled. The men continued to make the trenches impregnable, and were contented. It was in some ways a curiously happy time.

The New Zealanders and the Australians were generally clothed by the sunlight, which fitted them, better than any tailor, with a red-brown skin, and only on ceremonial occasions did they wear their belts and accoutrements.

Our sport was bathing, and the Brotherhood of the Bath was rudely democratic. There was at Anzac a singularly benevolent officer, but for all his geniality a strong disciplinarian, devoted to military observances. He was kind to all the world, not forgetting himself, and he had developed a kindly figure. No insect could resist his contours. Fleas and bugs made passionate love to him, inlaying his white skin with a wonderful red mosaic. One day he undressed and, leaving nothing of his dignity with his uniform, he mingled superbly with the crowd of bathers. Instantly he received a hearty blow upon his tender, red and white shoulder, and a cordial greeting from some democrat of Sydney or of Wellington: "Old man, you've been amongst the biscuits!"

He drew himself up to rebuke this presumption, then dived for the sea, for, as he said, "What's the good of telling one naked man to salute another naked man, especially when neither have got their caps?"

This month was marked by a feature that is rare in modern warfare. We had an armistice for the burial of the dead, which is described in the diary.

On the peninsula we were extremely anxious for an armistice for many reasons. We wished, on all occasions, to be able to get our wounded in after a fight, and we believed, or at least the writer was confident, that an arrangement could be come to. We were also very anxious to bury the dead. Rightly or wrongly, we thought that G.H.Q., living on its perfumed island, did not consider how great was the abomination of life upon the cramped and stinking battlefield that was our encampment, though this was not a charge that any man would have dreamed of bringing against Sir Ian Hamilton.

*Diary. Wednesday, May 19th, 1915.* Kaba Tepé. General Birdwood told me to go to Imbros to talk to Sir Ian Hamilton about an armistice, if General Godley would give me leave.

*Thursday, May 20th, 1915.* Kaba Tepé. Have been waiting for four hours in Colonel Knox's boat, which was supposed to go to Imbros. Turkish guns very quiet. . . . Hear that Ock Asquith and Wedgwood are wounded. A liaison officer down south says: "When the Senegalese fly, and the French troops stream forward twenty yards and then stream back twenty-five yards, we know that we are making excellent progress." There is a Coalition government at home. We think that we are the reason of that; we think the government cannot face the blunder of the Dardanelles without asking for support from the Conservatives.

*6 p.m.. "Arcadian."* Found George Lloyd. Have been talking to Sir Ian Hamilton with regard to the armistice. . . . Clive Bigham was there. He lent me some Shakespeares.

*Friday, May 21st, 1915.* Kaba Tepé. Saw Sir Ian Hamilton again this morning. The Turks are said to have put up a white flag and to have masse behind it in their trenches, intending to rush us. Left with four "Ardadians."

There was a parley yesterday while I was away. The Turks had put up some white flags, but it was not a case of bad faith as the "Ardadians" believed. We are said to have shot one Red Crescent man by mistake. General Walker went out to talk to the Turks, just like that. Both sides had, apparently, been frightened. I walked back to Reserve Gully with the general, to see the new brigade. The evening sun was shining on the myrtles in all the gullies, and the new brigade was singing and whistling up and down the hills, while fires crackled everywhere.

*Saturday, May 22nd, 1915.* Kaba Tepé. S.B. was sent out yesterday to talk to the Turks, but he did not take a white flag with him, and was sniped and bruised. . . . This morning, suddenly, I was sent for.

S.B. and I hurried along the beach and crossed the barbed wire entanglements. We went along by the sea, through heavy showers of rain, and at last met a fierce Arab officer and a wandery-looking Turkish lieutenant. We sat and smoked in fields splendid with poppies, the sea glittering at us.

Then Kemal Bey arrived, and went into Anzac with S.B., while I went off as hostage.

S.B. and Kemal Bey, as they went, provided the Australian escort with much innocent laughter. Our barbed wire down to the sea consisted only of a few light strands, over which the Turk was helped by having his legs raised high for him. S.B., however, wished him, as he was blindfolded, to believe that this defence went on for at least twenty yards. So the Turk was made to do an enormously high, stiff goose-step over the empty air for that space, as absurd a spectacle to our men as I was to be, later, to the Turks. The Australians were almost sick from internal laughter.

*Diary.* Kemal Bey asked for a hostage, and I went out. They bandaged my eyes, and I mounted a horse and rode off with Sahib Bey. We went along by the sea for some time, for I could hear the waves. Then we went round and round—to puzzle me, I suppose—and ended up in a tent in a grove of olives, where they took the handkerchief off, and Sahib Bey said: "This is the beginning of a life-long friendship."

At that moment, as I was riding along, the soldier who was supposed to be leading my horse had apparently let go and had fallen behind to light a cigarette or pick flowers. I heard Sahib Bey call out: "You old fool! Can't you see he's riding straight over the cliff?"

I protested loudly as I rode on, blind as fate.

We had cheese and tea and coffee, Sahib Bey offering to eat first to show me that it was all right, which I said was nonsense. He said: "It may not be political economy, but there are some great advantages in war. It's very comfortable when there are no exports, because it means that all the things stay at home and are very cheap."

He tried to impress me with their well-being. He said he hated all politicians and had sworn never to read the papers. The Turks had come sadly into the war against us, otherwise gladly. They wanted to regain the prestige that they had lost in the Balkans. . . . He said, after I had talked to him:

"There are many of us who think like you, but we must obey. We know that you are just and that Moslems thrive under you, but you have made cruel mistakes by us, the taking of those two ships and the way in which they were taken."

He asked me a few questions, which I put aside. He had had a conversation with Dash the day before, when we parleyed. Dash is a most innocent creature. He had apparently told him that G.H.Q. was an awful bore, and also the number of Turkish prisoners we had taken. . . .

*Sunday, May 23rd, 1915.* Kaba Tepé. We landed a month ago today. We now hold a smaller front than then. Also the *Albion* had gone ashore. The rest of the fleet has left; she remains a fixture. All the boats are rushing up to tow her off. The Turks are sending in a hail of shrapnel. . . . It will be a bad business is they don't get her off. . . . They have got her off, thank the Lord, and everyone is breathing more freely.

We wonder if all the places with queer, accidental names will one day be historical: Johnson's Jolly, Dead Man's Ridge, Quinn's Post, The Valley of Death, The Sphinx, Anzac—by the way, that's not a name of good omen, as *anjak* in Turkish means barely, only just—Plugge's Plateau. Plugge is a grand man, wounded for the second time. The New Zealanders are all most gallant fellows. . . .

The big fight ought to come off, after the armistice. Two more divisions have come up against us. All quiet last night, but a shell came into the New Zealand hospital on the beach and killed four wounded men and a dresser and some more outside. It's these new guns whose position we still do not know.

*Tuesday, May 25th, 1915.* Kaba Tepé. We had the truce yesterday. I was afraid something might go wrong, but it went off all right. Skeen, Blamey, Howse, V.C., Hough and I started early.

Skeen offered me breakfast but, like a fool, I refused. He put some creosote on my handkerchief. We were at the rendezvous on the beach at 6.30. Heavy rain soaked us to the skin. At 7.30 we met the Turks, Miralai Izzedin, a peasant, rather sharp, little man; Arif, the son of Achmet Pasha, who gave me a card, *Sculpteur et Peintre* and *Etudiant de Poésie.* I saw Sahib and had a few words with him but he did not come with us. Fahreddin Bey came later. We walked from the sea and passed immediately up the hill, through a field of tall corn filled with poppies, then another cornfield; then the fearful smell of death began as we came upon scattered bodies. We mounted over a plateau and down through gullies filled with thyme, where there lay about 4000 Turkish dead. It was indescribable. One was grateful for the rain and the grey sky. A Turkish Red Crescent man came and gave me some antiseptic wool with scent on it, and this they renewed frequently. There were two wounded crying in that multitude of silence. The Turks were distressed, and Skeen strained a point to let them send water to the first wounded man, who must have been a sniper crawling home. I walked over to the second, who lay with a high circle of dead that made a mound round him, and gave him a drink from my water-bottle, but Skeen called me to come on and I had to leave the bottle. Later a Turk gave it back to me. The Turkish captain with me said: "At this spectacle even the most gentle must feel savage, and the most savage must weep."

The dead fill acres of ground, mostly killed in the one big attack, but some recently. They fill the myrtle-grown gullies. One saw the result of machine-gun fire very clearly; entire companies annihilated— not wounded, but killed, their heads doubled under them with the impetus of their rush and both hands clasping their bayonets. It was as if God had breathed in their faces, as *"the Assyrian came down like the wolf on the fold."*

The line was not easy to settle. Neither side wanted to give its position or its trenches away. At the end Skeen agreed that the Turks had been fair. We had not been going very long when we had a message to say that the Turks were entrenching at Johnson's Jolly. Skeen had, however, just been there and seen that they were doing nothing at all. He left me at Quinn's Post, looking at the communication trench through which I had spoken to the Turks. Corpses and dead men blown to bits everywhere. Richards was with me part of the time: easy to get on with; also a gentleman called indifferently by the men Mr. or Major Tibbs. A good deal of friction at first. The trenches were 10 to 15 yards apart. Each side was on the *qui vive* for treachery. In one gully the dead had got to be left unburied. It was impossible to bury them without one side seeing the position of the other. In the Turkish parapet there were many bodies buried. Fahreddin told Skeen he wanted to bury them, "but," he said, "we cannot take them out without putting something in their place."

Skeen agreed, but said that this concession was not to be taken advantage of to repair the trench. This was a difficult business.

When our people complained that the Turks were making loopholes, they invited me into their trench to look. Then the Turks said that we were stealing their rifles; this came from the dead land where we could not let them go. I went down, and when I got back, very hot, they took my word for it that we were not. There was some trouble because we were always crossing each other's lines. I talked to the Turks, one of whom pointed to the graves. "That's politics," he said. Then he pointed to the dead bodies and said: "That's diplomacy. God pity all of us poor soldiers."

Much of this business was ghastly to the point of nightmare.

I found a hardened old Albanian *chaoush* and got him to do anything I wanted. Then a lot of other Albanians came up, and I said: *"Tunya tyeta."*[4]

I had met some of them in Janina. They began clapping me on the back and cheering while half a dozen funeral services were going on all round, conducted by the chaplains. I had to stop them. I asked them if they did not want an Imam for a service over their own dead, but the old Albanian pagan roared with laughter and said that their souls were all right. They could look after themselves. Not many signs of fanaticism. One huge, savage-looking Anatolian looked curses at me. Greeks came up and tried to surrender to me, but were ordered back by the Turks pretty roughly.

Considering the number of their men we had killed, they remained extraordinary unmoved and polite. They wouldn't have, if we had been Russians. Blamey came to say that Skeen had lost H. and wanted me, so he, Arif and I walked to the sea. The burying had not been well done. It was sometimes impossible to do it. . . . As it went, we took our rifles from the Turkish side, minus their bolts, and gave the Turks their rifles in the same way. . . .

Our men gave cigarettes to the Turks, and beyond the storm-centre at Quinn's Post the feeling was all right. We sat down and sent men to look for Skeen. Arif was nervous and almost rude. Then Skeen came. He told me to get back as quickly as possible to Quinn's Post, as I said I was nervous at being away, and to retire the troops at 4 and the white-flag men at 4.15. I said to Arif: "Everybody's behaved very well. Now we must take care that nobody loses his head. Your men won't shoot you and my men won't shoot me, so we must walk about, otherwise a gun will go off and everybody will get shot." But Arif faded away.

I got back as quickly as possible. Blamey went away on the left. I

---

4. The usual Albanian greeting.

then found that the Turks' time was eight minutes ahead of ours, and put on our watches. The Turks asked me to witness their taking the money from their dead, as they had no officer there. They were very worried by having no officer, and asked me if anyone were coming. I, of course, had no idea, but I told them I would see that they were all right. They were very patient. . . .

The burying was finished some time before the end. There were certain tricks on both sides.

Our men and the Turks began fraternizing, exchanging badges, etc. I had to keep them apart. At 4 o'clock the Turks came to me for orders. I do not believe this could have happened anywhere else. I retired their troops and ours, walking along the line. At 4.7 I retired the white-flag men, making them shake hands with our men. Then I came to the upper end. About a dozen Turks came out. I chaffed them, and said that they would shoot me next day. They said, in a horrified chorus: "God forbid!"

The Albanians laughed and cheered, and said: "We will never shoot you."

Then the Australians began coming up, and said: "Goodbye old chap; good luck!"

And the Turks said: *"Oghur Ola gule gule gedejekseniz, gule gule gele-jekseniz"* (Smiling may you go and smiling come again).

Then I told them all to get into their trenches, and unthinkingly went up to the Turkish trench and got a deep *salaam* from it. I told them that neither side would fire for twenty-five minutes after they had got into the trenches. One Turks was seen out away on our left, but there was nothing to be done, and I think he was all right. A couple of rifles had gone off about twenty minutes before the end but Potts and I went hurriedly to and fro seeing it was all right. At last we dropped into our trenches, glad that the strain was over. I walked back with Temperley. I got some raw whisky for the infection in my throat, and iodine for where the barbed wire had torn my feet. There was a hush over the Peninsula. . . .

*Wednesday, May 26th, 1915.* Kaba Tepé. This morning I was talking to Dix, asking him if he believed there were submarines. "Yes," he said, and then swore, and added: "There's the *Triumph* sinking."

Every picket-boat dashed off to pick up the survivors. The Turks behaved well in not shelling the survivors. There was fury, panic, and rage on the beach and on the hill. I heard Uncle Bill, half off his head, saying: "You should kill all enemies. Like a wounded bird, she is. Give them cigarettes. Swine! Like a wounded bird. The swine!"

He was shaking his fist. Men were crying and cursing. Very different from yesterday's temper.

This afternoon I went round past Monash Gully, towards Kaba Tepé, and bathed. I got shelled, and came back over the ridges having a beastly time from the shrapnel which hunted me.

We have now got a sap under Quinn's Post. The flies and ants are past endurance.

*Thursday, May 27th, 1915.* Kaba Tepé. A very wet night. I wish the Turks would forget how to shoot. Here we are for an indefinite period without the power of replying effectively and with the knowledge that we are firmly locked outside the back door of a side-show. . . .

Went with the general to General Russell's trenches. They are very much improved. The men call an ideal trench a Godley-Braithwaite trench; that is, tall enough for General Godley and broad enough for Colonel Braithwaite. Bathed. Charlie Bentinck arrived. His destroyer lay just off the beach and was shelled. Some sailors and five soldiers killed. Forty-eight wounded. Very unfortunate. If they had come yesterday, it would have been all right—a quiet day, though we had thirty men sniped. The *Majestic* reported sunk off Helles. Off to Mudros to get stores.

*Friday, May 28th, 1915.* Mudros. Left after many delays, and slept on deck. Very cold. It's a pretty tall order for the French to put black Senegalese cannibals into Red Cross uniform. . . .

*Saturday, May 29th, 1915.* Lemnos. Drove across the island to Castro. There was a delightful spring half a mile from Castro and a café kept by a Greek. His wife had been killed by the Turks. Great fig-trees and gardens. I met two naval officers, who told me Wedgwood had died of wounds. I am very sorry; he was a very fine man. I admired him a lot. Castro is beautiful, with balconies over the narrow streets, half Turk and half Greek, and shady gardens. I bathed in a transparent sea, facing Athos, which was gleaming like a diamond. I watched its shadow come across the eighty miles of sea at sunset, as Homer said it did. I found a Greek, who had been Cromer's cook. He said he would come back and cook for me, if there was no danger. He said he knew that G.H.Q. cooks were safe, but his wife would not let him go on to the Peninsula. He said her idea of warfare was wrong. She always thought of men and bullets skipping about together on a hillside.

*Sunday, May 30th, 1915.* Mudros. I bathed before dawn and went back to Mudros with masses of mosquito-netting, etc. Turkish prisoners of the French were being guarded by Greeks. It was rather like monkeys looking after bears. They were uniforms that were a cross between Ali Pasha of Janina and Little Lord Fauntleroy. I saw H., who had been on the River Clyde. He looked as if he were still watching the sea turn red with blood, as he described the landing on Gallipoli. Jack was sick, and I had to leave him with my coat. Went and saw my friend the Papas of the little Greek church on the hill.

*Monday, May 31st, 1915.* Anzac. I saw Hutton this morning, slightly wounded. Bathed at the farthest point towards Kaba Tepé, but had to fly with my clothes in my hand, leaving my cigarettes. . . .

*Wednesday, June 2nd, 1915.* Kaba Tepé. Had a picturesque examination of a Greek peasant this morning. It was a fine picture, with the settling of the blue sea and the mountains. The man himself was patriarchal and biblical, surrounded by tall English officers and half-naked soldiers. Last night we sent up bombs from Japanese mortars by Quinn's. It sounded beastly. This morning I went to Reserve Gully with the general. Monash's Brigade is resting there for the first time for five weeks. The general, looking like a Trojan hero, made them a fine speech from a sort of natural throne in the middle of the sunlit amphitheatre, in which they all sat, tier after tier of magnificent-looking fellows, brown as Indians. Bullets swept over all the time, sometimes drowning the general's voice. . . . Have just heard that Quinn is killed. I am very sorry. He was a fine, jolly, gallant fellow.

*Friday, June 4th, 1915.* Anzac. Nothing doing. George Lloyd came over. Very glad to see him. This morning I went with Shaw to the extreme left, through fields of poppies, thyme, and lavender. We saw a vulture high overhead, and the air was full of the song of larks. At Helles there was a savage attack going on. There was very bad sniping. In some places the trenches are only knee-high; in other places there are no trenches and the Turks are anything from four to eight hundred yards off. Yesterday seventeen men were hit at one place, they said, by one sniper. At one place on the way, we ran like deer, dodging. The general, when he had had a number of bullets at him, also ran. Sniping is better fun than shrapnel; it's more human. You pit your wits against the enemy in a rather friendly sort of way. A lot of vultures collecting.

*Saturday, June 5th, 1915.* Anzac. Examined sixteen prisoners. Food good, munitions plentiful, morale all right. The individuals fed up with the war, but the mass obedient and pretty willing. No idea of surrendering. They think they are going to win. There was one Greek, a Karamanly, who only talked Turkish. He did not say until tonight that he was wounded. The flies are bad.

*Sunday, June 6th, 1915.* Anzac. Went to the service this morning with the general, in the amphitheatre. The sermon was mainly against America for not coming into the war, and also against bad language. The Chaplain said he could not understand the meaning of it. The men laughed. So did I.

*Monday, June 7th, 1915.* Kaba Tepé. This morning the land was sweet as Eden and there was the calm of the first creation. H. has been made a new Uriah the Hittite, but not because of Mrs. H. Last night I was invaded by mice. There is tremendous shelling going on now. This afternoon S.B., Onslow and I climbed a hill and had a beautiful view. Everyone is rather ill and feverish. I have no news about Jack. The intelligence office had been moved to a higher and safer place. Pirie Gordon, poor chap, has gone sick a long time ago. I rather liked the stuffy old place, which was called "The Mountain Path to the Jackal's Cave."

The attack last night failed, but the drone of the rifles went on unceasingly, like the drone of a dry waterfall. We shall not get to Constantinople unless the flat-faced Bulgars come in.

Yesterday I lunched with Temperley at the H.Q. Of Monash Valley. Times have changed: it's fairly safe going there through a long sap they have dug, and the noise is less bad.

Colonel —— had seen a lot of the Crown Prince in India, and said he was a very good fellow. Dined with Woods, Dix, S.B., and Edwards. Lots of champagne for once; a very good dinner.

I went to No. 2 outpost with the general. There is a sap all the way now. Only one sniper the whole way. The Turkish birds were singing beautifully as we went. There was also a Turkish snake, which I believed was quite harmless, but Tahu killed it. The men are getting pretty tired. They are not as resigned as their the thousand brother-monks over the way at Mount Athos.

*Friday, June 11th, 1915.* Kaba Tepé. The Australians and the New Zealanders have given up wearing clothes. They lie about and bathe and become darker than Indians. The general objects to this. "I suppose," he says, "we shall have our servants waiting on us like that." The flies are very bad, so are the mice, and so is the shelling. . . .

*Sunday, June 13th, 1915.* Kaba Tepé. A lot of mules and several men hit yesterday. Last night, S.B. and I were on the beach, when a man on a stretcher went by, groaning rhythmically. I thought he had been shot through the brain.

Later on I went into the hospital to find a wounded Turk, and found that this man had never been hit at all. He had been doing very good work till a shell exploded near him and gave him a shock. Then he went on imitating a machine gun. Some men in a sap up at Quinn's have been going off their heads.

Awful accounts of Mudros: flies, heat, sand, no water, typhoid. Today are the Greek elections.

Am dining with H. Woods. "The beach" now says that Ot has been poisoned by the Greek guides, who he ill-treats and uses as cooks. I shouldn't wonder. The shelling is bad. I am going to make a new dugout to get away from the flies and mice. The Turkish prisoners will do this. I pay them a small sum.

*Tuesday, June 15th, 1915.* Kaba Tepé. Colonel Chauvel[5] has pleurisy, Colonel Johnston[6] enteric. The sea's high and the navy depressed. . . . One man and two mules killed in our gully this morning; the body of one mule blown about 50 yards both ways.

*Wednesday, June 16th, 1915.* Kaba Tepé. Rain. I was to have gone to Helles with Woods to see Dedez, but no boats went; it was too rough. I was going to talk about spies to S.B., when General Cunliffe Owen said to me: "Wait a bit. The shelling is too bad. We will go along together."

---

5. Commanding 1st Australian Light Horse Brigade.
6. Commanding New Zealand Infantry Brigade. Afterwards killed at battle of Messines in 1917.

But I was in too much of a hurry. A shell fell in the gully as I crossed, and Woods came out to see where it had hit. It went into Machono-chie's dugout, where H. Was, and blew him out of his dugout, black and shaken. It destroyed his furniture. I felt sorry for him. Ot tried to turn him out of the intelligence dugout, but we protested. The general has come back with the latest casualty lists from France. . . .

*Thursday, June 17th, 1915.* Helles. Thirty men killed and wounded on the beach today. This morning I came to Helles with Woods. As we got there a submarine had two shots at one of our transports by us. I was to have seen Dedez, but he had gone off to see Gouraud. George Peel walked in and took me round the beach, two miles on. We climbed on to the headland, in what he called "the quiet track of the Black Marias." He talked of every mortal thing—the future of Liberal and Socialist, the possibility of touching the heart of the people, the collapse of Christianity, our past and our policy. I left him and walked back across thyme and asphodel, Asia glowing like a jewel across the Dardanelles in the sunset. At night I talked late and long with Dash. Every Department is jealous, everyone is at cross-purposes, no co-operation between the War Office and the Foreign Office.

Walked in the morning to the H.Q. of the R.N.D. with Whittall. We were shelled most of the way in the open landscape. There was no cover anywhere. It felt unfamiliar. I was unfavourably impressed with the insecurity of life in this part of the world, and wished for Anzac. In the evening we drank *mavrodaphne* and tried to get rid of—

*Friday, June 18th, 1915.* Kaba Tepé. I left Helles in the middle of very heavy shelling, a star performance. A lot of horses killed this morning. A submarine popped up last night. As we came back to Anzac the Turks shelled our trawler and hit her twice, but without doing any damage.

Shelling grew worse at Anzac, and sickness began to make itself felt. Men were sent across to Imbros when it was possible to rest.

*Diary.* On June 25th I went across to Imbros with H. Woods and the Greek miller, Nikolas. Hawker was there, and E. of Macedonia. E. is very unpopular. If he takes a dislike to a man he digs around his dugout, until it falls in on him. The chief R.A.M.C. officer, an Irish-

91

man, was mourning over the ruins of his home. We slept uncomfortably on the ground, with flies to keep us warm.

As I was writing this a shell burst outside my dugout, a lot of shrapnel coming through, and one bullet glancing off the typewriter, which has just come. At the same time Jack was hit across the gully going from my dugout to his. Conolly, the escort, and I carried him down, after binding his leg up, under heavy fire. Then I nipped back to get some of his stuff to take off, but on going back to the beach found that he had gone. Many men hit on the beach. Thousands of flies on the wounded. The general's blankets riddled with bullets. They have our range, pat. Two days ago Colonel Parker had his chair and table smashed while he was in his dugout. He left it to have tea with Wagstaffe. There he was reading when another bullet tore his paper in two. I have been covered with dirt several times in the last days. L.S. Amery came with K. I only saw him for a minute, worse luck, but he is coming back tomorrow, I hope, when we can have a talk. G.H.Q. turned up in force, and walked about like wooden images.

We have a clerk here, Venables. He has got tired of writing, and, wanting to change the pen for the sword, borrowed a rifle and walked up to the front line at Quinn's Post. There he popped his head in and said: "Excuse me, is this a private trench, or may anyone fire out of it?"

The sound of battle has ended. Men are bathing. The clouds that the cannonade had called up are gone, and the sea is still and crimson in the sunset to Imbros and Samothrace.

*Tuesday, June 29th, 1915.* Anzac. We have advanced 1000 yards down at Helles, but no details yet. Many men shot here yesterday by the Anafarta gun. I should think this gun had as good a tale of killed and wounded as any gun in the war. Every day it gets its twenty odd on the beach. The Australians attacked on the right yesterday. Fifty killed and wounded; they think the Turks suffered more heavily. I went with the general to the extreme left. Terrific heat. We came to a valley filled with thyme and lavender, which the Maoris are to inhabit. The men were bathing beyond Shrapnel Point. They say the Turks let them. I had two letters—one two months old, a curious one to receive here, from an Englishwoman, wife of the ex-Grand Vizier of Afghanistan. He was a progressive man, and is therefore in an Afghan prison. She wants work for her son. Wants him to be a saddler, a job a lot of men here would like. All my stuff looted coming from Egypt.

Men are practising bomb-throwing, all over the place. They are mostly half-naked, and darker than Red Indians. It's a day of blessed peace, but there's a lot of feeling about the Anafarta gun, and bathing is stopped on the beach till night.

*Wednesday, June 30th, 1915.* Anzac. Last night I went down to the hospital and was inoculated for cholera by C., a witty man. A trench had been blown in, and men were lying groaning on the floor, most of them suffering from shell-shock, not wounds, but some of the wounds horrible. . . . I asked C. Why the wounded men were not sent to Cyprus instead of Mudros. He said: "Because it's a splendid climate and there is heaps of water."

The chief doctor at Mudros is useless, the second—(with regard to the second doctor I regret that the diary is libellous.) Anyway, what is certain is that the condition of the sick and wounded is awful. This morning it's very rough, and I can't get out to Jack at the hospital ship, as prisoners are coming in. . . .

*July 1st, 1915.* Anzac. I examined the prisoners, amongst them a tall Armenian lawyer, who talked some English. I asked him how he had surrendered. He said: " I saw two gentlemen with their looking glasses, and came over to them."

By this he meant two officers with periscopes. He said that the psychology of the Turks is a curious thing. They do not fear death, yet are not brave. . . .

No water came in yesterday. The storm wrecked the barges and the beach is covered with lighters. We got brackish water from the hill. I could not get to Jack for work.

At lunch I heard there were wounded crying on Walker's Ridge, and went up there with Zachariades. We found a first-rate Australian, Major Reynell. We went through the trenches, dripping with sweat; it was a boiling day, and my head reeled from inoculation. We had to crawl through a secret say over a number of dead Turks, some of whom were in a ghastly condition, headless and covered with flies. Then out from the darkness into another sap, with a dead Turk to walk over. The Turkish trenches were 30 yards off, and the dead lay between the two lines.

When I called I was answered at once by a Turk. He said he could not move. . . . I gave him a drink, and Reynell and I carried him in, stumbling over the dead among whom he lay. I went back for my water-bottle, but the Turks began shooting as a warning, and I had to go back into the trench.

An awful time getting the Turk through the very narrow trench. I got one other, unwounded, shaming dead. We threw a rope, and in he came.

The taking of the second Turk was a curious episode that perhaps deserves a little more description than is given by the diary. The process of catching Turks fascinated the Australians, and amongst them an R.A.M.C. doctor who came round on that occasion. This officer prided himself upon neatness and a smart appearance, when the dust and heat of the Dardanelles had turned everyone else into scallywags. After he had attended to the first wounded man, he pointed out the second Turk lying between our trenches and the Turks' and only a few yards from either. "You go out again, sir," said the Australians; "it's as good as a show."

I, however, took another view. I called out to the Turk: "Do you want any water?"

"By God," he whispered back, "I do, but I am afraid of my people."

We then threw him a rope and pulled him in. He told us that the night before he had lost direction in the attack. Fire seemed to be coming every way, and it had seemed to him the best plan to fall and lie still amongst his dead comrades. The doctor gave him some water, with which he rinsed his mouth, and I left him under the charge of the R.A.M.C. doctor. This is what happened subsequently. They had to crawl back through the secret sap, from which the bodies of the dead Turks had by that time been removed and left at the entrance. The Turk was blindfolded, but he saw his dead comrades, over whose bodies he had to step, he leapt to the conclusion that it was our habit to bring our prisoners to one place and there to kill them. He gave one panic-stricken yell; he threw his arms round the neck of the well-dressed officer; they fell and rolled upon the corpses together, the Turk in convulsions of fear clinging to the neck of the doctor, pressing his face to the faces of the dead till he was covered with blood and dust and the ghastly remains of death, while the soldiers stood round saying to the Turk: "Now, don't you carry on so."

*Diary. Friday, July 2nd, 1915.* Anzac. This morning I had a magnificent bathe with General Birdwell. At night a great storm blew up. The lightning played in splendid glares over Imbros and Samothrace.

The sea roared, the thunder crashed, and rain spouted down. After a time that stopped and a cloud, black as ink, came down upon us like a pall.

Yesterday morning me the two Whittalls going to Helles with General de Lotbiniere and his periscopes.

I went off to the *Sicilia* to see Jack, and had a lot of trouble about a pass. I saw Jack. He said they had re-bound his leg on the beach, but that it had not been looked at for eighteen hours on the boat. It had swelled to double its size. Then a doctor came and said the bandage had been done too tight, and there was a chance of his losing his leg. I felt absolutely savage. . . . Saw General House, V.C., on shore and got him to promise to do what he could. We had a bad time going home. We were slung off the ship in wooden cases. It was very rough indeed, and when the wooden case hit the flat barge it bounced like anything. Then we were towed out on this flat barge, open to the great waves and shrapnel, to a lighter, and left off Anzac for a couple of hours. The Turks sent a few shells, absent-mindedly. Finally, a trawler brought us off, very angry.

S. dined, a scholarly fanatic, interesting about the next war, which he thinks will be with Russia, in fifteen years. A lot of people going sick.

I saw Cox tonight, who said that this is the worst storm we have had. We have only one day's water supply. We could have had as much as we had wanted, but many of the cans stored on the beach are useless, as they have had holes knocked in them by the shrapnel. We are not as abstemious as the Turks, who had been lying for so many hours under the sun, and shall suffer from thirst badly.

*Saturday, July 3rd, 1915.* Anzac. Macaulay has come as our artillery officer. I dined with him and H. Woods last night. Yesterday it rained. Jack's boat has gone. We are being badly shelled here. I shall have to change my dugout, if this goes on. The guide Katzangaris has been hit in the mouth.

*Sunday, July 4th, 1915.* Saw the Maoris, who had just landed. General Godley made them a first-class speech. They danced a fine Haka with tremendous enthusiasm in his honour when he had finished. They liked digging their dugouts, and seemed to like it when they came to human remains. . . . More people going sick. Doctor F. Told me that he and another doctor had asked to be allowed to help on board the hospital ships where they have more wounded than they can deal with, short-handed as they are, but have been refused permission by the R.A.M.C.

There has been a great explosion at Achi Baba. Macaulay saw a transport of ours sunk this afternoon. . . . G.L. came ashore with depressing accounts of Russia. He is probably going to come on this beach. Hope he does. Went off and bathed with Macaulay. Saw Colonel Bauchop, who promised me a present of some fresh drinking-water tomorrow.

*Monday, July 5th, 1915*. Kaba Tepé. A breathless, panting morning, still and blue and fiery hot, with not a ripple on the sea. Colonel Bauchop, commanding the Otago Mounted Rifles, was shot in the shoulder last night. This morning we have had an exhibition of "frightfulness" in the shape of vast shells. They burst with a tremendous roar that echoes to the sky and across the sea for more than a minute. Their case of bullets fall over the sea in a great area. They started by striking the sea and raising great columns of water. Now they burst and fall on land and sea.

It has had the great result of getting rid of Mr.. Lock, the Socialist Czech, from the doorway of my dugout. He was an undergraduate at —— and afterwards a Labour candidate. Now he is Colonel P.'s cook.

The transport that Macaulay saw go down was French. Six lives lost. The explosion down south was a French ammunition store. This shelling makes one's head ache.

*Tuesday, July 6th, 1915*. Kaba Tepé. Yesterday I went to Quinn's Post with General Godley in the morning. There was a fair amount of shelling. They had just hit thirteen men in Courtney's before we got there. We went into a mine that was being dug towards and under the Turkish trenches. At the end of the sap the Turks were only six to eight feet away. We could hear them picking. The time for blowing in had very nearly come. These underground people take it all as a matter of course. I should hate fighting on my stomach in a passage two feet high, yards under the ground. The Turks were throwing bombs from the trenches, and these hit the ground over us, three of them, making it shudder. Down below they talk in whispers. We went round the trenches. Saw none so fine as last time, when we came to the Millionaires' Sap, so called because it was made by six Australians, each the son of a millionaire.

In the afternoon I tried to sleep, but there was too much shelling. Kyumjiyan was hit, and has gone; S.B. was grazed. It was 11.2 shells filled with all kinds of stuff. We answered with a monitor whose terrific percussions shook my dugout, bringing down dust and stones. A submarine appeared, and all the destroyers were after her. Then two aeroplanes started a fight as the sun set down towards Helles, appearing and vanishing behind crimson clouds. Captain Buck, the Maori doctor and M.P., dined with us, to wind up an exciting day.

This morning is like yesterday. No breath of air, but the day is more clear, and Samothrace and Imbros look very peaceful. Early again the shelling began. As I was shaving outside three shells hit the beach just in front. I wasn't watching the third, but suddenly heard a great burst of laughter. At the first shell a bather had rushed back to his dugout; the shell had come and knocked it in on the top of him, and he was dug out, naked and black, but smiling and none the worse. "Another blasted sniper," he said, which made the men laugh.

Active preparations are being made to fight the gas, as the intelligence says it is going to be used. Am going out with the general at 9.30. Was sent to get Colonel Parker, but found him sick, and under pretty heavy fire, having a new dugout built. Came back and stood with the general, Thoms and others outside headquarters. A shell burst just by us, bruised the general in the ribs, and filled his eyes with dirt. Went out with Colonel Anthill and Poles. Talked of arranging a truce to bury the Turkish dead on our parapet. They said that otherwise our men must get cholera; the heat and sand and flies and smell is awful. We met Colonel Bauchop with his arm in a sling, but the bullet out of his shoulder, and Colonel White with his head still bandaged. The Australians very cheerful.

*Wednesday, July 7th, 1915.* Kaba Tepé. A fierce, expectant dawn. We shelled furiously at 4.30 a.m. Now absolute peace on a glassy sea. Last night Bentinck, Jack Anderson and I bathed. I was at the end of the pier; as I was beginning to dress a shell burst very close, the smoke and powder in my face. I fled half dressed; Colonel P. rose like Venus from the sea followed with nothing. A calm Marine gave me my cigarette-holder.

One of the prisoners reported that on the occasion of the armistice Turkish staff officers had put on Red Crescent clothes in order to have a look at our trenches. . . . No news of Jack.

The Turks put up five crosses yesterday, all of which we shot down. I first thought it was probably Greeks or Armenians who wanted to surrender, and telephoned to Courtney's to see if I could get into touch with them, but now I think it's probably Turks who were anxious to make us shoot at the sign of our own religion. In this they succeeded.

Colonel Johnson, Commanding the New Zealand Infantry Brigade, gone sick. I persuaded the mess to get inoculated for cholera. Last night I dined with Woods and Macaulay. They told Eastern stories, and we had a very contented time, drinking *mavrodaphne* and looking at the sea.

The Turks shelled a little after eight, in answer to our tiresome provocative monitor fire. This morning Tahu arrived from Egypt with letters. The Turks are bombing something cruel from Kaba Tepé. . . . It's a beautiful sight—a sea like lapis-lazuli and a burning sun, with columns of water like geysers where the shells hit. A good many men hit here today.

*Saturday, July 10th, 1915.* Kaba Tepé. I went with General Godley to the Triad, and dined with Admiral de Robeck. Took the general's things to put them on board the picket-boat, but as I got there a shell struck her and knocked a hole in her. There was another one, and we sat and waited uncomfortably in this till he came. . . . Found Alec Ramsay on board. Slept in Commodore Roger Keyes' cabin. Very comfortable. He was very kind. Went to G.H.Q. and had lunch with L. and Bob Graves.

*Sunday, July 11th, 1915.* Felt much better. Went ashore and saw Colonel Hawker and the Turkish prisoners. . . . Came back late at night, after some very jolly days. Best week-end I ever spent. The Turks have asked for another armistice in the south. This has been refused. If they attack, they will have to do it across their own dead, piled high, and this is not good for morale.

By this time the persecutions of the interpreters had greatly diminished. They were still badly treated by a man called Ot, but to a large extent they had won the respect of the troops by their behaviour. The chief interpreter was an old Greek of some sixty-two or sixty-three years, Mr. Kyriakidis, who was given a medal for conspicuous gallantry at the bombardment of Alexandria and had served with General Stuart's unfortunate expedition. He was a gentleman, and one of the straightest men I have met. His simplicity, courtesy, and unfailing courage had gained him many friends. He was also endowed with considerable humour.

A relation had sent me a gas mask, at that time a rarity at Anzac. I did not believe that I should need it, and made a present of it to the first man I met, who happened to be Mr. Kyriakidis. He went down and played poker with the other interpreters on the beach. He put on my respirator as a poker mask, with much swagger. This put the fear of death into the interpreters, who sent a deputation to G.H.Q. intelligence, insisting that they should also be provided with masks.

*Monday, July 12th, 1915*. Kaba Tepé. By the way, an unhappy shadow was shot yesterday, an interpreter of whom we none of us knew anything, and who was on no list. Things are not very comfortable. The fire is increasingly heavy. All the air is full of thudding and broken echoes. No one minds anything much, but high explosives. . . . The hospitals are being moved. They had too many casualties where they were before.

*Tuesday, July 13th, 1915*. Kaba Tepé. Tremendous fire around Achi Baba yesterday. French advanced 150 and we 200 yards. Don't know what the losses were. I went with Macaulay and Woods to No. 3 Post, to Bauchop's Fountain. They can snipe there very close, and killed a man a couple of days ago, two yards off under the olives, and wounded his mate, who crawled back into the sandy way. On both sides there is tall wild lavender and what M. calls pig's parsley.

We crawled down a sandy path to the sea, M. rather sick. Met the general going back, who told us not to bathe. In the evening Tahu got out his gramophone and we had some good songs when the shooting was not too much.

Ramadan began today. George Lloyd arrived this afternoon and said they wanted to send me to Tenedos for a special job.

Yesterday evening General Godley went to Courtney's Post. As he got there the Turks shelled with heavy stuff, killing and wounding about twenty men. Reynell came to see me. I like him very much indeed.

*Diary. Sunday, July 18th, 1915*. Kaba Tepé. They are now shelling the pier, and killed a doctor, cutting off both his legs, and several other people, when I was bathing from the pier. Everybody is again going sick. The situation is changing. Every night we are landing guns. The moon is young now and growing. It seems, therefore, reasonable to expect that we cannot land forces of men that take time before the nights are moonless; that is, in about a month's time the preparations ought to be ready.

A few days ago we had an attack on Achi Baba, won about 400 yards and lost about 5000 men. Two battalions got out of touch and were lost for a considerable time. The *Imbros Journal, Dardanelles Driveller*, or whatever it's called, said *"their return was as surprising as that of Jonah from the belly of the whale."* Good, happy, author!

A German Taube over us throwing bombs and also heavy stuff, but not much damage lately. George Lloyd was here this afternoon, and while we talked a shell burst and hit four men.

*Monday, July 19th, 1915.* Kaba Tepé. My dugout has now become a centre for Australian and New Zealand officers, all good fellows. I had it made small on purpose, so that no one would offer to share it with me, and that makes it less convenient for the crowd that now sit in it. Two old friends come when the day's work is over, and grow sentimental by moonlight; both ill and, I am afraid, getting worse. All the talk is now about gassing. It is thought that they will do it to us here. As usual, new troops are reported to be coming against us.

*Tuesday, July 20th, 1915.* Kaba Tepé. There is always something fresh here. Now a lot of sharks are supposed to have come in. During the last two days there has been absolute silence, no shelling at all, nothing but the sound of crickets and at night a singsong chorus as the men drag up the great tanks prepared for water. S.B. Yesterday worked out a theory to prove that the Turks were to attack us last night.

1. No gunfire yesterday; the reason being they (the Turks) were moving troops. They didn't want us to fire at their troops, therefore didn't draw fire by shooting at us.

2. Ulemas have come down. There must be a special reason for this.

3. 10,000 coming up. Gas being prepared.

All this means an attack on Anzac. To wipe us out would be a great feather in their cap. I am inclined to doubt another great attack. . . . Tempers all a bit ruffled. General Birdwood is sick. The heat is fierce and the stillness absolute. This afternoon I heard from Dedez, who asked me to go to Tenedos for a time. . . .

*Wednesday, July 21st, 1915.* Imbros. On Wednesday I went over to G.H.Q. and met old friends among the war correspondents. Met some of the New Zealanders who had come over for a rest, but were coming back for the expected attack. Meanwhile, they had been kept on fatigue most of the time, and were unutterably weary. At Imbros I was ordered to go to Tenedos and Mytilene.

*Thursday, July 22nd, 1915.* Came back to Anzac in the same boat with Ashmead Bartlett and Nevinson, war correspondents, and got leave to take them round in the afternoon.

Later on, during one of the worst days of the Suvla fighting, I met my friend Nevinson picking his way amongst the wounded on their stretchers under fire. "After this," he said, decisively, "I shall confine myself strictly to revolutions."

*Diary. July 23rd.* Started for Imbros and went in the *Bacchante* pinnace, which was leaking badly from a shell hole. There were six of us on deck, and one man was hit when we were about a hundred yards out. We put back and left him on shore.

*Saturday, July 24th.* Imbros. Went for a ride on a mule, and had a bathe.

At this point in the campaign, though the morale was excellent, depression began to grow. There was a great deal of sickness, form which practically no one escaped, though it was less virulent in its form than later in the summer. I had been ill for some time, and was very anxious to avoid being invalided to Egypt, and was grateful for the chance of going to the islands for a change of climate and light work, for the few days that were sufficient to give another lease of health.

The feeling that invades almost every side-show, sooner or later, that the home authorities cared nothing and knew nothing about the Dardanelles, was abroad. The policy and the strategy of the expedition were bitterly criticized. I remember a friend of mine saying to me: "All this expedition is like one of Walter Scott's novels, upside down." Walter Scott generally put his hero at the top of a winding stair, where he comfortably disposed, one by one, of a hundred of his enemies. "Now," he said, "what we have done was, first of all to warn the Turks that we were going to attack by having a naval bombardment. That made them fortify the Dardanelles, but still they were not completely ready. We then send a small force to attack, to tell them that we really are in earnest, and to ask them if they are quite ready. In fact, we have put the man who ought to be, not the hero, but the villain of the piece, at the top of the corkscrew stair, and we have given him so much notice that when the hero attacks the villain has more men at the top of the circular stair than the hero has at the bottom. It's like throwing pebbles at a stone wall," he said, mixing his metaphors.

*Diary. Sunday, July 25th, 1915.* On the Sea. I left for Tenedos; a most beautiful day. We have just been to Anzac, very burnt and wounded amongst the surrounding greenery. Pretty peaceful there, only a few bullets coming over.

Perhaps the record of a sojourn in the Greek Islands on what was really sick-leave, as the work was of the lightest, should not be included in a war diary, but the writer looks back with amusement and pleasure to days that were not uneventful. They were passed with friends who were playing a difficult and most arduous part, and whose services, in many cases, have not received the recognition that was their due.

It was pleasant once again to be lord of the horizon, to have space through which to roam, and lovely hills and valleys to ride across in the careless, scented air of the Mediterranean summer, with the sea shining a peacock-blue through the pines. It is this space and liberty that men cramped in a siege desire, more than the freedom from the shelling of the enemy's guns. There was much, too, that was *opéra bouffe* in the Islands, that made a not unpleasant contrast to the general life at Anzac.

If there was spy mania on the Peninsula, it was multiplied tenfold, and quite reasonably, on the Islands, where part of the population were strongly pro-Ally, another part pro-German, while others were anti-British by the accidental kind of ricochet. These were the royalist followers of King Constantine, who hated Venizelos, and consequently the friends of Venizelos, Great Britain and France.

The situation on the Islands was one with which it was extremely hard to cope. We were very anxious to safeguard the lives of our men, and to prevent information going to the enemy, and, at the same time, not to pursue German methods. It was unceasing work, with a great strain of responsibility. There was an inevitable *va et vient* between the Peninsula and Imbros. From Imbros boats could slip across to Tenedos, Mytiline or the mainland. The native *caïques* would drop in at evening, report, be ordered to stay till further notice, and would drift away like ghosts in the night. Men, and women, performed remarkable feats, in appearing and disappearing. They were like pictures on a film in their coming and their going. Watchers and watched, they thrust and parried, discovered and concealed, glowed on the picture and darkened.

Anatasio, a Serbian by birth, was one of our workers, conspicuous for his quickness and intelligence. At the outbreak of the war he had already been five months in an Austrian prison at Cattaro, but the prospect of battle stimulated his faculties, and he escaped. One day at luncheon, I asked him where it was that he had learned Italian, which he did not talk very well.

"While I was in prison at Smyrna," said he.

"What for?" said I.

"For stabbing a Cretan," said he, and added that he would rather be five years in prison in Turkey than one in Austria.

Then there was Avani, one of the most vivid personalities that I have ever met. He was a poet and a clairvoyant, a mesmerist and a masseur, a specialist in rheumatism and the science of detection, once a member of General Chermside's *gendarmerie* in Crete, and ex-chief of the Smyrna fire brigade. The stories of him are too many, and too flamboyant, to tell.

*Diary.* Avani mesmerized the wife of the Armenian *dragoman.* Unfortunately it went wrong. Her obedience to his volition was delayed and she only obeyed his commands in the wrong company some hours after.

He had given proof of rare courage, and also considerable indiscretion. On one occasion, armed to the teeth, he burst into a perfectly innocent house at night, and, revolver in hand, hunted a terrified inhabitant. His only evidence against this man was, that when he had been caught and hurled to the ground and sat upon, his heart had beaten very fast, which would not happen, insisted Avani, if he had not been guilty of some crime.

Amongst our opponents were the romantic but sinister Vassilaki family, two brothers and three lovely sisters. Talk about them in the Islands was almost as incessant as was talk about shelling on the Peninsula.

*Diary. Monday, July 26th, 1915.* Tenedos. Yesterday I was very ill, and again today, but was injected with something or other and feel better, but weak. Tried to sleep yesterday, but one of our monitors at Rabbit Island bombarded hugely, shaking the bugs down on me. This place is clean, but there are bugs and some lice. Last night I dined with the Governor, Colonel Mullins, and a jolly French doctor, and Thompson, who has fallen ill. Am carrying on for him at the moment.

*Tuesday, July 27th, 1915*. Tenedos. Went to the trenches at Tenedos. They face the enemy. That is the most military thing about them. Thompson went out to see the inhabitants. I was going with him, but felt worse and went to rest. The Turks here are in a very bad way. We do not allow them to work. It is inevitable. They mayn't fish or work at the aerodrome.

*Wednesday, July 28th, 1915*. Tenedos. Interpreted for the Governor of Tenedos, who, like Jupiter, rules with might, in the afternoon. In the evening I saw the Mufti, who had a list of starving, widows and indigent. . . . Last night the Cretan soldiers started ragging the Turks and singing, till I stopped them. They were quite good.

Still ill, but better. Had a beautiful walk in the evening, and a long talk with the Greek refugees working in the vines by the edge of the sea. The old patriarch addressed me all the time as *chorbaji*—that is, possessor of the soup, the headman of the village.

*Thursday, July 29th, 1915*. Tenedos. Yesterday I rode over to the French aerodrome, coming late for luncheon, but had coffee with about twenty French officers, all very jolly. Promised to let me fly over the Dardanelles. I went on to the Cretans in a pinewood. Their officer, a Frenchman, very keen on a show in Asia Minor. . . . The elder Vassilaki has been arrested. His brother saw him go by in a trawler. Am going to Mytilene, then return after three days, and leave here on Tuesday for Anzac. No news of anything happening. Tenedos is a beautiful town in its way, surrounded by windmills, with Mount Elias in the background. Its streets are narrow, picturesque, and hung with vines that make them cool and shady. At the end of the town there is a very fine old Venetian fortress, but its magnificence is outside; inside it is furnished with round stone cannon-balls, ammunition for catapults. In the last war the Greeks took the island, but one day a Turkish destroyer popped her nose in. All the Greeks fled, and the Mufti and the Moslems went and pulled the Greek flag down. Then in came a Greek destroyer, and the Turkish one departed. The

Mufti and the Turks were taken off to Mudros, where he and they were beaten. He narrowly missed being killed. . . .

*Friday, July 30th, 1915.* Tenedos. Slept very badly again. Had a letter from the O.C. Poor Onslow killed, lying on his bed by his dugout. A good fellow and a fine soldier. Aden nearly captured. I prophesied its capture in Egypt. I shall be recalled before anything happens.

The radiant air of Tenedos gave health as it did in Homeric times, and I left with the desire that others should have the same chance as myself of using that beautiful island as a hospital; but all the pictures there were not bright. Under the wind-mills above the shining sea there were the motionless, dark-clad, desolate Moslem women, sitting without food or shelter. Their case, it is true, was no harder than that of the thousands of Greek refugees who had been driven from their homes, but these at any rate were living amongst kindred, while the unfortunate Moslems were without help or sympathy, except that which came from their enemies, the British.

*Diary. Friday, July 30th, 1915.* Mytilene. I left by the Greek boat yesterday. On the boat I met a man who might be useful as an interpreter, Anibal Miscu, Entrepreneur de Travaux Publiques, black as my hat, but talks English, French, German, Italian, Spanish, Turkish, Greek, Arabic, Bulgar, Russian, and something else. The boat was stopped by our trawler, No.—, and searched for contraband of war. The Greeks were furious. I landed at Mytilene, not having slept much and felling bad. Avani said they had tried to bribe him to allow some raisins through, and kicked up the devil of a row. He seemed to think that the raisins were dynamite. He was left guarding the raisins, all night, I believe, with his revolver.

I was given a warm welcome by Compton Mackenzie at Mytilene. He, fortunately for me, had been sent there by G.H.Q. I found several old friends—Heathcote-Smith, the consul, whose work it would be impertinent for me to praise, and Hadkinson, whom I had last seen at my own house in England, where he was staying with me when the Archduke Franz Ferdinand had been murdered. Hadkinson had passed most of his life on his property in Macedonia. Of the eastern and southern languages he talked Greek, Italian, Turkish, Bulgarian, Serbian, and Albanian. His voice was as delightful as his knowledge of Balkan ballads was wide, and his friends made him sing the endless songs of the mountaineers. His personality had carried him through experiences that would have been disastrous to most men; battles decisive in European's history had raged in front of his doors, while his house had remained untouched; brigands of most of the Balkan races had crossed his farm, rarely driving off his stock, and most of the local peasantry in their misfortunes had come to him for help, for advice, doctoring or intercession. Until the European War had crashed upon the world, Hadkinson had been a good example of the fact that minorities, even when they are a minority of one, do not always suffer.

The people of Mytilene, at that time, were very pro-English, though the officials were of the faction of King Constantine. The desire I frequently heard expressed was that Great Britain should take over Mytilene, as she did the Ionian Islands, and that when Mytilene had been put in order it should be restored to Greece.

*Diary. Friday, July 30th, 1915.* Mytilene.—and Hadkinson have gone out with a motor-boat and a machine gun. The Vassilakis, or some of them, have been deported. Vassilaki to Imbros and the beautiful sisters to Mudros. . . . It's a blazing, burning day.

*Saturday, July 31st, 1915.* Mytilene. A gaming-house. Moved from my first hotel to a larger and more disreputable one. Lunched with Hadkinson and Compton Mackenzie.

. . . . At Thasos the Greeks have arrested our agents under the orders of Gunaris. Have worked, and am feeling better.

*Later.* The three Miss Vassilakis have not gone to Mudros. They turned up this morning, and I was left to deal with them. Not as beautiful, except one, as I had been led to believe. They got Avani out of the room and wept and wept and wept. I told them their brother would be all right. . . . They wanted to know who prevented them from leaving. I said it was the Admiral. That good man is far away.

*Sunday, August 1st, 1915.* Mytilene. Avani went off with the three Miss Vassilakis, in hysterics, last night. They were very angry with us. It seems probable that we shall have a landing on the mainland here to divert attention from the Peninsula. Sir Ian Hamilton is coming down to have a look. A good deal of friction over the blockade. The present system causes much inconvenience to all concerned.

They were enchanting days of golden light or starlit darkness, while one drank health almost in the concrete from the hot pine-scented air and the famous wine of Mytilene. The conditions of others was unfortunately less happy. There were some 80,000 Greek refugees from the mainland, for who the Greek government had done practically nothing, while the patriotic Greek communities of England and America had not had the opportunity of relieving their necessities. We all did what we could to help these people.

There was another question allied to this to be considered: whether a Greek expeditionary Force, largely composed of these refugees, should be sent into Asia Minor. The danger of such a campaign to the native Greeks was obvious; mainly for this reason it was not undertaken. But while no expedition occurred, there was much talk about one. The fact that Sir Ian Hamilton had come was widely known. It was said that great preparations were being made, and these rumours probably troubled the Turks and kept troops of theirs in a non-combatant area.

*Diary. Sunday, August 1st, 1915.* Mytilene. Lunched with Mavromati Bey. He was very heroic, saying he preferred to die rather than to lie under the German yoke, but there were no signs of a funeral at luncheon, which was delicious.

Dined with Hadkinson, and was taken ill, but got all right and went off with him on the motor-boat *Omala* after dinner. H. said that for a long time he had felt that I was coming, and had ordered a lamb for me to be executed the following day; told the cook, too, to get some special herbs. The object of our journey was to find a wonderful woman, lithe as a leopard and strong as a horse, and put her somewhere near Aivali to gain information.

*Monday, August 2nd, 1915. Omala* off Moskonisi. At dawn this morning we came to Moskonisi, luminous in the sea. A decrepit shepherd led a flock of sheep along the beach. His name is Panayotis and he has a Homeric past; he killed two Turkish guards who courted a beautiful sister-in-law before marriage. Then he killed two others for a pusillanimous brother-in-law after marriage, and he has also sent two other Turks to their rest, though H. does not know the reason for their death.

Hadkinson had collected a large band of Palikaris, but the motor-boat only held a few, the cream of them. He had English names for most of them—Little John, Robin Hood, etc. They were tall men with very quick, clever eyes and lithe movements, picturesquely dressed. One of them had a cross glittering in his *kalpak*, and A.M. (for Asia Minor) on both sides of the cross. He said to me, pointing to Aivali: "There is my country; we are an orphan people. For 150 years we have shed our blood and given our best to Greece. Now in her hour of triumph and in our day of wretchedness she denies us help. May she ever be less!"

Another Greek had been to Mecca as a soldier and stayed there and in the Yemen for some years. The Captain was a quiet man, but apparently very excitable. They were delighted with their army rifles. The woman, Angeliko Andriotis, did not turn up at Gymno, so we went on to Moskonisi, the men often playing on a plaintive flute, and sometimes singing low together. At breakfast, soon after dawn, we had a sort of orchestra.

We arrived opposite to Aivali. The Turks have sunk three *mauna*. . . . Hadkinson saw one of their submarines.

The situation at Aivali is curious. It lies at the head of a bay. Above it there are hills, not high hills, but high enough, the men said who were with us, to prevent its being bombarded by the Turks. They looked at it with longing eyes. Their families were there. They kept on cursing the "black dogs" and saying they would eat them. There were 35,000 people in Aivali, now only 25,000; 10,000 have left lately. The sword of Damocles hangs over the rest of them, for they might be sent off into the interior at any moment. We went on to the channel between Moskonisi and Pyrgos. There we found the child of the woman, who was sent with a note to her. Men were moving in the olives and the scrub some distance off, whom the Greeks said were their own compatriots.

The boy, who was thirteen, took the letter and put it under his saddle. He went off calmly to get past the Turks, without any air of adventure about him. The others realized the stage on which they were acting, and swaggered finely. I got off on Pyrgos with Hadkinson, and went to a small, rough chapel, where they were bringing the *eikons* back in triumph.

The beauty of it all was beyond words. I bathed on a silver sand in transparent water between the two islands. Moskonisi, by the way, doesn't mean the Island of Perfume, but takes its name from a great brigand who practically held the island against the Turks about thirty years ago.

After a time the boy returned with a letter from his mother, and a peasant with binoculars. He and the peasant both said that they had seen a great oil-pool in Aivali Bay. We thought that this must be from a submarine, and dashed round there at full speed, but found nothing. Then we decided to come home. We picked up some of the men we had dropped *en route*; and they brought us presents of *gran* Turco, *basilica* and sweet-scented pinks. Then they played their flutes as the sun set, and Hadkinson sang Greek, Bulgarian and Turkish songs, singing the *Imam's Call* beautifully and, to the horror of his Greek followers, reverently.

We might have bagged the twenty-five Turks, or whatever the number there were, quite easily, but H. Thought this would have produced reprisals. He was probably right.

*Tuesday, August 3rd, 1915.* Mytilene. We got back last night after dinner and heard that Sir Ian Hamilton, George Lloyd, and George Brodrick had been here. . . . One of the poor Whittall boys very badly wounded. They were a fine pair.

*Wednesday, August 4th, 1915.* Mytilene. Yesterday we heard that the Turks had sent the town-crier to the equivalent of the capital of Moskonisi to say that any Greek going beyond a certain line would be put to death. Miss Vassilake turned up, and said that she and her sister would come with me to Tenedos. I said they couldn't.

We dined with General Hill and his Staff and slept on the *Canopus*. . . . Mackenzie no better. . . . A good deal of friction at Tenedos. Athanasius Vassilaki has escaped, and everyone is annoyed. Some men have been arrested for signalling.

*Thursday, August 5th, 1915.* Tenedos. Most of the officers sick. I was asked to stay on at Tenedos, but felt I must get back at once. Christo says that it's dull here, and Kaba Tepé is better than this house. Turkish guns have been firing at our trawlers. A couple of men wounded. Examined a man just escaped for Constantinople. Constantinople is quite cheery: theatres, carriages, boats, etc. The Germans say we can't hold out on the Peninsula when the bad weather comes.

Then I examined a Lebanon French soldier who had arrested a child and an old man for signalling. . . .

Here there are some pages of my diary missing, but the events that occurred are still vividly in my mind.

109

In company with other officers I went first to Imbros, hearing the thunder of the guns from Helles. In passionate haste we tried every means to get to the Peninsula for the great battle. I left Christo to follow with my kit, if he could, with the future doubtful before him, and no certainty, except that of being arrested many times.

In the harbour at Imbros on that night there was a heavy sea, and in a small, dancing boat we quested through the darkness for any ship sailing to Anzac. One was found at last that was on the point of sailing, and off we went.

The instructions of my friend Ian Smith were to get to Suvla, and luck favoured him, for at dawn we lay off Suvla, and a trawler took him ashore.

Along the heights and down to the seashore the battle growled and raged, and it was difficult to know what was the mist of the morning or battle smoke. I got off at Anzac, which was calm, realizing that I had missed the first attack.

*Diary. Saturday, August 7th, 1915.* Kaba Tepé. I went out to headquarters, which are now beyond Colonel Bauchop's old headquarters. He, poor fellow, had just been hit and was said to be dying. Dix[7] again wounded in the leg and Cator killed when he had just been promoted. I saw the general; on the way out I met 300 Turkish prisoners and was ordered to return and embark them. We came to the pier on the beach, then three shells fell on and beside it; both S.B. and I thought we were going to have a very bad time, packed like sardines, with panicky prisoners. Embarking them took time; we were all very snappy, but we got them off. I was glad to find S.B. and Woods. All the dugouts here are desolate. I saw General Birdwood, who was very sad about Onslow.[8] He talked of the water difficulties. He was cheerful, as usual, and said he thought we should know which way things were going by 5 o'clock. S. was less cheerful.

I went back to headquarters, a weary trudge of two hot, steaming miles, past masses of wounded. The saps were constantly blocked. Then back to Anzac for a few hours' sleep, till I can get my kit.

*Sunday, August 8th, 1915.* Near Anafarta. Slept badly last night at Anzac. The place was very desolate with everyone away. I got up before a clear dawn and went out to the observation post, where I found

---

7. Naval beach-master.
8. His A.D.C., a Captain in the Indian Lancers, who had been killed.

General Godley and General Shaw. Our assault began. We saw our men in the growing light attack the Turks. It was a cruel and beautiful sight, for it was like a fight in fairyland; they went forward in parties through the beautiful light, with the clouds crimsoning over them. Sometimes a tiny, gallant figure would be in front, then a puff would come and they would be lying still. We got to within about forty yards of the Turks; later we lost ground. Meanwhile, men were streaming up, through awful heat. There were Irish troops cursing the Kaiser. At the observation post we were being badly shelled. The beauty of the place was extraordinary, and made it better than the baldness of Anzac, but we were on an unpropitious hillside, and beyond there were mules and men, clustered thickly.

Then I was sent back to Kaba Tepé, where I found a lot of wounded prisoners, who had not been attended to. I woke a doctor who had not slept for ages. He talked almost deliriously, but came along and worked like a real good man. I saw General House, V.C., and suggested attaching one doctor to the prisoners, so that we should not get contagious diseases.

Returned to Bauchop's Post and examined a couple of Germans from the *Goeben*. Got a good deal of information. Then I was telephoned for to interrogate a wounded Greek, who had, however, got lost. I went back outside the hospital, where there were many wounded lying. I stumbled upon poor A.C. (a schoolfellow), who had been wounded about 3 a.m. the day before, and had lain in the sun on the sand all the previous day. He recognized me, and asked me to help him, but was light-headed. There were fifty-six others with him; M. and I counted. It was awful having to pass them. A lot of the men called out: *"We are being murdered."* The smells were fearful.... I went down a sap to the north to find the Greek. Fierce shelling began. The sap was knocked down in front and behind.

I came to a field hospital, situated where the troops were going through. There no one knew where Taylor's Hollow, the place where the Greek was supposed to be, was. While I was there shelling was bad. Several of the wounded were hit again. One man was knocked in on the top of me, bleeding all over. I returned to meet Thoms, who said he knew the way. We ran the gauntlet....

I had a curious, beautiful walk, looking for the wounded Greek, going to nineteen hospitals. Many wounded everywhere. First I saw one of our fellows who had met ten Turks and had ten bayonet wounds. He was extremely cheerful. Then a couple of Turks in the shadow of some pines, one dying and groaning, really unconscious. I offered the other water from my bottle, but he refused because of his companion, using Philip Sidney's words in Turkish.

Men were being hit everywhere. After going by fields and groves and lanes I came back to where the wounded were lying in hundreds, in the sap going to the sea, near Bauchop's Fountain. There a man called to me in French. He was the Greek I was looking for, badly wounded. He talked a great deal. Said 200,000 reinforcements were expected from Gallipoli. No gas would be used here. . . .

*Monday, August 9th, 1915.* No. 3 outpost. Slept uncomfortably on the ground. Went before dawn to observation post; returned to examine prisoners. Had an unsuccessful expedition with Hastings to find some guns which he said had been lost between the lines.

Bullets came streaming down our valley, and we put up a small wall of sacks, 3 feet high, behind which we slept. I was sitting at breakfast this morning listening to Colonel Manders[9] talking, when suddenly I saw Charlie B. Put his hand to his own head and say: "By G—, he's killed!"

Manders fell back dead, with a bullet through his temple, he was a very good fellow.

Sir Ian Hamilton came ashore. I saw him for a moment. Then to Kaba Tepé; going and coming one passes a lone of bodies, some dreadful, being carried for burial. Many still lying out. The last wounded have been more pitiful than anything I have seen. Cazalet is badly wounded; I hope he will recover; he is a good boy. Colonel Malone was killed last night and Jacky Hughes wounded. Lots of shelling.

Coming back I had to go outside the crowded sap, and got sniped. Thoms and I had a very lively time of it.

Came back for Manders' funeral. I was very fond of him. General Godley read a few sentences with the help of my electric torch, which failed. Four others were buried with him. Later I saw a great shell strike the grave. A cemetery, or rather lots, growing up round us. There are dead buried or half buried in every gully.

*Tuesday, August 10th, 1915.* No. 3 outpost. Christo arrived with my kit and some grapes last night. While we were eating these, two men, one of whom was our cook, were hit, and he being the second cook, it was decided to change our quarters, as a lot of bullets streamed

---

9. A.D.M S., New Zealand Division.

down the gully and we had been losing heavily. I was called up in the night to see about some wounded. The general had said they had better go by boat, because of the difficulty of the saps, but there were no boats, and Manders' death had caused confusion at the hospital. The doctor on the beach said he could not keep the wounded there any longer, because of the rifle fire. I woke Charlied B. We got 200 men from the Canterbury reinforcements. They had been fighting without sleep since Sunday morning, but evacuated about 300 wounded to below Walker's Ridge. There were no complaints. The Turks still had to be left. They called to me at night and at dawn. I gave them drinks, and later, after sunrise, shifted them into the shade, which made them cheerful. The general had not slept for three nights. The day went badly for us. We lost Chunuk Bair, and without it we cannot win the battle. The Turks have fought very finely, and all praise their courage. It was wonderful to see them charging down the hill, through the storm of shrapnel, under the white ghost wreaths of smoke. Our own men were splendid. The N.Z. Infantry Bridade must have ceased to exist. Meanwhile, the condition of the wounded is indescribable. They lie in the sand in rows upon rows, their faces caked with sand and blood; one murmur for water; no shelter from the sun; many of them in saps, with men passing all the time scattering more dust on them. There is hardly any possibility of transporting them. The fire zones are desperate, and the saps are blocked with ammunition transport and mules, also whinnying for water, carrying food, etc. Some unwounded men almost mad from thirst, cursing.

We all did what we could, but amongst so many it was almost impossible. . . . The wounded Turks still here. I kept them alive with water. More prisoners in, report another 15,000 men at Bulair and a new Division, the 7th, coming against us here. I saw General Cooper,[10] wounded, in the afternoon, and got him water. His Staff had all been killed or wounded. . . .

If the Turks continue to hold Chunuk Bair and get up their big guns there, we are, as a force, for worse off than at Anzac. What has happened is roughly this: we have emerged from a position which was unsatisfactory, but certain, into one that is uncertain but partly satisfactory. If the Turks have the time to dig themselves in, then we are worse off than before, because we shall again be held up, with the winter to face, and time running hard against us, with an extended front. The Turks will still have land communications, while we shall

---

10. Irish Guards, commanding 29th Irish Brigade.

only have sea communications, and though we ourselves shall be possibly better off, because we shall now have a harbour, the Turks some time will almost certainly be able to break through, though possibly not able to keep what they take. But the men at Helles will not be freed as our move proposed to free them.

I thought one of the wounded Turks had cholera today. There is very little water, and we have to give them water out of our own bottles. We have a terrible view here: lines of wounded creeping up from the hospital to the cemetery like a tide, and the cemetery is going like a live thing to meet the wounded. Between us and the sea is about 150 yards; this space is now empty of men because of the sniping. There are a number of dead mules on it, which smell horribly but cannot be moved. A curious exhibition of sniping took place just below us this evening, about 50 yards away. Two men were on the open space when a sniper started to shoot at them. They popped into a dry well that practically hid them, but he got his bullets all round them—in front and behind and on the sides. They weren't hit. The camp watched, laughing.

*Thursday, August 12th, 1915.* No. 3 outpost. At 4.30 in the morning I got up and walked with the general. We went up to Rhododendron Ridge to have a look at the Turks. It is a steep, beautiful walk, and a glorious view—trees everywhere and cliffs. We are fastening the cliffs up, and camouflaging the trenches.

I took Nikolas the miller round the observation post in the morning. A new Division is supposed to be against us, the 8th. In the afternoon walked into Anzac to get a drink of water as have had fever and a cruel thirst. The dugouts smell, and washing's difficult. Anglesey gave me excellent water.

*Friday, August 13th, 1915.* No. 3 outpost. Nothing doing. Bullets singing about, but nobody's getting hit. The heat's ferocious, and everybody's feeling ill. Macaulay's wounded.

Worked yesterday morning, also started on new dugout. In the afternoon went with Turkish papers to Anzac. I saw C. He said that this beach for cruelty had beaten the Crimea. . . . Savage feeling with the R.A.M.C. . . .

Streams of mules took water out in the evening as the sun set. I met several men with sunstroke coming in. I saw George Hutton, Royal Welsh Fusiliers, who has become a colonel. He had a hand-to-hand bayonet tussle with a Turk, in the last fight. Another man came up, and killed the Turk with his bayonet. Then, he said, the man, instead of pulling his bayonet out, dashed to another man and asked him for his bayonet, saying: "I have let mine in the Turk."

The battle-cries, by the way, were for the Turks the sonorous, deep-voiced *"Allah, Allah,"* and *"Voor"* ("God, God," "Strike"); while the New Zealanders used often to shout: *"Eggs is cooked."* This apparently irrelevant, unwarlike slogan had its origin in Egypt. There, on field days in the desert, when the men halted to rest, Egyptians would appear magically with primitive kitchens and the cry of *"Eggs is cooked!"*

*Diary. Monday, August 16th, 1915.* No. 3 outpost. Christo will spit on my razor-strop; otherwise he is a good servant. . . . Bathed with Charlie B. Yesterday afternoon. . . . I don't think we want Roumania in. If she had no ammunition and takes a very bad knock from Germany, it would give Germany a very strong strategic position. The Turks who have come in do not really seem very disheartened.

At about this time the expeditionary force entered upon a new phase. The agony of the struggle had passed its crisis. Both sides sat down grimly, to wait for the winter. In many ways our position had distinctly improved. There was more room, and space banished the sense of imprisonment that had afflicted us. The country was not as battle-scarred as Anzac, and walking over the heights at sunset was a feast of loveliness.

We moved our headquarters again, and I went up to a large dugout in what had been a Turkish fort. The troops quartered in this fort were an Indian field battery and sixty-three New Zealanders, all that was left of their battalion. These men had been in the first landing. They had, everyone of them, had dysentery or fever, and the great majority were still sick and over-ripe for hospital.

As time went on, and illness increased, one often heard men and officers say: "If we can't hold the trenches with sound men, we have got to hold them with sick men." When all was quiet, the sick-list grew daily. But when the men knew that there was to be an attack, they fought their sickness, to fight the Turk, and the stream to the hospitals shrank.

I admired nothing in the war more than the spirit of these sixty-three New Zealanders, who were soon to go to their last fight. When the day's work was over, and the sunset swept the sea, we used to lean upon the parapet and look up to where Chunuk Bair flamed, and talk. The great distance from their own country created an atmosphere of loneliness. This loneliness was emphasized by the fact that the New Zealanders rarely received the same recognition as the Australians in the Press, and many of their gallant deeds went unrecorded or were attributed to their greater neighbours. But they had a silent pride that put these things into proper perspective. The spirit of these men was unconquered and unconquerable. At night, when the great moon of the Dardanelles soared and all was quiet except the occasional whine of a bullet overhead, the voices of the tired men continually argued the merits of the expedition, and there was always one end of these discussions: "Well, it may all be a—mistake, but in a war of this size you will have mistakes of this size, and it doesn't matter a d— to us whether we are for it here or in France, for we came out to do one job, and it's nothing to us whether we finish in one place or another." the Turks were not the only fatalities in those days.

We were now well supplied with water, but food of the right kind was a difficulty. It was very hard to obtain supplies for sick men, and here, as always, we met with the greatest kindness from the navy.

Horlick's malted milk and fruit from the Islands did us more good than anything else. Relations of mine in Egypt sent me an enormous quantity of the first, which I was able to distribute to the garrison of the fort. Later, when I was invalided, I bequeathed the massive remnants to a friend who had just landed. Greedily he opened my stores, hoping for the good things of the world—tongues, potted ham and whisky—only to find a wilderness of Horlick's malted milk.

Our position had at last been appreciated at home, and we were no longer irritated, as in the early days by the frivolity and fatuousness of London. Upon one occasion, shortly after the first landing, one of the illustrated papers had a magnificent picture entitled, if I remember right, *The Charge that Won Constantinople.* The picture was of a cavalry charge, led quite obviously by General Godley—and those were the days when we were living on the edge of a cliff, where only centipedes could, and did, charge, and when we were provided with some mules and my six donkeys for all our transport.

There was a remarkable contrast between our war against the Germans and the Turks. In France the British soldier started fighting good-naturedly, and it took considerable time to work him up to a pitch of hatred; at Anzac the troops from the Dominions began their campaign with feelings of contempt and hatred, which gradually turned to respect for the Moslems. At the beginning the great majority of our men had naturally no knowledge of the enemy they were fighting. Once, looking down from a gun emplacement, I saw a number of Turks walking about, and asked why they had not been shot at

"Well," said one man, "it seems hard on them, poor chaps. They aren't doing any harm."

Then up came another: "Those Turks," he said, "they walk about as if this place belongs to them."

I suggested that it was their native land.

"Well," he said, "I never thought of that."

*Diary. Monday, August 16th, 1915.* No. 2 outpost. It's curious the way the men speak of the Turks here. They still can't be made to wear gas helmets, because they say the Turks are clean fighters and won't use gas. . . .

It's good to be high up in this observation post, above the smells, with a magnificent view of hill and valley. We shoot from here pretty often at the Turkish guns. Last night the Dardanelles droned on for hours. This morning the machine guns on both sides were going like dentists' drills. Today it's absolutely still, with only the whirr of aeroplanes overhead.

Bartlett turned up tonight. He had not much hope. . . . Poor Bauchop is dead. News came tonight. . . . A gallant man.

On Wednesday, August 18th, I was sent to G.H.Q. at Imbros, and heard a full account of the tragic battle down at Helles, and the condition of the wounded at Mudros.

When men have gone to the limits of human endurance, when blood had been spilled like water, and the result is still unachieved, bitter and indiscriminate recrimination and criticism inevitably follow. But Anzac had one great advantage. Our leaders were able to see General Birdwood and General Godley every day in the front trenches with themselves, walking about under fire as if they had been on a lawn in England, and the men knew that their own lives were never uselessly sacrificed.

The work of many of the doctors on the Peninsula was beyond all praise, but there was black rage against the chiefs of the R.A.M.C. at Imbros and in Egypt. The anger would have been still greater if their attitude of complacent self-sufficiency had been known.

*Diary. Thursday, August 19th, 1915.* No. 3 outpost. Returned to the Peninsula with Bettinson and Commander Patch, and Phillips, the navigator. When we had come up to the fort I told them not to show their heads at the observation post, as the fort did not belong to me, and I did not want to become unpopular. I got Perry, Captain of the fort, and he sat them down on the parapet, showing them the lines of our trenches. While we talked, a sniper shot at Patch, just missing him, and hitting the parapet beside him. They were very pleased, though the others said I had paid a man to shoot in order to give them fun. Perry said in a friendly way: "That's a good sniper; he's thirteen hundred yards off, so it was a pretty decent shot." then he talked to them, and they felt what anyone must feel talking to these men. They gave us a lot of things, and are sending all sorts of things tomorrow for the men here.

*Friday, August 20th, 1915.* No. 2 outpost. Last night was the first cold night. This morning I went out with the general, who was like a bulldog and a cyclone. We met Birdweed, who was there to see the last Australians arrive, 17th and 18th Brigades, in Reserve Gully. They looked a splendid lot, and it did one's heard good to see them. Some more officers from the *Bacchante* turned up with stores, and special cocoa for me. I was just going off to find Perry when I met him. He is off out; there is a fight tomorrow. I gave him the cocoa. He was glad to have it. . . . The men are all tired out with heat and dysentery, and digging, and fighting. The general and I went up to Sazli Beit Deri. I didn't think it over safe for him.

*Saturday, August 21st, 1915.* No. 2 outpost. Work in the morning. Was to have gone with the general in the afternoon, but prisoners came in to be examined. They said: "Curse the Germans! We can't go on. There are no more men left."

One of them was killed by their own fire after I left. G.L. Came to luncheon. Charlie B., he and I started off together, I feeling pretty bad. It was very hot. We went at a great pace over two or three ridges and across valleys, our guns thundering about us. Finally, I felt so bad I let them go on, and came back. . . . The battle developed and the shooting was fierce and general. While I hunted for General Monash's headquarters I met Colonel A.J., who was rather worried. We had a close shave. . . . I left him, and had an odd adventure. . . . Went home alone through deafening noise, all the valleys under fire. . . . Got at last into a shallow *nullah* that led into a regular gully, and so home.

That day I saw an unforgettable sight. The dismounted Yeomanry attacked the Turks across the salt lakes of Suvla. Shrapnel burst over them continuously; above their heads there was a sea of smoke. Away to the north by Chocolate Hill fires broke out on the plain. The Yeomanry never faltered. On they came through the haze of smoke in two formations, columns and extended. Sometimes they broke into a run, but they always came on. It is difficult to describe the feelings of pride and sorrow with which we watched this advance, in which so many of our friends and relations were playing their part.

*Diary. August 21st.* Charlie B. and G.L. came back all right. . . . The Turks had come over in three waves down Chunuk Bair. The first two were destroyed by naval fire; the third got home into our trenches. Charlie B. Was full of admiration for one old fellow whom he had seen holding up his finger and lecturing to the men when they hung back. Hutton is wounded again.

*Sunday, August 22nd, 1915.* No. 2 outpost. Last night, or this morning at 1 o'clock, I was called up. They said there were 150 Turks in one place and others elsewhere, anxious to surrender. I took the miller, Zachariades and Kyreakidis out to headquarters. Sent back Kyriakidis and the miller, as there was nothing doing and I wanted to keep Kyriakidis. Went on with Zachariades and guides sent by Poles to Colonel Agnew to his H.Q. There we lay on the ground, very cold. They said the Turks had wished to surrender, but there had been no interpreter, and they had been fired on. The Turks were then attacking heavily. Eastwood telephoned that they had fourteen prisoners. I went back to see if they could give any news about our immediate front.

Everyone worried. The — Battalion of Australians had gone wrong. Nobody knew where they were. I sent my escort to try and find them. The Hampshires, who ought to have arrived, had not come. . . . They came along gradually.

We attacked at about four in the morning. The Turkish fire tarried a little, then got furious. We went towards Monash, and met the Hampshires, very tired and way-worn. Bullets sang very viciously, and burst into flame on the rocks. There was a thunder of rifle fire and echoes in the gullies, men dropping now and then. Lower down the gully I found the Hampshires running like mad upwards to the firing line; beyond this a mixed crowd of men without an officer. . . . My guide, wild as a hawk, took us up a ridge. I fell over a dead man in the darkness and hurt my ankle. We had to wait. There seemed a sort of froth of dust on the other side of the ridge, from the rifle fire, and I told the escort to take us down and round the ridge across the valley. He admitted afterwards we had no chance of crossing the other way. In the valley the bullets sang. We came to the half-*nullah* where I had taken such unsatisfactory cover in the afternoon. There we waited a bit, and then ran across the hundred yards to the next gully. Zachariades and the escort grazed. Found the prisoners; the other Zachariades examined them. . . . Spent bullets falling about, but the Greeks never winked. A surrendered Armenian could only tell us that the Turks were very weak before us. The rifle fire died away in the end, and we walked back at dawn, getting here by sunrise. The examined more prisoners till about 11, and slept till 1.

The position is still indefinite. It's on the same old lines, on the hills we are the eyebrows and the Turks are the forehead.

*Monday, August 23rd, 1915.* No. 2 outpost. Perry is wounded, but not badly I hope, in the arm. There is hardly anyone in the fort. The interpreter question becoming very difficult. They are all going sick. Had a quiet evening last night, and read on the parapet. It will be very difficult to keep these old troops here during the winter. The Australians and New Zealanders who have been here a long time are weak, and will all get pneumonia. There was a great wing blowing and the sound of heavy firing. I went to Anzac today, and found men bombing fish. They got about twenty from one bomb, beautiful fish, half-pounders.

*Tuesday, August 24th, 1915.* No. 2 outpost. General Shaw has gone sick to England; General Maude has taken his place. He commands the 13th. He and Harter dined here last night. Longford was killed, Milbanke said to be killed or wounded, and the Hertfordshires have suffered.

This morning we talked about the winter seriously and of preparations to be made. I am for a hill-side. The plain is a marsh and the valley a watercourse. We ought to have fuel, caves for drying clothes, cooking, etc., and mostly this hill is made of dust and sand. A great mail came in last night, but the machine guns got on to the men as they passed by the beach in the moonlight, killed some and wounded five men. So there are the mails lying now, with the machine guns playing round them. . . .

I advised Lawless yesterday at Anzac to move out from the beach, lest the sea should rise and take him like a winkle from his shell.

Saw D. today. He has a curious story to tell of the other night, when I was telephoned for. He said I was called three hours too late. A lot of Turks had come out of their trenches, some unarmed and some armed, and some with bombs. He had gone out and pointed his revolver at one of them, who shouldered arms and stood to attention. Some of the Turks came right up, and the New Zealanders said: "Come in here, Turkey," and began pulling them into the front trench. D. Had feared that the Turks, who were about 200, might rush the trench, and had waved them back and finally fired his revolver and ordered our fellows to fire. It was a pity there was no one there who could talk. Later I saw Temperley, who said when we took Rhododendron Ridge there were 250 Turks on the top. They piled their arms, cheered us and clapped their hands.

Tonight I went to Chaylak Dere with the general and saw General Maude, and his Staff, who looked pretty ill, also Claude Willoughby, who was anxious to take the Knoll by the Apex.

There was a tremendous wind, and dust-storms everywhere. In the gullies men were burying the dead, not covering them sufficiently. My eyes are still full of the dust and the glow of the camp-fires on the hill-side, and the moonlight. It is an extraordinary country to look across—range after range of high hills, precipice and gully, the despair of generals, the grave and oblivion of soldiers.

********

Here the diary stops abruptly, and begins again on Saturday, September 23rd.

*Saturday, September 23rd, 1915.* No. 2 outpost. After writing the above I had a bad go of fever, and was put on to hospital ship. Went aboard with General Birdwood, General Godley, and Tahu Rhodes. The generals had come to inspect the New Zealand hospital ship, which was excellent. That night there was a very heavy fire. I felt some friend of mine would be hit on shore, and the next morning I found Charlie B. on board, not badly wounded, hit in the side.

My friend Charlie B. Had a temper, and was often angry when others were calm, but in moments of excitement he was calm to the point of phlegm. When we were off Mudros there was a great crash, and a jarring of the ship from end to end. I went into Charlie B.'s cabin and said: "Come along. They say we're torpedoed. I'll help you."

"Where are my slippers?" he asked. I said: "Curse your slippers."

"I will not be hurried by these Germans," answered Charlie B., and he had the right of it, for we had only had a minor collision with another boat.

At Mudros the majority of the sick and wounded on our hospital ship were sent to England, but my friend and I were luckily carried on to Egypt.

*Diary. September 23rd.* There was a remarkable man on board the *Manitou,* Major K. He had led 240 men into a Turkish trench; three had returned unwounded, but he got most of his wounded back with eighteen men. The Adjutant was killed on his back. He himself had already been wounded twice. Finally, he left the trench alone, and turned round and faced the Turks at 200 yards. They never fired at him, because he said, "they admired me." This officer found a D.S.O. waiting for him in Egypt and has since earned the V.C. in France, for which he had been previously recommended in South Africa. He and I returned to the Dardanelles together while he still had a long, unhealed bayonet wound in his leg.

At Alexandria, fortunately for myself, I had relations who were working there. I went to the hospital of a friend. It was a great marble palace, surrounded by lawns and fountains, and made, at any rate, gorgeous within by the loves of the gods, painted in the colours of the Egyptian sunset on the ceilings.

The Englishwomen in Alexandria were working like slaves for the wounded and the sick. They did all that was humanly possible to make up for the improvidence and the callousness of the home medical authorities. Thanks to their untiring and unceasing work, day and night, these ladies saved great numbers of British lives.

One day the *sultan* came to inspect the hospital where I was a patient. For reasons of *toilette,* I should have preferred not to have been seen on that occasion by His Highness, but the royal eye fixed itself upon my *kimono,* and I was taken aside for a few minutes conversation.

*Diary.* (Subsequently written on the Peninsula.) The *sultan* said that he was very grieved about the Conservative party, because of the coalition, I suppose, and also about Gallipoli. There I cordially agreed.

**\*\*\*\*\*\*\*\***

I went up to Cairo for a few days, and found the city and life there very changed. Shepheard's was filled with the ghosts of those who had left on and since April 12th.

In Egypt the danger of the canal had passed, but anxiety had not gone with it. There was much doubt as to what the Senoussi would be likely to do and what consequences their action would have. They had little to gain by attacking, but all knew that this would not necessarily deter them. I was in Cairo when Fathy Pasha was stabbed, and those in authority feared for the life of the *sultan.*

My friend Charlie B. and Major K. and I left Alexandria in brilliant moonlight. Our boat could do a bare twelve knots an hour. On the journey rockets went up at night, S.O.S. signals were sent us, all in vain: we were not to be seduced from our steady spinster's course to Mudros. When we again reached that place we found our sister ship, the *Ramadan,* had been torpedoed.

**\*\*\*\*\*\*\*\***

*Diary.* (Written September 23rd.) General Godley was on the Lord Nelson. He had been sick for some time, and had been taking three days off. Roger Keyes desperately anxious to go up the Dardanelles, come what may. He is the proper man to do it, but I think it's only singeing the King of Spain's beard.

At Imbros the general, Charlie B. and I had a stormy row ashore and a long walk to G.H.Q., where I found Willy Percy, who had been badly wounded, now recovering. I saw Tyrrell, G.L., and Dedez. The news had just come through of Bulgaria's mobilization, but they did not know against whom. I wonder if the Bulgars will attack both the Serbs and the Turks. That would be a topsy-turvy, Balkan thing to do, and might suit their book. We ought to have had them in on our side six months ago. From G.H.Q. we came back to Anzac. The general has had my dugout kept for me in the fort, where Christo and I now live in solitude, for all the rest are gone. I found a lot of new uniforms and a magnificent cap. When I put this on Christo cried violently: "No, no, no, not until we ride into Constantinople as conquerors."

H.Q. are on the other side of the Turkish fort, in a tiny valley across which you can throw a stone. They have all the appearance of a more comfortable Pompeii, and are scarcely more alive; it is the quietest town I have ever seen; there lies in front a ridge of valley, a dip of blue sea, and good deal of the Anafarta plain. The first night on arriving the cold was bitter, also next morning. Pleurisy has already started. This morning the general went up to the Apex and behind it. He was not at all pleased with the fire trenches. He nearly drove C., the officer at that moment instructing the Australians, mad first by criticising everything—I thought pretty justly—and then by standing about in view of the Turks and not worrying about shells or bombs. I did my best to get him in. The Australians were all laughing at C. for his caution and fussiness. Incidentally, one of the big mortar-bombs fell in the trench as we arrived. Hastings is intelligence officer. It's luck to have got him.

*Sunday, September 24th, 1915.* No. 2 outpost. A lovely morning. There was a bracing chill of autumn and yet warm air and a smiling, southern look across Anafarta Plain, with great hills on the other side, stately and formidable. Swallows everywhere. Up till now it's been very silent. I thought that the noise of war was past, but bullets and shells have been whining and moaning over us. At Anzac yesterday morning they had about twenty men hit by one shell, and I saw a lot of mules being dragged down to the sea as I went in. We walked through the "Camel's Hump," with Colonel Chauvel and Glasgow, on to No. 1 outpost, now deserted, with the beautiful trench made by the six millionaires. I wonder what has happened to them all.

Cazalet, of whom I had grown very fond, is dead, Hornby's missing. I was very sad to hear that Reynell was killed on the night of the 27th, when we left. A fine man in every way. His men worshipped him. . . .

A lot of French transports were leaving Egypt as we left, maybe for Asia. We shall do nothing more here unless we have an over-whelming force. We have never done anything except with a rush. Directly we have touched a spade we have ceased to advance, and have gone on adding bricks to the wall which we first built and then beat our heads against.

This morning we had a service in the valley, which is extraordinarily beautiful. The flies are awful, horrible, lethargic; they stick to one like gum. The men in the trenches are wearing the head-dresses that Egypt has sent. I went with the general in the afternoon to Anzac. We walked back as shelling began. We had one whizz round us, and a man fell beside me on the beach. I heard a tremendous smack, and thought he was dead, and began to drag him in to cover, but he was all right, though a bullet had thumped him.

The flies and their habits deserve to live in a diary of their own. They were horrible in themselves, and made more horrible by our circumstances and their habits. They lived upon the dead, between the trenches, and came bloated from their meal to fasten on the living. One day I killed a fly on my leg that made a splash of blood that half a crown would not have covered.

*Diary. Monday, September 27th, 1915.* No. 2 outpost. Last night F. Dined. He said that the Indians could get back from Mudros if they gave the hospital orderly ten *rupees*. The hospital orderly would then certify them as having dysentery. Most of them did not want to go back, some did. When they were reluctant about fighting he thought it was due to the fact that it was Moslems they were against. This morning the general and I went round Colonel Anthill's trenches. Billy H. was there, as independent and casual as ever. He came out here as a sergeant and is now acting-brigade-major. I am giving him a shirt.

Billy H. was not the only member of his family who was independent. His father, a well-known Australian doctor, on one occasion gave one of the chiefs of the British R.A.M.C. his sincere opinion about the treatment of the sick and wounded. After a while the chief of the R.A.M.C. said: "You don't seem to understand that it is I who am responsible for these things."

"Oh yes, I do," said the Australian doctor, "but it's not you I'm getting at; it's the fool who put you there."

*Diary. Tuesday, September 28th, 1915.* No. 2 outpost. Last night I dined with S.B. And H. Woods. Walked back through a still, moonlit night, with the sea and the air just breathing. Very bright stars. We sent up flares. The general was ill this morning, so did not go out. The Greek interpreters have been called up for mobilization. This Greek mobilization ought to do some good about the German submarines. Last night at Anzac they had iron needles dropped from aeroplanes. I always objected to this. This morning over our heads there was a Taube firing hard at something with a machine gun. It produces an unpleasant impression, I suppose because it is unfamiliar, to hear the noise straight above one. Two bombs were dropped—at least, I suppose they were. They fell with a progressive whistle, but not close to us; another big one, however, and 8-inch one, I believe, from the Dardanelles, fell with a tired and sensuous thud just over the ridge.

*Wednesday, September 29th, 1915.* No. 2 outpost. The general went out at nine this morning, P. and I with him. He went to the Apex and round. In the evening Kettle and I talked in the fort.

*Friday, October 1st, 1915.* No. 2 outpost. Yesterday morning General Godley, General Birdwood, de Crespigny and I went round the trenches, Apex, Anthill's, etc., from 9.30 until 3. A very hot day; I wish that generals were a hungrier, thirstier race. We had some light shelling, into which the generals walked without winking or reason, though they made us take intervals.

G.L. Has gone home. Ross turned up last night; glad to see him again. He said that a statement was to be made almost at once, and that we weren't going to be here for the winter. He had a notion that the Italians were going to take our place. . . .

This morning there was a very heavy mist; the hills and the sea were curtained in it. My clothes were wringing wet. The Greek interpreters have been called up by the Greek mobilization and have gone to Imbros, some of them to try to avoid going. They have, says Christo, *kria kardia* (cold feet). Xenophon, in a moment of enthusiasm, changed Turkish for Greek nationality. He now speaks of the days of his Ottoman nationality with a solemn and mournful affection, as of a golden age. He envies his cousin, Pericles, who was not so carried away. Kyriakidis is too old to go, thank goodness.

Going into Anzac with the general, and glad to be quit of the trenches. It's a weary business walking through these narrow mountain trenches, hearing the perpetual iteration of the same commands. The trenches are curiously personal. Some are so tidy as to be almost red-tape—the names of the streets, notices, etc., everywhere—and others slums.

*Later.* I went into Anzac with the general to see General Birdwood, but he had gone out to see the bombardment from the sea. The general went off to the New Zealand hospital ship, *Mahino.* I went to get P. off, who was ill. The general and I had a very philosophical talk coming back. There was a radiance over Anzac; the sunken timber ship shone against the sunset, with the crew half of them naked. Shells screamed over us, and in the headquarters hollow parts of them came whimpering down.

*Saturday, October 2nd, 1915.* No. 2 outpost. This morning General Godley, Colonel Artillery Johnson and I went round to see the guns, all across the Anafarta Plain. Yesterday they had been shelling a good deal and had killed some Ghurkhas. . . . We trudged about in the open, the Turkish hills in a semicircle round us. We kept about fifty yards apart. . . . I thought it very risky for the general; however, nothing happened. Have been meeting various school acquaintances these days. . . .

*Sunday, October 3rd, 1915.* The general and Charlie B. went to Suvla. I lunched with S.B. and H. Woods. We played chess. A good deal of shelling. A fair number hit. . . .

*Monday, October 4th, 1915.* Changed my dugout this morning with an infinity of trouble. I didn't like doing it; it involved men standing on the roof, and if one of them had been hit I should have felt responsible. However, we did it all right. I stole some corrugated iron, and am well off. This morning the Turks had a fierce demonstration. The bullets kicked up the dust at the mouth of the gully. Colonel Artillery Johnson just missed being hit, but only one man struck. They shelled us with big stuff that came over tired and groaning, bursting with a beastly noise and torrents of smoke. General C. lunched. He said people sent curiously inappropriate stores sometimes. In the middle of the summer they had sent us here mufflers and cardigan jackets, and two thousand swagger canes. These were now at Mudros. Chauvel has taken over command while the general is sick. He borrowed all my novels.

*Tuesday, October 5th, 1915.* General C.O. turned up. He said we are going to attack through Macedonia. Heaven help us! Bulgaria has been given twenty-four hours' ultimatum by Russia.
Went into Anzac, to go by boat to Suvla. Met C., who was at W—— (my private school). He said there was no boat. I went on and played chess, coming back through one of the most beautiful evenings we have had, the sea a lake of gold and the sky a lake of fire; but C. and I agreed we would not go back to Anzac or to W——, if we could help it.

*Wednesday, October 6th, 1915.* I was going into Suvla with Hastings, but in the morning a Turkish deserter, Ahmed Ali, came in. He promised to show us two machine guns, which he did (one German, immovable, and the other Turkish, movable), and seven guns which he had collected; this he failed to do, and also to produce three more comrades by firing a Turkish rifle as a signal.

In the afternoon I had a signal from S.B. to say he was leaving, sick, for Egypt. I walked in to see, and found he had gastritis. . . .

*Thursday, October 7th, 1915. N.Z. and A.H.Q.* This morning we went up with Ahmed Ali, and lay waiting for the Turkish deserters until after six. One Turkish rifle shot, a thicker sound than ours, was fired at Kidd's Post, but no Turks came. Ahmed Ali was distressed. The dawn was fine; clouds of fire all over the sky.

The Turkish deserters and prisoners were put through a number of inquisitions. There was first of all the local officer, who had captured the Turk and was creditably anxious to anticipate the discoveries of the intelligence. Then there was G.H.Q., intensely jealous of its privileges, and then Divisional H.Q., waiting rather sourly for the final examination of the exhausted Turks.

The Turkish private soldiers, being Moslems, were inspired rather with the theocratic ideals of comradeship than by the *esprit de corps* of nationality, and spoke freely. They were always well treated, and this probably loosened their tongues, but Ahmed Ali was more voluble than the majority of his comrades, and I append information which he supplied as an illustration of our examinations and their results. The two sides of Turkish character were very difficult to reconcile. On the one hand, we were faced in the trenches by the stubborn and courageous Anatolian peasant, who fought to the last gasp; on the other hand, in our dugouts we had a friendly prisoner, who would overwhelm us with information. "The fact is you are just a bit above our trenches. If only you can get your fire rather lower, you will be right into them, and here exactly is the dugout of our captain, Riza Kiazim Bey, a poor, good man. You miss him all the time. If you will take the line of that pine tree, you will get him."

*Diary. Saturday, October 9th, 1915. A. and N.Z.. H.Q.* Ahmed Ali proposed coming to England with me when I went there. . . . Last night we had bad weather; a sort of whirlwind came down. It whizzed away the iron sheeting over my dugout and poured in a cascade of water, soaking everything. Iron sheeting was flying about like razors; it was not possible to light candles. Finally, Ryrie came and lent me a torch, and I slept, wet but comfortable, under my cloak. Our people and the Turks both got excited, and heavy rifle fire broke out, as loud as the storm. An angry dawn, very windy and rifles crackling.

********

At this point the diary ends, for the writer was evacuated on the hospital ship, and did not return to active service for several months. Of all those who had sailed from Egypt with General Godley on April 12th, the general himself remained the only man who saw the campaign through from the first to the last day, with the rare exception of a few days of sickness.

# Kut

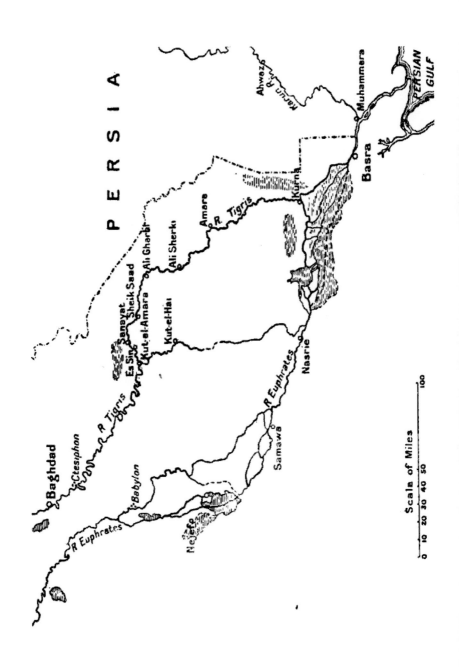

PERSIA

PERSIAN GULF

Ahwaz R. Karun

Muhammera

Basra

Kurna

R. Tigris

Amare

Ali Gharbi

Ali Sherki

Sanayat

Es Sin

Sheik Saad

Kut-el-Amara

Kut-el-Hai

Nasrie

R. Euphrates

Samawa

Baghdad

Ctesiphon

R. Tigris

Babylon

Nejeff

R. Euphrates

Scale of Miles

0  10  20  30  40  50                    100

# Kut, 1916

After some months or convalescence, I was passed fit for active service. Admiral Wemyss, Commander-in-Chief of the East Indian Fleet, had done me the honour to ask me to serve under him, when I was well again, as his liaison and intelligence officer. I accepted very gladly, for I knew how devoted to him were all those who served Admiral Wemyss. The unappreciative War Office showed no reluctance in dispensing with my services, but my orders got lost, and it was only late in February when I left. When my weak qualifications in the way of languages were put before the Department concerned, the brief comment was: "This must be an immoral man to know so many languages."

About this time the question was perpetually debated as to whether war should be made mainly on the one great front or *en petits paquets*; that is, practically all over the globe. "Hit your enemy where he is the weakest," said some, while others were violently in favour of striking where he was strongest.

When I left England, she was in a curious state of official indecision. It would then have been, obviously, greatly to our advantage had we been able to get the Turks out of the war, for the collapse of Bulgaria would almost certainly have followed. On the other hand, Russia had been promised Constantinople and the church of Santa Sophia, and while these promises held it was idle to think that the Grand Turk would compromise or resign his position as head of Islam. So the dread in the minds of Englishmen of friction with Russia was unconsciously adding square leagues to the British Empire, by forcing us reluctantly to attack an unwilling foe. In the end, we chose both Scylla and Charybdis, for the Turks remained in the war, Russia went out. Yet we survived, victoriously. *Allah is greatest.*

The story of this campaign is the most difficult to tell. The writer was in a humble position, but in a position of trust, and can only record what he saw and the things with which all men's ears were too familiar in Mesopotamia.

*Diary. Monday, February 28th, 1916. S.S. Mooltan.* Off Marseilles. The Germans are by way of not torpedoing our boats until Wednesday, but today is St. Leander's Day, not a good day, on the sea, at this time of year. They have torpedoed four boats these last days near Marseilles. We are off the coast of Corsica, dull and unattractive. . . . John Baird is here. . . .

*Wednesday, March 1st, 1916. S.S. Mooltan.* yesterday J.B., Captain Cummings, and I went ashore at Malta. We heard of the torpedoing of the *Maloja* off Dover. I saw Admiral Limpus, and old friend; then dined with Admiral de Robeck. I saw R.K. He still wants to go up the Dardanelles. This seems to me to be a war of ants and attrition, and no one ought to think of the glory of the army of the navy before winning the war. I do not think he cares if he is at the bottom of the sea, as long as the country and the navy is covered with imperishable splendour. He talked about the blizzard as if it had been a zephyr. You can't beat that sort. A lot of old admirals rolled up. They had rejoined long past the age as commanders of sweepers, or in any and every kind of capacity. The spirit of their Elizabethan ancestors was not more tough or fine than theirs. . . . Left J.B. and Jack Marriott.

*Monday, March 6th, 1916.* Ismailia. We landed without incident from the *Mooltan.* The last day, at luncheon, there were two tremendously loud bangs, the lids of hatches falling; they sounded exactly like cannon shot. Nobody moved at lunch, which I thought was good. Am staying with O'Sullivan. He has been eighteen years in Central Africa. Tonight I went to the club and found Kettle, alive, whom I thought dead—very glad to find it wasn't true—and lots of Anzacs. Then went for a walk with the admiral; I understand why men like serving him. Afterwards tea with General Birdwood and a yarn about the Peninsula. All the men from Anzac talk of it with something like reverence. I dined with General Godley. I have been doing work between the navy and the army; found them very stiff. Yesterday they said: "What can you want to know?" Also, in my humble opinion, what they are doing is wrong.

*Friday, March 10th, 1916.* Cairo. Back again at Zamalek. They have sown a proper, green, English lawn instead of the clover which we put in for economy. Saw C. in the evening. Agreed that for the time being our Arab policy was finished. . . . If the Russians go ahead and threaten Constantinople, the French agreement may stand. If, on the other hand, they cannot get beyond Trebizond, then Arabia will probably be a confederation, perhaps nominally under the Turks. The powers would probably look favourably at this, as it would be a return to the bad old principle. It would constitute one more extension of the life of the Turk, outside Turkey, made miserable to him and his subjects, during which all his legatees would intrigue to improve their own position. They would go on fermenting discontent amongst the subjects of the Turk, and when it did not exist they would create it. It is the old cynicism that this war had done nothing to get rid of. On the other hand, if annexation follows there will be two results: first, the population in the annexed French and Russian spheres will be rigorously conscripted. I think we ought to do our best to prevent the Arabs being the subjects and victims of high explosive powers. They themselves don't realize what it means, and simply look forward to the boredom of having to beat their swords into ploughshares and take up the dullness of civilization. The second result is that we shall have vast, conterminous frontiers with France and Russia, and that we shall be compelled to become a huge military power and adopt the Prussianism that we are fighting. There ought to be a self-denying ordinance about annexation. We should none of us annex.

*Wednesday, March 8th, 1916.* Cairo. I arranged for Storrs to come down the Red Sea with the commander-in-chief. In the evening I saw the *sultan* at the palace. He prophesied that the Russians would be in Trebizond in eight days, and that we should be in Solloum in the same time; he put our arrival at Baghdad at the end of May. The snows were melting, he said, and the waters of the Tigris and Euphrates rising; the Turks might be cut off and might have to surrender. . . . He said we did not understand the Moslems or what was their fraternity. In his hall he had two signs, "God and His prophet," and the other, "I live by God's will." Any Moslem who entered saw these, and knew him for his brother. He would rather have been a farmer, dressed as a farmer, and, he added, rather quaintly, sitting in his automobile, amongst his fields, than in his Palace with interviews before him all day long.

He had accepted the Throne when it had been offered to him after consideration, because the good of Egypt was bound up in our success, and as *sultan* he could help us. He regretted he had not been allowed to help more. He was loyal, but neither we, nor any man, could buy his honour. We could throw him over at any moment. So be it; he knew what his honour and individual dignity demanded. General Maxwell, he said, understood the Moslems. Even the Duke of Connaught could hardly have done better in Egypt. He, the *sultan*, had deplored Gallipoli, both before and after. We English were *bons enfants*, but did not understand the east. He gave many messages to his friends, especially General Birdwood.

*Thursday, March 9th, 1916.* Cairo. Saw Jaafar Pasha, a prisoner. He was wounded by a sword thrust in the arm. They had had a good old-fashioned mêlée. He was just off shopping, taking his captivity with great philosophy. It was beautiful weather. The Bougainvillea was purple and scarlet all over the house. It looked as fairylike as a Japanese dwelling.

*Friday, March 10th, 1916.* Cairo. The admiral came up on Thursday night. I lunched with General Maxwell. Bron came. He said his leg troubled him flying, but he loved it. I saw his colonel, who told me that he was worried, as if he fell in the desert he was done, as he could not walk great distances like the others, with his wooden leg.

I have got a *Who's Who*, for Arabian, but I want a *Where's Where*.

*Saturday, March 11th, 1916.* Ismailia. The Australians have been having high old times in Cairo. We have to pay for their extraordinary fine fighting qualities, but it's a pity that they can't be more quiet. . . . They admire General Birdwood, who's got a difficult job. We owed a lot to their initiative at Anzac, when all their officers were killed. Salutes, after all, matter less than fighting. In peace they resent General Godley's discipline, and that's natural, but it's inevitable, and they know it, when it comes to fighting. Charlie Bentinck came down with us, going home; I hope he gets there all right.

*Tuesday, March 14th, 1916.* Ismailia. Maxwell is not definitely recalled. . . . It's a pity to take away the man whose name is everything in Egypt. On Saturday I dined with the admiral and Potts of the Khedive's yacht. Like Jimmy Watson, he was very fond of his ex-chief. Sunday I lunched with the admiral and General Murray, and saw my old friend Tyrrell. Yesterday the admiral left with Philip Neville for Solloum. I should have liked to have been in that show.

Here are criticisms and indiscretions, which are better left lying at the bottom of a drawer. . . .

All are very sad about Desmond Fitzgerald's death. There was no one quite like him. He would have played a great part. He was extraordinarily fine, too fine to be a type, though he was a type, but not of these times. I shall never forget him during the retreat, always calm and always cheerful. Bron came, and we had a long talk.

*Wednesday, March 15th, 1916.* Cairo. This morning I saw Jaafar Pasha for a minute. He is becoming less and less a prisoner. Was off to shop, and said that he heard that Cairo was a nice town. He was unmoved by the war. I said to M. that the war ought to prevent one's pulses ever fluttering again. M. said to me: "Yes, unless it makes them flutter for ever."

Here there followed naval, strategical, political and commercial considerations which are irrelevant to this published diary.

*Diary. March 15th, 1916.* Went to the citadel to see the old *sheikh.* It was a lovely day of heat, fresh winds, clear air and flowers everywhere.

*Wednesday, March 22nd, 1916.* Ismailia. I have neglected my diary. Yesterday I went and said goodbye to General Birdwood. General Godley, he and everybody went to see Maxwell off. It was a very remarkable demonstration; all were there—red hats and *tarbouches,* blue gowns and the khaki of the private soldier. We were all downhearted at his going.

Today I rode with Temperley through the groves of Ismailia, out by the lagoon. The desert was in splendid form. The Australians were bathing everywhere and French sailors were paddling. I lunched with General Russell. . . . I dined with General Godley. All the talk was of Mesopotamia. Someone said at dinner that no securely beleaguered force had ever cut its way out. I could only think of Xenophon, who, General Gwynne said, quite truly, was not beleaguered, and also of Plevna, that didn't get out.

*Sunday, March 26th, 1916.* Cairo. This morning we leave for Mesopotamia, by the Viceroy's train. He arrived yesterday, having been shot at by a torpedo on the way. The soldiers are becoming discontented. Their pay is four months due, and when they get it they are paid in threepenny bits for which they only receive twopence in exchange. Hence their irritation. Tommy Howard's brigade has nearly all got commissions. There are now forty-seven officers and only enough soldiers left for their servants. Saw Uncle Bob G., who reminded me of Sayid Talib, the Lion of Mesopotamia and the terror of the Turks, with whom on one occasion I travelled from Constantinople. Sayid Talib once wanted to get rid of a very good *vali* of Basrah. He went round to all the keepers of *hashish* dens and infamous houses and got them to draw up a petition: *"We, the undersigned, hear with anguish that our beloved vali is to be removed by the merciful government. He is a good man, has been just to all, and most just to us, who now implore the mercy of the Sublime Porte."* Constantinople was in a virtuous mood. The experts of Basrah were summoned. They expressed their horror at the support which the *vali* was receiving from all the worst elements in the town. The *vali* was removed. Sayid Talib scored. He was on our side, and remained in Basrah, but we made him a prisoner and sent him to India, I believe.

*Monday, March 27th, 1916.* H.M.S. *Euryalus.* Gulf of Suez. Yesterday, Sunday, the Prince of Wales, the Viceroy, General Birdwood and the High Commissioner travelled down to Ismailia. Storrs and I were also of the company. General Godley was at the station to meet the Prince, and a lot of others.

*Tuesday, March 28th, 1916.* H.M.S. *Euryalus.* I wonder what situation we shall find in Mesopotamia. Willcocks in Cairo said that the Arabs were feeding Townshend's people. "In the old days," he said, "Elijah was fed by the ravens—that is, *orab*, which means Arabs as well as ravens." That was how he explained that miracle.

It's getting very hot. I am working at Hindustani. The staff here are all first class. It's luck to find Colonel de Sausmarez, who was on the *Bacchante*, now promoted.

*Thursday, March 30th, 1916.* H.M.S. *Euryalus.* Took a bad fall down the ladder. Storrs sleeps in a casemate. The only ventilation is through a gun whose breech has now been closed. Have been writing précis and political notes. We are bound to make mistakes in dealing with the Arabs, but they need not matter if they are passive mistakes; they can be corrected. If they are active, they are much harder to remedy.

. . . Our people divide the world into two categories. The Ulstermen, the Serbs and the Portuguese are good, loyal people, because they are supposed to put our interests first, whereas the Bulgars, the Arabs, etc., are beastly traitors, because sometimes a thought of self-interest crosses their minds.

It's raining hard this morning and it's cooler. Hope to get into the trenches at Aden, but doubt there being time. Am learning Hindustani. A number of the same words mean different things. *kal* means yesterday or tomorrow, *i.e.* one day distant; but on the other hand *parson* means the day after tomorrow or the day before yesterday. This must occasionally make muddles about appointments.

*Friday, March 31st, 1916.* Aden. Got up early this morning and went over to the Northbrook. The Turks at Lahej are being bombarded. The admiral's going part of the way to see it. Six seaplanes off. A heavy, hot, grey day. The Turks are fighting well. There is no ill-will here. They say the Turk is a member of the club, but has not been in it lately. We are feeding the Turks and they feed us. Caravans come and go as usual. There are great difficulties in the way of blockade. We can't hit our enemies without also hitting our friends, and yet if we do nothing our prestige suffers.

A conference this morning. Fifty years ago Colonel Pelly said that the Turks were like the thirty-nine articles; everyone accepts them, but nobody remembers them or what they are. India seems extremely apathetic about Aden. We left early this morning. Last night I saw Colonel Jacob, who has been twelve years at Aden and in the *hinterland*. In the evening I went with the brigadier to the Turkish prisoners. They said they had surrendered because life was impossible in the Yemen. They had been six to seven years without pay, had had bad food and perpetual fighting. Then they had been put on a ship to go back to their families, then taken off again and sent to fight us. Human nature could not stand it, they said. They liked their commander, Said Pasha, who was good to the soldiers, but they complained of their non-commissioned officers. . . .

We seem to be perpetually changing our officers here. This C.O. Is the fifth in a short time. Jacob is the only man who talks Arabic, and there is not a soul who talks Turkish. Wrote to Egypt to get an interpreter.

*Sunday, April 2nd, 1916.* H.M.S. *Euryalus.* we are steaming through a grey-black gloom, like an English autumn afternoon, only the thermometer is 92 and there are no rooks cawing. There are lowering skies everywhere. Talked about Arabia yesterday with the admiral.

Have been re-reading Whigan's *Persia* and other Gulf books. Wish that I had George Lloyd's memoranda. The present position is unsatisfactory. We have policed and lighted and pacified this Gulf for a hundred years, and we are entitled to a more definite status. We ought to have Bunder Abbas. Otherwise, if the Russians come down the Gulf to Bunder Abbas, they hold the neck of the bottle of the Persian Gulf and we shall be corked in our own bottle; they would be on the flank of India; they would be fed by a railway, while our large naval station would be cooking away in Elphinstone's Inlet (which is only another name for a slow process of frying), where we should have battle casualties in peace time from the heat. Elphinstone's Inlet to Bushire is a poor *Wei-hai-wei* to a first-rate Port Arthur. Then, if the Russians come down, any defensive measures which we may be forced into taking will appear aggressive when the Russians are on the spot. They would not appear aggressive now. We have a prescriptive right to Bunder Abbas, which we ought to strengthen. It doesn't involve territorial annexations.

*Monday, April 3rd, 1916.* H.M.S. *Euryalus.* last night I had a long and rather acrimonious argument with ―― and ―― on the question of Arab policy. They said: "You must punish the Arabs if they don't come in on our side."

I said: "You have no means of punishing them. All you can do is to antagonize them."

There is news of a Zeppelin raid on London. Everybody is anxious.

*Tuesday, April 4th, 1916.* H.M.S. *Euryalus*, Muskat. Last night I had my fourth Hindustani lesson, a very easy one. Jack Marriott is extraordinarily quick at languages. My teacher said that his affianced wife is fourteen and that he kept her in a cage at Bushire. Talked with the admiral and Captain Burmester. . . .

Today is a wild day, Arabia crouching, yellow like a lion, in a sand storm, and spray and sand flying in layers on the ship. All the land is lurid and the sea foaming and the sky black. If only there had been some sharks at sea and lions on shore, it would have been a perfect picture. This afternoon it cleared and became beautiful. We passed a desolate coast with no sign of life, where it looked as if a man would fry in half an hour in summer. A few *dhows* on the sea were all we saw. My last journey here came back vividly and the time at Bahrein after we were wrecked in the Africa.

Wireless came into Basrah to say the spring offensive was beginning. We put into Muskat. I found that the resident, Colonel Ducat, was a neighbour. There has been a row at Chahbar, and the *Philomel*, which we expected to find here, has left, telegraphed for this morning. The news here is that the tribes intend to attack Muskat, but it's not believed. We went ashore this evening, and a Beluchi boy took the admiral and all of us round. The people who had not been to the east before were enchanted by the quiet, the scent of musk, and the evening behind the *sultan's* palace. Last time I was here was on Christmas day, with Leland Buxton. I was very sick, carrying a huge bag of Maria Teresa dollars. The Portuguese forts and the names of the ships that come here, painted in huge white letters on the cliffs, are the remarkable things about the place. There is a sort of a silent roll-call of the ships. The men like writing their names up in white letters. Matrah is round the corner, and looks bigger than Muskat. You have got to get to it by boat. Muskat itself is completely cut off. I saw a straight-looking Arab from Asir who had been with the Turks and had information, and asked the agent to send him on to Aden.

*Wednesday, April 5th, 1916.* Muskat. Came ashore early this morning. Then came the admiral and his staff, and we went to the *sultan's* house. He had about thirty followers. We drank sherbet like scented lip-salve, and the sailors didn't like it. The admiral and the *sultan* talked. Later the *sultan* came here with seven A.D.C.'s and a nephew who talked very good English, which he had learned at Harrow. The *sultan* has got a lot of rather nice-looking little horses and a monstrous goat with ears that are about 3 feet long. The *sultan* gets 5 per cent of the customs of this place. Jack Marriott went to see a prisoner in the Portuguese fort. He was *sheikh* of a village in which a murder had been committed. They had failed to catch the murderer, and so the *sheikh* had to suffer imprisonment himself. Not a bad plan, really. It's the old Anglo-Saxon idea. That sort of thing discourages men from pushing for power and makes them very energetic, for their own sakes, when they have power. Everything seems quiet in the *hinterland*. These people here are Bunhas, who cheat the *sultan*, slim aristocratic Arabs, and gorilla-like negroes. They are mostly armed to the teeth. Sheets of rain fell this afternoon.

*Thursday, April 6th, 1916.* Persian Gulf. We left early this morning. Some very fine king-fish were brought aboard, about 4 feet long. Great heat. We had an excellent telegram about Gorringe's offensive in Mesopotamia; the Turks driven back. The admiral in great spirits. I am tremendously glad, because I have always felt that we were coming to a tragedy. I remember the telegram read out to us at Anzac and the cheers—"The Turks are beaten! The way lies open to Baghdad!"— and our enthusiasm and the disappointment after it, and I did not think this would succeed. Hanna, on the left bank of the Tigris, is reported taken. That ought to open Sinn on the right bank.

*Friday, April 7th, 1916.* Persian Gulf. . . . Today we were told by wireless telegram that we had a slave of the *sultan's* on board. Quite true; so we have. . . . He said he had been with the *sultan* eight years and that if he were sent back he feared for his throat. He drew his finger across it very tenderly, and everybody roared with laughter. I do not see that the *sultan* has a leg to stand on. If the man went to him eight years ago, he went either of his own free will, in which case he can leave, or he was sold, and we do not recognize anything except bondage, no traffic in slavery.

The *Philomel's* prisoners have been transferred to us. One of them looks like an old nobleman. His name is Shah Dulla. He held up Chahbar for 4000 *rupees*, like other old noblemen, and was captured with seven bearded patriarchs by the *Philomel* fours days ago. They are dignified people.

Saturday, April 8th, 1916. H.M.S. *Euryalus.* Bushire. A very cold morning with a clear sky. It's a nuisance having lost all my coats. Here I leave Edward. I hope he will be all right. He is to follow by the first opportunity with the other servants and my kit. McKay, who is a jolly fellow, will look after him. The news this morning is that we have again improved our position and have taken the second Turkish line. The Russians are advancing. There was a fight here a couple of nights ago. Our Agent, his brother and four *sepoys* were killed last night at Lingah.

*Sunday, April 9th, 1916.* H.M.S. *Imogene.* Shat-el-Arab. Yesterday Commodore Wake came aboard. . . . He said that an officer had put land-mines down, and that some time after this officer had been re-called. People in Bushire naturally wanted him either to remove or mark his land-mines, but he said that they were all right, as they were only exploded by electricity. The following night, however, there were loud explosions when dogs gambolled over these mines, so people still walk like Agag, and walking is not a popular form of exercise round Bushire. Today we are in a brown waste of waters that I remember well, a dismal *Hinterland* to a future Egypt. We passed a hospital ship early this morning, in these yellow shallow waters. It reminded me of the Dardanelles, but there it was much better, for there the sea and sky were beautiful and the climate, by comparison, excellent.

Ages ago, in Egypt, Machel used to talk of ghosts. This ship conjures them up all right—trips with Sir Nicholas and the children to the island and many other people, some of them still in Constantinople. Sir Nicholas would have been surprised if he could have seen the name of his yacht written on the rocks at Muskat, and, as the admiral said, he would not have liked anyone else in command of his yacht, here or in any other waters. Townshend has telegraphed some time ago to say he could only hold out until April 1st. Here we are at the 9th.

*Monday, April 10th, 1916.* H.M.S. *Imogene.* Kurna. Yesterday we arrived at Basra. It looked very beautiful and green, but we only had a short time. Everything seemed in a state of great confusion. Two generals came aboard. They said we had taken two out of three lines of the trenches that we had got to take in the first attack. Then our men had been checked. We ought to have taken the third line last night. The Sinn position still remains to be taken. If we had been successful last night (and we ought to have heard this morning), we have got a chance of relieving Townshend. If not, I am afraid there is not much chance. . . . The doctors are being pretty hotly criticized, also the Royal Indian Marine, though how they can be expected to know this river I can't see. Apparently they asked for iron barges from India and were given wooden barges that the banks and the current continually break. They asked here for one type of river-craft from home, and were told they must have another. Lynch out here says that Lynch in London has never been consulted, though they deny this at home. The troops have only two days' supplies. The soldiers in Basra were cheerful; the wounded also, for the first time, were cheerful, because they thought it had been worth it and that we are going to succeed. . .

There is a great storm getting up. The river's a vast rolling flood of yellow water, palm trees beyond and again beyond that, marshes and glimpses of a skeleton land, with marsh Arabs always in the background, like ghouls, swarming on every battlefield, killing and robbing the wounded on both sides. The Turks, they say in Basra, had said: *"Let us both have a truce and go for the Arabs and then we can turn to and fight again."* Nureddin, the Turkish commander-in-chief, is supposed to have been at Harrow with Townshend. I should think that it was really a pension at Lausanne. I saw P.Z. Cox yesterday. He and Lady Cox were very good to me years ago in the Gulf. . . . The Russians have not yet met any considerable Turkish force. If we do not relieve Townshend, and have to fall back, we shall be attacked by all the Arabs, who are well armed. They say a Royal Commission is being sent to India because at home they anticipate a failure here and want a scape-goat, which they have already provided in Nixon.

I dined with Gertrude Bell, Millborrow, whom I had last seen at Bahrein, and Wilson, whom I had known before. We transferred here at Kurna from the *Imogene* on to a tiny admiralty gunboat, as usual leaving all our kit. Dick Bevan says that he has a vision of perpetual landings and expeditions until we arrive in China, with always the same troubles, too few mules, too many A.P.M.'s, etc. This is a war threshold to conjure up dreams and visions. It would be hard to find one more tragic. It's a curious fate that sends us a second time, unprepared, to one of the richest countries in the world that, like Egypt, has combined fertility and desert, with a stream controlling its future.

*Tuesday, April 11th, 1916.* H.M.S. *Snakefly*. Monday night we got off the *Imogene* on to the *Snakefly*, one of the twelve Admiralty gunboats built for this expedition. The Admiralty don't seem able to stop building them, now they've started. They were sent out here in pieces, then put together. One has been taken by the Turks.[1] The *Snakefly* draws 2 feet 9 inches only. Webster is her captain. We slept on deck all right. We saw practically no traffic at first on the river, and could not understand why we did not pass boats coming back empty for supplies. We passed many Indian troops, mainly on the left bank of the river; also isolated stations with telegraph-masters as chiefs. These men go out two or four miles into the desert with only a couple of rifles. These small posts contain the maximum of boredom and anxiety, because there is nothing to do, and if any force of Arabs came along they would be done in. An enterprising Indian sentry fired at us in the night. We passed dour, scowling Arabs in villages and groups on the bank with flocks and herds, buffaloes and goats, men more savage than the Philistines, but armed with rifles.

---

1. Taken back after.

An almost endless column of our cavalry wound its way through marsh and desert, over the green grass, and here and there fires sent up their smoke where meals were cooked. It struck me as more curious than the Australians round the Pyramids. At 6 p.m. we reached Ali Gharbi. I talked to an officer of the —the Punjabis. They were all very depressed at the failure of Aylmer's attack on the 8th March. . . . Townshend was the man they swore by. The 4th Devons, where John Kennaway is, are said to be at the front. There are flies that bite like bulldogs everywhere. Each night we have had lightning over towards Kut like a sort of malignant and fantastic Star of Bethlehem to light us on.

*Wednesday, April 12th, 1916.* H.M.S. *Snakefly.* last night the weather broke. The admiral's got a cabin about 6 feet long by 2½ across. He put his head out of the window and said: "Would any of you fellows like to come in?"

It was a beastly night. Our clothes are the thinnest tropical khaki, and they tear like a woman's veil. There was no shelter. I got into a conning-tower, like a telescope, but finally walked about. There seemed to be people's faces everywhere on deck, though there was a lot of water. I kept my dictionary dry. Now it's fine and bright. At seven this morning, when I had gone below, a boy scout of eighteen, one of the crew, went overboard. He was rescued almost at once, and swam lightly and gallantly. He was lucky. Today is the 12th, my lucky day, but I have only got one extra shirt and one blanket, and a Turkish dictionary for a pillow. . . .

Everything seems greater and greater chaos. . . . We started this campaign against one of the great military powers of the world with two brigades of Indians, who ought not to have been used at all, if it could have been avoided, on this ground, which to them is holy. We started with the wrong type of boat, and also Indian generals who looked on the expedition as a frontier campaign. . . . If we fail to relieve Townshend, I suppose the best thing to do would be to cut our losses and retire to Kurna and hold that line, but if we do that the Turks can fortify the river and make it impregnable. We ran onto the bank last night, and stayed there. We spent an uncomfortable wet night, but got off all right this morning. There was an encampment close by. We couldn't make out if they were friends or enemies; the admiral didn't bother. We all want a clean pair of socks and fewer mosquitoes.

*Thursday, April 13th, 1916.* Near Sanayat. It was at noon yesterday that we arrived at Ali Gharbi. The admiral saw General Lake. We are cruelly handicapped by lacking transport and not being able to get in. In the afternoon I crossed the river and saw General Gilman at Felahiya. I was very glad to see him again. He had been on our left with the 13th Division at Anafarta. One of the best men I have met. We had a long talk. . . . Then I came back with Dick Bevan. What's happened is this: we got in such a state about Townshend being able to hold out till the end of January that we rushed up troops and attacked without the possibility of making preparation for the wounded, ambulances, etc., and we failed. . . . Townshend had got 5,000 Arabs with him, and the *bouches inutiles* have told enormously, but T. has apparently promised these people his protection and nothing will make him send them away, and he's right. The strain on the men with him has been very great indeed; some of the older men are very sick. No one thinks that he's got a dog's chance of getting out. The —th were badly cut up at Anafarta, but they kept their keenness, and at the beginning of this show their officers could not keep them back, *on the 8th of March.* The fight on the 9th of April was very bad luck. All the men were very cold and tired. A hot cup of coffee might have made the whole difference. . . . We shall have to face a lot of trouble with the Arabs and look out for Nasryah, which could be cut off by marsh Arabs from Basra way and turned into another Kut. Most people think that the line that we ought to defend is Nasryah—Amara—Ahwaz. The admiral's going to Nasryah. I suggested his taking General Gillman, and he is off too. Everyone is raging against the economy of India, especially a man called Meyer, the treasury member for the Council of India. He is said to have refused to give any help. In this flat land they need observation balloons; none forthcoming. They asked for transport from May to Christmas, and then got one launch. . . .

I saw the admiral in the evening. He was cheered after talking to General Gorringe. We walked by the river. We met some of the Black Watch—clean, smart men. There was a great bridge of boats, without rails, swaying and tossing in the hurricane and covered with driven foam from the raging yellow water. Across this there lurched Madrassis, Sudanese, terrified cavalry horses, mules that seemed to think that there was only water on one side, and that they would be on dry land if they jumped off on the other. We are out of range, but shelling is going on and one can fix points in the landscape by bursts. The eternal flatness is depressing. This morning I saw Leachman, the political officer. He had had a lot of adventures in Arabia—a very good fellow, whom everybody likes, which is rare. . . . He was against our going farther back than Sheikh Saad, both from the point of view of strategy and also because it would be playing a low game on our own friendlies. The Arabs on the bank between Sheikh Saad and Ali Gharbi are, apparently, past praying for.

This afternoon I went out with the admiral. . . . Townshend has been telegraphing today. His men are dying of starvation. The whole situation is pitiful. Here the troops have been on half rations for some time. Our boats are many, but insufficient. They are of every kind, from an Irawaddy steamer to the steamers of the Gordon Relief expedition and L.C.C. Boats. We met some of the 6th Devons, and I asked them if the way the admiral was going was safe. They said: "We be strangers here, zur," as if they were Exeter men in Taunton. . . . The rain is making the relief practically impossible. Last night there was heavy firing and we advanced 2,000 yards, but the main positions are still untaken. Tonight met Percy Herbert, very useful, as my tropical khaki is coming to pieces.

*Friday, April 14th, 1916.* H.M.S. *Stonefly*. . . . A furious wind got up and drove mountains of yellow water before it, against the stream. The skies were black. Captain Nunn, the senior naval officer, wanted to go to Sheikh Saad. I wanted to go to H.Q. To see Colonel Beach, chief of the intelligence, who has written to me to come. We got off with difficulty into the stream. It was like a monstrous snake, heaving and coiling. We only drew 3 feet and we were very top-heavy with iron, and I thought we were bound to turn over. I said so to Singleton, the captain, who said: "I quite agree. It serves them d——d well right if we do, for sending us out in this weather."

This thought pleased him, though it did not satisfy me. Nunn said it was the worst weather he had seen in the year. I got off at Wadi thankfully, and went to see Beach, but it was not all over yet. He wanted to go and see how the bridge of boats was standing the strain. The end of the bridge of boats had been removed to let the steamers through, though there were none passing. It was twisting like an eel trying to get free, and going up and down like a moving staircase in agony. There was foam and gloom and strain and fury and the screaming of the timber, but the bridge held. The engineers were calmly smoking their pipes at the end, wondering in a detached way if it would hold. I prefer fighting any day to this sort of thing. Then I went walking with Beach. He asked me to be ready in case Townshend wanted me. I dined with General Lake, General Money, Williams, and Dent; capital fellows. Had an interesting time after dinner. The future is doubtful. If we have to retire, we shall have a double loss of prestige, Kut gone and our own retreat. When we want to advance later, we shall find all our present positions fortified against us. A retreat will also involve the abandonment of our friendlies. This campaign has taught me why we have been called *perfide Albion*. It's very simple. We embark upon a campaign without any forethought at all. Then, naturally we get into extreme difficulties. After that, we talk to the natives, telling them quite truthfully that we have got magnificent principles of truth, justice, tolerance, etc., that where the British Raj is all creeds are free. They like these principles so much that they forget to count our guns. Then, principles or no principles, we have got to retreat before a vastly superior force, and the people who have come in with us get strafed. Then they all say *"perfide Albion,"* though it's really nobody's fault—sometimes not even the fault of the government.

I slept on the *Malamir*, on deck. It was very wet in the night, but I kept fairly dry.

*Saturday, April 15th, 1916. Malamir.* I went and saw the Turkish prisoners in one of the most desolate camps on earth; some Albanians amongst them. They said there were munitions factories in Bagdad, that 4,000 Turks had gone to Persia—they did not know if it was to the oilfield at Basra or against the Russians. It's Basra and the oilfield that are important to us.

Lunched aboard the *Malamir*. General Lake was very kind. I went off on an Irawaddy steamer, a "P" boat. The captain told appalling stories of the wounded on board after Ctesiphon. It took them seventeen days to Amara, which sounds incredible. They had to turn back three times at Wadi and return to Kut, because they were heavily attacked at Wadi by Kurds. General Nixon had to turn back, too. The transport was so overcrowded that men were pushed overboard. I met an Indian political officer on board. . . . (and again). . . . He said one thing to me that was not indiscreet. Once at Abazai he had seen a Pathan wrestling. Before he wrestled he held up his hands, and cried an invocation: *"Dynamis"* ("Might"). He thought it must have come from the days of Alexander. He had been in the Dujaila fight

148

on March 8th, and talked about it, unhappily. He also said that the corruption of the Babus at Basra was awful.

On board our ship there were piles of bread without any covering, but a swarming deposit of flies; good for everybody's stomach.

*Sunday, April 16th, 1916.* Half a day's food is being dropped daily by aeroplanes in Kut. . . . I met a very jolly Irish officer, a V.C. He said that when the war broke out he, and many like himself, saw the Mohammedan difficulty. They had themselves been ready to refuse to fight against Ulster; why should Indians fight the Turks? We were fighting for our own lives, but the quarrel did not really concern Indians. They might have been expected to be spectators. Then the orders came for them to go to France. They called up the Indian officers and said to them: "Germany has declared war, and on second thoughts, a *jehad*. She quarrelled with England first and then pretended she was fighting for Islam." The Indian officers agreed, and came along readily. They were then ordered to Mesopotamia. They again called upon the Indian officers, who said: "We would sooner go anywhere else in the world, but we will go, and we will not let the regiment down." They were told to go to Baghdad, and were willing to go, though their frame of mind was the same. . . . Then I went off to interrogate prisoners. It was tremendously hot. The prisoners were under a guard of Indians, and I found it hard to make the Indians understand my few words of Hindustani. The prisoners' morale seemed good. They said they were not tired of the war and that they did not think of disobeying orders, for that, they said, would be awful and would make chaos. They thought that what pleased God was going to happen, and they were inclined to believe that that would be victory for the Turks. They said twenty-seven guns had come up in the last eight days, 17 cm. and 20 cm. If that's the case, they can shell us out of here. I told the admiral, and in the evening we talked. We met General Gorringe. . . . I am tremendously sorry for these men here. Last year the God of battles was on our side. We ought not to have won, by any law of odds or strategy, at Shaiba, at Ctesiphon, or Nasriyah, but we did. They won against everything, and now the luck has turned. They have brought Indian troops to fight on holy soil for things that mean nothing to them. They have been hopelessly outnumbered by the Turks. They have been starved of everything, from food to letters, not to speak of high explosives. They have been through the most ghastly heat and the

149

most cruel cold, and they are still cheerful. I have never seen a more friendly lot than these men here. They have always got something to say when you meet them. The weather has changed and it's very fine, with a beautiful wind and clear skies, but there are no scents, like in Gallipoli, of thyme and myrtle. It's a limitless bare plain, green and sometimes brown mud, covered by an amazing mixture of men and creatures: horses and mules and buffaloes, Highlanders, Soudanese and Devons, Arabs and Babus. Camp fires spring up, somehow, at night by magic. We generally have a bombardment most days, but no shells round us.

*Monday, April 17th, 1916.* H.M.S. *Waterfly.* Harris is captain. While we were having breakfast this morning a German aeroplane flew over and bombed us ineffectually. Bombs fell a couple of hundred yards away in camp, not doing any damage, but they'll get us sometime, as we are a fine target, three boats together.

*Tuesday, April 18th, 1916.* H.M.S. *Waterfly.* Last night the admiral went to Amara. He left Jack Marriott, Philip Neville, Dick Bevan and me here. There was no work down there and a lot here. Last night we did well, took about 250 prisoners and the Bunds that are essential to us. If the Turks have these and want to, they can flood the country to the extent of making manoeuvring impossible. There was peace yesterday at the crimson sunset. Then after that came the tremendous fight. Guns and flares blazed all along the line. Now comes the news that we have lost the Bunds and the eight guns we had taken. The position is not clear. We are said to have retaken most of the positions this morning.

The prisoners; morale here is much better than in Gallipoli. I asked an Arab if he was glad to be a prisoner. He said that he was sorry, because his own people might think that he hadn't fought well, but that he was glad not to have to go on fighting for the Germans. Jack Marriott wrote for me while I translated. The prisoners could not or would not tell us anything much about the condition of the river. This morning I had an experience. I walked out through tremendous heat to where the last batch of officer prisoners were guarded in a tent. As I came up, I heard loud wrangling, and saw the prisoners being harangued by a fierce black-bearded officer. I said: "Who here talks Turkish?" and a grizzled old Kurd said: "Some of us talk Kurdish and some Arabic, but we all talk Turkish." I picked out Black-beard and took him apart from the others, whom I saw he had been bullying. He was a schoolmaster and a machine-gunner, and fierce beyond words. He began by saying sarcastically that he would give me all the information I wanted.

"You have failed at Gallipoli," he said. "We hold you up at Salonica, and you are only visitors at Basra. I do not mind how much I tell you, because I know we are going to win."

I answered rather tartly that it was our national habit to be defeated at the beginning of every war and to win in the end, and that we should go on, if it took us ten years.

"Ah, then," he said, "you will be fighting Russia."

I did not like the way this conversation was going, and said to him: "Do you know the thing that your friends the Germans have done? They have offered Persia to Russia. How do you like that?"

"The question is," he said, "how do you like it?" He then said that he was sick of the word *German*, that Turkey was not fighting for the Germans, but to get rid of the capitulations. He said they had four Austrian motor-guns of 24 cm. coming in a few days. I congratulated him. In the end he became more friendly, but I got nothing out of him. One prisoner had a series of fits: I think it was fright. He got all right when he was given water and food. The river has given another great sigh and risen a foot and a half. We have crossed over from the right to the left bank. It's a black, thundery day. Much depends on today and tonight.

*Good Friday, April 21st, 1916.* H.M.S. *Waterfly*. I have had no time to write these last days. This morning is a beautiful morning, with a fresh north wind. When we first came here Townshend was supposed to be able to hold out until the 12th. Now the 27th April is the last date. All the reports that we have been getting from the Turks are bad. Masses more men and guns coming up, heavy calibre guns. Still, Townshend is getting some food. . . . The *Julnar* is to go up in a few days, when the moon is waning. It is very difficult to get information from the prisoners, without running the risk of giving things away. Costello is chief of the intelligence here, a capital fellow.

The Royal Indian Marine, freed from the obstruction of India, seem to have done pretty well. A lot of the boats and barges sent here have been sunk on the way. The Admiralty goes on building these river Fly boats like anything. The *Mantis* with Bernard Buxton captain, draws 5 feet and was intended for the Danube in the days

151

when we were going to have taken Constantinople. On Wednesday, the 18th, we fired a good deal from the *Waterfly*. We are not well situated for firing. . . .

The Dorsets and Norfolks, the Oxfords and the Devons, have done the most splendid fighting. Twenty-two Dorsets save the whole situation at Ahwaz. Harris, who is only twenty-five, had been through all this. He was the first up here, with Leachman. It's awfully bad luck on Townshend, being shut up again, the second time counting Chitral. On Wednesday there was a tremendous fire. It sounded like a nearer Helles. The Turks are three miles from us. They lollop down mines that go on the bank, but this morning one was found close by the ship.

I examined a Turk this morning, who said that three army Corps were coming up under Mehemed Ali Pasha. I asked him if they could outflank us on the Hai, to try and turn this place into a second Kut. "That," he said, "has always been my opinion."

Yesterday, the 20th, I went to H.Q. in the morning, then talked to Dick and got maps revised and borrowed a horse for the afternoon from Percy Herbert, and got another from Costello for B.

Here I should explain that I had promised my friend B., the sailor, to take him up into the front-line trenches. He had never been in a front trench before, and was determined to see what it was like.

*Diary.* General Gillman gave B. and me luncheon. Then B. and I rode out to the camp of the 18th Division, where I found Brownrigg, now become a colonel, with malaria. I congratulated and condoled. I asked if we could get into the front trench, and Colonel Hillard said it was unhealthy. B. said that didn't matter, and I asked exactly how unhealthy. Hillard said there were no communication trenches and we should be under machine-gun fire at 80 yards. No rations were being sent up till nightfall, but still, of course, if we wanted to go, we could. B. was passionately anxious to go; I was not. We walked down a shallow communication trench, which we soon had to leave, because of the water, and then across the open to a beastly place called Crofton's Post, an observation post in the flat land, with a few sandbags and mud walls. They had dug a kind of shelter about 6 feet deep below it. It stood about 20 feet high. The Turks were eight to nine hundred yards away. We passed other observation posts, these simply a ladder rising from the flat land, and men like flies on it. It's incredible that the Turks leave these places standing or that they allow people to walk about in the open in the way in which they do. Coming out, we passed a lot of quail and partridge and some jolly wildflowers, but also the smells of the battlefield.

After we had been at Crofton's Post a little while, a furious bombardment of the Turks by us began. I cursed myself for not having asked what the plans of the afternoon were going to be. B. was delighted. Shells rushed over our heads from all sides. I heard the scream of two premature bursts just by us. They raised filthy, great columns of heaving smoke. It was a wonderful picture; the radiant and brilliant light of the afternoon, the desert out by the river, the gleam of the gun flashes and the smouldering smoke columns.

The Ghurkhas fought very well two nights ago, they said here. They used up all their ammunition and what Turkish rifles they could get and then they fought with *kukries*. At one place an unfortunate mistake happened. We mistook the Indians for Turks, and we bombarded each other.

We went back almost deafened by our own guns, B. reluctant to leave. I expected a heavy Turkish return bombardment every minute, which would have been unpleasant without any cover, but beyond the ticking of a machine gun nothing happened. Found General Maude having tea. His casualties have been heavy—nineteen officers killed and wounded in the last ten days, simply trench work, no attacks. He said it was putting a very heavy strain on the new army.

The more I see of this foul country, the more convinced I am that we are a seafaring people, lured to disaster by this river. The River Tigris has been a disaster and a delusion to us. These lines are untenable without two railways, one across to Nasriyah and the other up to Baghdad. At the present moment, we can be cut off if the river falls or if they manage to put in guns anywhere down the river and sink a couple of our boats, or even one, in the narrows, and so block the channel. We have got no policy. We came here and we saw the Tigris and we said: "This is as good as the sea, and up we will go," and now it will dry up and we shall get left.

Lawrence arrived at Wadi on Wednesday. Had some talk with him; I am very glad to see him. Got a letter from John Kennaway yesterday—he is down at Sheikh Saad—asking me to go there. I can get no news about Bobby Palmer. Am afraid there is no doubt; he must be killed; am very sad for his people.

*Easter Sunday, April 23rd, 1916.* H.M.S. *Greenfly.* a curious morning, with the whole of Pushti Kuh standing blue and clear. The last two foreigners who visited that place were given the choice of embracing Islam or of being pushed over the precipice. They chose the precipice.

Yesterday morning we attacked. The 19th Brigade, the Black Watch, the 20th and the 28th. We took two trenches, but were driven back to our own. I was sent *post-haste* to H.Q. for news. There was a great sand-storm and men and artillery going through it like phantoms. Overhead it was lurid. One could hardly breathe for the sand. High columns of it rushed across the desert. The repulse looks as if the end's very close. I came back to the admiral and was sent back again. This time they said there was a truce, and if the admiral would give permission, I was to go to the front at once. I came back and found the admiral and went on shore. I got a horse and rode up to the front as fast as I could, passing many dead and wounded. I went to General Younghusband and asked if I could be of any use to him. He said the truce was ending. The Turks had pushed out white flags, which was decent of them. We had done the same. A staff officer came in to say that the Turks were taking our kit, and he wanted to fire on them. I was anxious we should not do so without giving warning.

We discussed the possibility of the Turks letting Townshend and his men come out with the honours of war, to be on parole till peace. I said that I could see no *quid pro quo*, and even if one existed, we, here, could not use it, because of our ignorance of the Russian situation. . . . The general said that the water had narrowed our front to 300 yards across which to attack. The Turkish trenches were half full of water and many of our men fell and got their rifles filled with mud. The Turks attacked again at once. He said there were not many troops who would do that when a brigade like the 19th had been through them. There's very little left of the 19th; beautiful men they were. I have talked to a lot of them these last days. I rode back on a horse that was always falling down. In the morning I crossed the river with the admiral and rode up to the front with Beach. There was shelling going on, but nothing came near. The river was gorgeous in the sunset. Overhead the sand-grouse flew. We talked about the future. . . . It seems to me that if we have got to retreat 130 miles it's less bad for prestige to do it in one go. The politicals' point of view is that you should not retreat at all, but that, of course, has got to depend on military considerations. The soldiers' point of view is that you should not do your retreat in one go, because you do not kill so many of the enemy as if you fall back from one position to another; but then, I suppose, that cuts both ways. None of these soldiers have had any decorations since the beginning of the war. One of them said to me it made them unhappy, because they felt that they hadn't done their duty. It's an infernal shame. I asked the man who had said this if he had any leave. He said: "Not much! I should have lost my job." That would have been quite a pleasure to a lot of men. . . .

Lawrence has gone and got fever; Nunn also has it. The atmosphere makes shooting difficult. Yesterday the Turks shot quite a lot at a mirage, splashing their bullets about in the Suwekki marsh. We often do the same. Curiously enough, I believe that we won the battle of Shaiba by virtue of a mirage. We saw a lot of Turks marching up against our position, and fired at them; these Turks were phantoms of men miles away; but it happened to be the only road by which they could bring up ammunition, and our firing prevented that. Tonight the *Julnar* goes up the river on her journey. She has less speed than they thought.

For various reasons I have barely mentioned the *Julnar* until now, though she had been very much in our thoughts. The *Julnar* was a river-boat, and for some days past she had been preparing to set out upon her splendid tragic mission. In her lay the last hope of General Townshend and his gallant force. Her freight was food, intended to prolong the resistance of the garrison until the relieving force was sufficiently strong to drive back the Turks and enter Kut. The writer of this diary has many heroic pictures in his mind, but no more heroic picture and no more glowing memory than the little *Julnar* steaming slowly up the flaming Tigris to meet the Turkish army and her fate. Her captains were Lieut. Firman, R.N., and Lieut.-Comdr. Cowley, R.N.V.R., of Lynch's Company, who had spent a long life navigating the River Tigris.

When Admiral Wemyss called for volunteers, every man volunteered, for what was practically certain death. Lieut. Firman and Lieut.-Comdr. Cowley were both killed, and both received posthumous V.C.s.

*Diary. April 23rd.* H.M.S. *Greenfly.* We are alongside the *Mantis.* I am sleeping in Firman's cabin. He is downstream, but he comes up tonight. Many men badly wounded yesterday, but all as cheerful as could be; one man with three bullets in his stomach, full of talk and oaths. Fifteen of the Dorsets have died in the nearest hospital and have been buried close by.

This afternoon an Easter service was held on board. The padre made a good sermon three minutes long. It was a wonderful sight—the desert covered with our graves, mirages in the distance and the river glowing in the sun. At the end of the service the *Julnar* arrived. Firman is an attractive, good-looking fellow. King, whom I met last year in Alexandretta, whither he had marched from Baghdad, is also here. When Buxton told the men of the hundred to one chance of the *Julnar*'s getting through, they volunteered to a man. Gieve waistcoats are being served out; the cannon's sounding while they are loading the *Julnar* and the Black Watch are playing on the bagpipes close by. Overhead go the sand-grouse, calling and the river and the desert wind are sighing. It's all like a dream. . . . Even if she does get through, I don't believe we can relieve Kut. The Turks will have time to consolidate their position and we shan't be sent enough men from home to take them. If this attempt fails, I suppose we shall fall back to Sheikh Saad. I see three points: (1) Political. Don't retreat. (2) Military. You've got to retreat, occupying as many positions as possible, in order to attrition the enemy. (3) If you do this last, you give the Turks the chance of saying they have beaten you in a number of battles. Probably retreat as little as possible is the best. A retreat may be more disastrous to us than the loss of Kut. While we hold Sheikh Saad, it's difficult for them to outflank us on the right bank, and while we have the *vali* of Pushti Kuh with us, they ought not to be able to get to Ahwaz. One wonders if they realize the supreme importance of Basra at home and that if we no longer hold it we do not hold the Indian Ocean.

*Monday, April 24th, 1916.* H.M.S. *Dragonfly.* Firman came last night, and I sat next to him at dinner. The *Julnar* could not start; she starts tonight.

I went ashore this morning and saw Leachman, then Colonel Beach. The flies are awful; one black web of them this morning; in one's hair and eyes and mouth, in one's bath and shaving-water, in one's tea and in one's towel. It's a great nuisance being without Edward and having to do everything oneself, besides one's work. It destroys all joy in war.

*Tuesday, April 25th, 1916.* H.M.S. *Greenfly.* A year ago today we landed at Anzac. Today is the day of the fall of Kut, though the surrender may not be made for some time. Last night the *Julnar* left. I saw old Cowley, an old friend. He is to pilot her. He has been thirty-three years on this river. He is a proper Englishman. He laughed and chaffed with Philip Neville and me on the *Julnar* before starting. Firman was very glad to have got the job, and felt the responsibility. Everybody wanted to go. The sailors were moved. No cheers were allowed. They pushed off, almost stationary, into the river, that was a glory of light with the graceful *mehailahs* in an avenue on both sides of it, with masts and rigging a filigree against the gorgeous sunset. The faint bagpipes and the desert wind were the only music at their going. . . . The admiral told me to be ready to go out at any moment. This morning Colonel Beach came aboard and told me to hold myself in readiness. He proposed going out to see the Turks with Lawrence and myself. He talked about terms. It's a very difficult thing to get terms when one side holds all the cards. If Townshend destroys his guns, as he must, I don't see what terms we have got. My own opinion is that Townshend would make better terms for himself with the Turks than we can get for him here. It will be difficult to stop the Arabs being shot and hung. We have got to do our best. . . .

The *Julnar* has grounded above the Sinn position. Nothing is known of what happened to the crew.

Wilfred Peek turned up here this afternoon, having seen John Kennaway down the stream. We have no terms to offer the Turks except money, general or local peace, or the evacuation of territory. I do not think the first is any good. We cannot offer the second because of ourselves and of Russia. The third might be all right, if it was not beyond Amarah. I hope in these negotiations we do not meet a Prussian Turk in Khalil.

After lunch I met Captain Potter. In the last attack this had happened: A corporal had gone mad, and, after rolling in filth, had come down the trench with a bomb in each hand, shouting out that he was looking for the —— Arabs. The parapet was low, about shoulder high, and there was a good deal of shrapnel and bullets coming in. The corporal threw the bomb into the middle of the officers' mess, killing one and wounding the colonel, knocking Potter and the others out. They collared the corporal, who had got a madman's strength. Then the attack followed. Potter went as soon as he recovered. They charged across 600 yards under machine-gun fire, up to their knees in mud. The Turks were in their third trench. The first and the second were filled with mud. Then the Turks ran out a white flag, which suited us very well, as it allowed our men in the Turkish trenches to get away, which otherwise they couldn't have done. He thought the Turks did it because they wanted to bring up reinforcements. He now commands a battalion of 84, all that are left of 650 men. He said they had reached the limit of human endurance. He had three officers, including himself, left. The Black Watch had been wiped out twice, and other regiments simply annihilated. I told him that I thought there would be no more attacks. He said a Turkish prisoner, a friend of his, had said to him: "Let's have a truce and both kill the Arabs."

Beach says there is no question of going out today. I went our shooting sand-grouse.

*Wednesday, April 26th, 1916.* H.M.S. *Mantis*. I am writing in great haste, till the sun goes down, as the *mehailahs* stream past on a river of fire, in the retreat that is beginning.

The news from home is good and bad. As usual, they are desperately optimistic, but more men are coming. We must, if we can, save the Arabs with Townshend. The last telegrams in were pitiful. Townshend quotes military precedents and other campaigns, and it's all mixed up with famine and the stinks of Kut. Wilfred Peek's his A.D.C. I am to try and get him a safe conduct to take Townshend's stuff up to him, also one for us. If Townshend does not make it clear that it's a return ticket, we shall all be kept. I saw General Lake this morning. Captain Bermester, the chief of the staff, Neville, Dick Bevan, and Millar all went off this morning. The admiral is coming back. I have received instructions about negotiations.

*Friday, April 28th, 1916.* H.M.S. *Mantis*. for the last two days I have been standing by to go to Kut, constantly dressing up for it and then undressing for the heat. A wave of great heat has come and the air is black with flies. Practically no firing, though they tried to shell us yesterday and an aeroplane dropped bombs near here. We have got very little to bargain with, as far as the Turks are concerned, practically only the exchange of prisoners. The operations of this force are not to be reckoned with as a bargaining asset. We are not to retire to save Townshend. Yesterday Townshend saw Khalil at 10 a.m., whom he liked. Khalil said that Townshend would have as great a reception in Turkey as Osman Pasha in Russia, but he demanded unconditional surrender, or that Townshend should march out of Kut. This last is equivalent to an unconditional surrender, and Townshend's men are too weak. We are all sorry for them.

Yesterday morning General Lake sent for me, and talked about the Turks. I said it was quite clear to me that the Turks would procrastinate, if it was only from force of habit, and the end of that must mean unconditional surrender. General Lake was calm. He had been made responsible for things for which other people are answerable. Townshend has telegraphed to say that he has only food for two more days and that Khalil has referred to Enver for better terms. . . . I still think Townshend would get better terms for himself than we shall get for him. He has made a desperately gallant fight of it, and his position had not been taken. Lack of food makes him surrender, not force of arms. We, the relieving force have been checked by the Turks, but I suppose all these men, Lake, Townshend, and Nixon, will be made scapegoats. In the last telegrams Townshend warns us that the Turks may attack. He says he cannot move out, and that even if he were able to get his weak men out the Turks would not have enough tents for them or transport them to Baghdad, and that there will be a terrible tragedy and that a lot of sick and wounded will die. . . . We are not in a position to insist on anything. One is more sorry for Townshend and his men than words can say.

*Sunday, April 30th, 1916.* H.M.S. *Mantis. The Events of Saturday:* Yesterday morning Colonel Beach came to the *Mantis* at seven and took me off. We rode across the bridge to General Younghusband's H.Q. Nothing that I have ever seen or dreamed of came up to the flies. They hatched out until they were almost the air. They were in myriads. The horses were half mad. The flies were mostly tiny. They rolled up in little balls, when one passed one's hand across one's sweating face. They were on your eyelids and lashes and in your lips and nostrils. We could not speak for them, and could hardly see.

We went into General Younghusband's tent. The flies, for some reason, stayed outside. He put a loose net across the door of the tent. They were like a visible fever, shimmering in the burning light all round. Inside his tent you did not breathe them; outside you could not help taking them in through the nose and the mouth. We left General Younghusband and went on to the front trenches, where we met Colonel Aylsmee. There Lawrence joined us. We three went out of the trenches with a white flag, and walked a couple of hundred yards

159

or so ahead, where we waited, with all the battlefield smells round us. It was all a plain, with the river to the north and the place crawling with huge black beetles and singing flies, that have been feeding on the dead. After a time a couple of Turks came out. I said: "We have got a letter to Khalil."

This they wanted to take from us, but we refused to give it up, and they sent an orderly back to ask if we might come in to the Turkish lines. Meanwhile we talked amiably. One of the Turkish officers, a Cretan, had left school five years ago and had been in five wars. He reckoned that he had been in 200 attacks, not counting scraps with brigands and *comitadjis*. The Turks showed us their medals, and we were rather chagrined at not being able to match them, but they and we agreed that we should find the remedy for that in a future opportunity.

Several hours passed. It was very hot. I was hungry, having had no breakfast. Again they asked us to give up our letter. I said that our orders were to deliver it in person and, as soldiers, they knew what orders were, but that Colonel Beach would give the letter up if their C.O. would guarantee that we should see Khalil Pasha. This took a long time. The Turks sent for a tent. A few rifle shots went off from our lines, but Beach went back and stopped it. The Turks sent for oranges and water, and we ate and drank. We had to refill these bottles from the Tigris, and up and down the banks were a lot of dead bodies from shot-wounds and cholera. After some time they agreed to Beach's proposal. We were blindfolded and we went in a string of hot hands to the trenches of the Turks. When it was plain going the Turks, who talked French, called: *"Franchement, en avant,"* and when it was bad going, over trenches, *"Yavash Dikatet."* We marched a long way through these trenches, banging against men and corners, and sweating something cruel. Beyond the trenches we went for half an hour, while my handkerchief became a wet string across my eyes. Then we met Bekir Sami Bey. He was a very fine man and very jolly, something between an athlete and old King Cole. He lavished hospitality upon us, coffee and yoghurt, and begged us to say if there was anything more he could get us, while we sat and streamed with perspiration. He told us how he had loved England and still did. He was fierceness and friendship incarnate. He said it was all Grey's fault, and glorified the Crimea. Why couldn't we have stuck to that policy? Then, as we were going off, I said that he would not insist on our eyes being bandaged, showing him my taut, wet rag of a pocket-handkerchief. He shouted with laughter and said: "No, no; you have chosen soldiering, a very hard profession. You have got to wear that for miles, and you will have to ride across ditches." Then he shook hands and patted us on the shoulder.

My eyes were bound, and I got on a horse that started bucking because of the torture of the flies. The Turk was angry and amused. I heard him laughing and swearing: "This is perfectly monstrous. *Ha, ha!* He'll be off. *Ha, ha!* This is a reproach to us."

I was then given another horse that was not much of an improvement, and off we three went with a Turkish officer, Ali Shefket, and a guard. Lawrence had hurt his knee and could not ride. He got off and walked, a Turkish officer being left with him. Colonel Beach and I went on. Then our eyes were unbound, though as a matter of fact this was against the orders I had heard given. The Turk Ali Shefket and I talked. He knew no French. He said to me: "Formerly the Arabs would not take our banknotes; now they take them. Once upon a time they would not take *medjids*; two days ago they took them. To what do you put that down?"

I knew he meant the fall of Kut, but it was not said maliciously. I said that I put it down to the beautiful character of the marsh Arabs, *"yerli bourda beule"* ("here the native are thus"). He laughed and agreed. We passed formidable herds of horses and mules, our road a sand track. The escort rode ahead of us. The heat was very great, but we galloped. The Turks we met thought that we were prisoners. They saluted sometimes at strict attention, sometimes with a grin, and later our Indians were told in return to salute the Turkish officers, who looked at them as black as thunder.

At last we come to Khalil's camp, a single round tent, a few men on motor-cycles coming and going, horses here and there and the camp in process of shifting. Later on, Khalil said that the flies bored him and that he meant to camp beside the river. Colonel Beach told me to start talking. I said to Khalil, whose face I remembered: "Where was it that I met your Excellency last?"

And he said: "At a dance at the British Embassy."

Khalil, throughout the interview was polite. He was quite a young man for his position, I suppose about thirty-five, and a fine man to look at—lion-taming eyes, a square chin and a mouth like a trap. Kiazim Bey, who was also courteous, but silent, was his C.G.S. We began on minor points. The Turks had taken the English ladies in Baghdad. Their husbands were sent across to Alexandretta, where

I met them last year; some of them, worse luck, are now prisoners again. We had Turkish ladies at Amara and also twenty-five Turkish civilian officials. This exchange was arranged. They were to meet each other at Beyrout.

I went on to speak of the *Julnar*. He said that there had been two killed on the *Julnar*. He was afraid it was the two captains. He was sorry. It made Beach and me very sad. I did hope they would have got through. Firman was a gallant man—he had had forty-eight hours' leave in four years—and old Cowley was a splendid old fellow. Well, if you are going to be killed, trying to relieve Townshend is not a bad way to end.

After that, I began talking of the treatment of the Arab population in Kut. I asked Khalil to put himself in the position of Townshend. I said that I knew that he could not help feeling for Townshend, whose lifelong study of soldiering was brought to nought through siege and famine, by no fault of his own. I said that the Arabs with Townshend had done what weak people always do: they had trimmed their sails, and because they had feared him, they had given him their service. If they suffered, Townshend would fell that he was responsible. Khalil said: "There is no need to worry about Townshend. He's all right."

He added that the Arabs are Turkish subjects, not British, and that therefore their fate was irrelevant, but that their fate would depend upon what they did in the future, not upon what they had done in the past. We asked him for some assurance that there would be no hanging or persecution. He would not give his assurance, for the reasons already stated, but said that is was not his intention to do anything to the Arabs. Then Lawence turned up.

We discussed the question of our sick and wounded. He said that he would send 500 of them down the river, but that he required Turkish soldiers for them in exchange. I said that he gained by having sound men instead of wounded. He wanted us to send boats to fetch these men. He said that he was sending them drugs, doctors, and food, and doing what could be done. Beach asked for the exchange of all our prisoners in Kut against the Ottomans that we had taken. He at first said that he would exchange English against Turk and Arab against Indian, because he had a poor opinion of the fighting qualities of the last two. I said that some of the Arabs had fought very well, and he would gain by getting them back. He then pulled out a list of prisoners of ours, and went through the list of Arab surrenders, swearing.

He said: "Perhaps one of our men in ten is weak or cowardly, but it's only one in a hundred of the Arabs who is brave. Look, these brutes have surrendered to you because they were a lot of cowards. What are you to do with men like that? You can send them back to me if you like, but I have already condemned them to death. I should like to have them to hang." That ended that. We must see that Arabs are not sent back by mistake.

He then said that he would like us to send ships up to transport Townshend and his men to Baghdad; otherwise they would have to march, which would be hard on them. He promised to let us have these ships back again. Colonel Beach said to me, not for translation, that this was impossible. We have already insufficient transport. He told me to say that he would refer this to General Lake. We then talked about terms and the exchange of the sick and wounded. On this, Khalil said he would refer to Enver or Constantinople as to whether sound men at Kut would be exchanged against the Turkish prisoners in Cairo and India. He did not think it likely. He was going to give us the wounded in any case, at once. He would trust us to give their equivalent.

*Guns*: Townshend had destroyed the guns. Khalil was angry and showed it. He said he had a great admiration for Townshend, but he was obviously disappointed at not getting the guns, on which he had counted. He said: "I could have prevented it by bombarding, but I did not want to."

Later, one of his officers said to me: "The Pasha's a most honourable man; all love him. He was first very pleased and said that Townshend should go free. After that something happened, I don't know what, and now Townshend will be an honoured prisoner at Stamboul."

Beach told me to say that we would willingly pay for the maintenance of the civilians and the Arabs of Kut. Khalil brushed this aside and returned to his proposal that we should send up boats to transport Townshend's sick and wounded to Baghdad. Beach whispered to me that we had not enough ships for ourselves at the present moment and no reserve supplies. . . .

Then we talked of the general situation and its difficulties. I asked him if all this business would be possible without an armistice. Khalil said very strongly indeed that he was entirely against an armistice and that he wanted his assurance given to General Lake that even if there was a general offensive the ships carrying the sick and wounded could still come and go. Beach told me to say that we had no idea of an armistice. Khalil, at this point, grew very sleepy. He apologised and said he had had a lot of work to do. He also said that he had seen Townshend that morning and that he was all right, but he had slight fever.

Our final understanding with Khalil was that we were to notify him when we were sending up boats, so that he might clear the river. He laughed and said that he had forgotten all about the mines, which we had not.

We ended with mutual compliments, and we said goodbye to him and Kiazim Bey. As we were leaving he called to me and said that he hoped we should be comfortable that night and that we were to ask for all we wanted. After more compliments, we shook hands and rode away, all the Turks saluting. I talked to Ali Shefket, who now seemed a fast friend, and said: "How angry the Germans would be if they could see the Turks and the English."

We rode on, and before sunset, came to the Turkish camp. There the three of us sat down and, as far as we could for the flies, wrote reports.

The Turks gave us their tents, though I should have preferred to sleep out. They gave us their beds and an excellent dinner. We all sat and smoked after dinner for a few minutes under the stars, with camp fires burning round us. *Muezzin* called from different places and the sound of flutes and singing came through the dusk. Then Colonel Beach decided that I had better stay and go to Kut, where I was to meet him and Lawrence, who would come up with the boats to take our prisoners away. I didn't believe that Khalil would accept this sort of liaison business. Beach wanted to go straight back, but would not let Lawrence or me. We pointed out that, if he got shot in the dark by our people, it would upset everything.

I dictated a French letter to Lawrence, asking for permission for me to stay and go across to Kut. I cannot think how he wrote the letter. The whole place was one smother of small flies, attracted by the candle. They put it out three times. B. and I kept them off Lawrence while he wrote. We got an answer at about two in the morning. Khalil said that it was not necessary. All this happened on April 29th.

*Today. April 30th.* We left at 4.40 this morning, and this time rode all the way with unbandaged eyes. We ended up on the river bank amongst dead bodies. We walked across to our front lines and Colonel Beach telephoned to H.Q. While he was doing this a Turkish white flag went up and we went out again. After several *palavers*, Ali Shefket came out and said that the river was clear of mines. Beach and Lawrence went back to H.Q.

Our boat could go up if it arrived by 2 o'clock in the afternoon. I, with the Cretan, the man of a hundred fights, Ali Shefket and others, went across. A fierce-bearded colonel came out, arrogant and insolent, talking German. He boasted that he knew Greek, but when I talked to him in Greek, he could not answer. He then harangued me in bad German, talking rot. I said, in Turkish: "Neither you nor I can talk good German, therefore let us talk Turkish."

"Yes," said the other Turks; "it's a much better language."

The ship tarried. At 5 o'clock in the evening she was in sight, but she could not have arrived for another hour. It was decided that we could do nothing that night and that she would have to be put off until next day. A monstrous beetle, the size of half a crown, crawled up my back. The Turks were as horrified as I.

*Monday, May 1st, 1916.* H.M.S. *Mantis.* I came back last night. I saw General Lake this morning to report. I think Khalil is going to play the game, but he has got something up his sleeve. A letter has come in from him. The ships, he said, could go. He wanted boats to send the prisoners to Baghdad. He was answered by General Money that His Excellency would understand that we ourselves needed all our boats. Beach went up this morning with two boats, but they stopped him at No Man's Land.

*Tuesday, May 2nd, 1916.* H.M.S. *Mantis.* Last night I went on the P— to go to Kut, with a rather tiresome padre. It rained and blew in the night, and was very uncomfortable on deck. I got up at four, and we started soon after. They opened the bridge of boats for us. A launch followed for me, for I was to get off before entering neutral territory.

At the neutral territory I found white flags and an Indian major, who was tired and nervous. All the way up the river there had been a curious feeling of expectancy and uncanniness; the Indians looked at us, shading their eyes from the rising sun, and our own troops stared. There was an uncomfortable, eerie feeling in the air. The major said the Turks refused to allow the boats to go on. I telephoned to Colonel Beach, who was leaving H.Q. He told me to do the best I could. . . . I took a white flag and went out into No Man's Land and found the man I had talked to before, the Cretan's brother. I asked what all this meant. This was neither war nor peace. He said that it was our fellows, who had been shooting on the right bank, and there was quite enough shooting while we talked to make one feel uncomfortable. I said that

Khalil had given his word that the boats could go up, even if there was an offensive. This was telephoned to Khalil. Our fellows began loosing off with a machine gun. The beastly colonel and the Cretan then came out to say that they had telephoned, and later the Cretan came again, alone, to say that our boats could not go through until the others had returned from Kut. He said it might not be necessary to send them up to Kut. We sat and talked in the great heat. I have given Ali Shefket Bobby Palmer's photograph and have asked him to make inquiries. He sent it back to me by the Cretan, who read me out what Ali Shefket had written me. It was to say that Bobby Palmer was killed. He spoke very kindly and very sadly. I am so sorry for his family.

I went back very tired and found a lot of men making up burying parties which, reluctantly, I sent back again. A lot of the bodies on the river-bank look as if they died of cholera. By the way, we have had a hundred and fifty cases in the last three days. Then I shaved on the deck of the launch, while the Turks looked on in the distance. Then I went and telephoned from the front line to Beach. He told me to bring all the four boats back, which I did. The only news is that the Turks have dug in below us near Sheikh Saad.

*Wednesday, May 3rd, 1916.* H.M.S. *Mantis.* You foul land of Meso-potamia! This morning bodies raced by us on the stream and I spent most of the day walking in the ruin of battle. I was sent for by General Gorringe and General Brown. They wanted to know why our boats had not come down from Kut. They said that the Turks had been shooting on the right and sent out white-flag parties, 200 men strong, to bury the dead. I said I thought it would be all right about the ships but I would go and see Khalil. The fact that they did not want us to send more ships showed that it was all right, but I thought they would probably like to nag us into doing something indiscreet, and asked the general if he would give orders that there should be no firing except under instructions, as long as they had our hostages. He sent me off to see the Turks.

I rode fast through suffocating heat, with an Indian orderly. At the bridge I found our two ships, the *Sikhim* and the *Shaba*, which had come through from Kut. They were banking above the bridge, which was being mended. This altered the whole situation, since the general had sent me out to complain that they had not been let through, and I galloped back. After a talk at H.Q., it was decided that I was only to thank Khalil.

I jumped the trenches and finally arrived at the main trench, where my horse stared down at a horrified circle, lunching. The circle said that no horses were allowed there and that none had ever been there, and that my horse, or rather Costello's, would be shot immediately by the Turks. So I went to General Peebles, who was lunching farther along in the same trenches, and he had her sent back. I then got a white flag and walked out. . . . I met a couple of Turks. They wanted us to send up two ships tomorrow, and were quite agreeable. I asked them, as a favour, not to send out again the colonel who talked German, as I couldn't stand him, and they said they wouldn't.

It was blazing hot; a Turkish officer and I sat out between the lines.

There is one incident not recorded in the diary that is, perhaps, worth mentioning, as it had a curious result that will find its place in the sequel to this journal, if it is ever published. On one of the occasions when I was talking to the Turks between the lines, a general fire started from the British and the Turkish trenches. The Turks, for the honour of their country, and I, for the honour of mine, pretended to ignore this fire, and we continued to discuss our business, but in the end the fire refused to be ignored, and, with loud curses, we fell upon the ground and there attempted to continue the discussion. I suggested to the Turks that the whole proceeding was lacking in dignity and that it would be better for each to retire to their own trenches and resume negotiations when circumstances were more favourable.

Next time I returned I was informed that one of the Turks had been hit whilst returning. I naturally said how sorry I was, and that I hoped they would not think it was a case of *mala fides*, as it might have happened to one of us, and wrote a note explaining my regret.

*Diary.* It was curious and bitter sitting in that peaceful field talking amicably with the Turks between the lines, with maize round us. The river murmured and the larks were singing, while the stiff clay held the knee-deep prints, like plaster of Paris, of the Black Watch and the others, who had charged across that foul field, when it had been a trap and a bog.

*Thursday, May 4th, 1916.* H.M.S. *Mantis.* Very tired today. I rode back last night from the Turks, very fast. The flies made it impossible to go slow, horses couldn't breathe. At the bridge, I found that the traffic was going the other way and had to hold up an unfortunate brigade to get across, hating to do it.

I met Green Armitage, who had just come from Kut. He had got Townshend's terriers, who barked like mad. He said that there were three Turkish officers on board the *Sikhim*, who were asking for me. I didn't know what to do, as I wanted to go to H.Q., but dashed on board and found they were Ali Shefket and Mehmed Jemal and Salahedin Bey, inspector to the Agricultural Bank of Smyrna. Our people on board wanted me to stay. I told them I would come back. I saw the sick and wounded Indians being carried away, terribly emaciated. I reported at H.Q., where, apparently, half a dozen entirely contradictory orders were being prepared for me. I then went back in a launch to the Turks, who were reported to be taking notes of our position from the bridge. On the *Sikhim* I found crowds of our officers with the Turks and a general jollification going on. I did not understand how or why they had been allowed to come down. All the intelligence came along to see what the Turks could tell them. I was fed-up with the whole business, and disliked the Turks being on deck. I said to them: "Of course, it's a pleasure to have you here, as guests, but we would much rather give you hospitality in London, for there we can show you everything, and, unfortunately, that's not the case here. So in future, if you please, Turkish officers will not accompany the boats down." They agreed to that.

The same tiresome padre came bumbling up again. I think he wanted to go to Kut for the adventure, and I had no sympathy, as he would have meant another mouth to feed. The Turks made no particular objection to his going, but they said there was already a clergyman there, so I told the padre he could go if he liked, but that if he went he ought to stay and let the other chaplain come back, as the other had had all the hardships of the siege. He thought I was brutal, but cleared out and gave no more trouble. It seems to me, however, that he runs a fair risk, like the rest of us, of being made a prisoner.

I wish the admiral was here. The Turks on board said that they had hung seven Arabs at Kut, which made me furious. I said that Khalil had said that he had no intention of doing that. The Turks said that these men were not natives, but vagabonds. . . .

Then they talked about the future. I said it would not be easy for Turkey to dissociate herself from Germany, even if they wanted to. They replied: "How long did it take the Bulgars and Serbs to quarrel?"

They said Khalil had sent messages, and I arranged that if there was any hitch I should be able to get straight through.

I did not sleep much. This morning I went up with them to Sanayat, where Husni Bey took their place. Then I came back by launch to the bridge and found a motor, which I took to H.Q.

At dinner tonight Reuter's came in, and the doctor, in a perfectly calm voice, read out to us that there now seemed some chance of checking the rebellion in Ireland. Somebody said: "Don't be a fool. Things are bad enough here. Kut's fallen and we shall probably be prisoners. Don't invent worse things."

The doctor said: "It's an absolute fact," and read it out again.

Then somebody said: "Those cursed Irish."

Then an Ulsterman leapt to his feet and said: "You would insult my country, would you?"

Then there was a general row. After that, everything seemed so utterly desperate that there was nothing to be done but to make the best of things, and we had an extremely cheerful dinner. We must have missed a lot of news. Let's hope this Irish business is the bursting of a boil. I am more afraid of the treatment than the disease.

*Friday, May 5th, 1916. H.M.S. Mantis.* Vane Tempest came back from Kut with unpleasant stories. He said that our officers had been looted at the point of the bayonet by the Arabs. He had seen four men hanging and one man hanged. This was a curious incident. This man, as he was going to execution, threw Vane Tempest his *tesbih* (his rosary), the ninety-nine Beautiful Names of God. Vane Tempest had still got it. It means *"I commend my cause to you. Take up my quarrel."* I told Vane Tempest if he was superstitious he ought never to part with it.

Now there is a new position created. They can float down all their guns and stores. There is a fight coming, but I wonder where. Eight hundred Turks and Arabs below Sheikh Saad, with three guns. The country is up behind us and we have only half a day's provisions in reserve. The guns are booming away behind us. It's going to very hard to hold this position. I wish Edward was here, and hope he is all right, with my kit. I want it badly, but I got some stuff from Percy Herbert this morning. We agreed that we had a most excellent chance of being cut off. . . . One is sorry for these men here. They are starving in every way, ammunition excepted. They are not even given cigarettes and have to pay six times their price to the Arabs. Last night the Arabs were looting all over the place. A man told me this morning that a sick officer in the 21st Brigade found five Arabs in his tent and lost everything. Lucky for him that was all he lost.

*Saturday, May 6th, 1916.* H.M.S. *Mantis.* Sheikh Saad. Yesterday my typewriter broke. A jolly mechanic more or less repaired it and refused money. "It's all for one purpose," he said.

H.Q. suddenly determined to come down to Sheikh Saad in the afternoon. General Gorringe and General Ratcliffe went off, strafing like mad. Then the *Mantis* sailed. I found Edward on board the *Blosse Lynch*, with 200 "sea-gulls," as he called the *sepoys.* He was very upset about the Irish news, but glad to have found me.

I walked at night with Bernard Buxton into the Arab village to find H.Q. A curious sight: Devons and Somersets, Ghurkhas, Arabs and frogs all mixed up together. The Somersets were very glad to meet a friend.

This morning, after going through the evidence with the other officers about Bobby Palmer, I sent a telegram to Lord Selborne. They did not doubt the evidence of the Turks that he was killed.

This morning I walked along the banks of the Tigris, while bodies floated down it. After a time I found the 4th Devons and John Kennaway, Acland Troyte and the rest, also a lot of people from home. Promised them cigarettes and that I would get messages home for them. The latest out were a bit depressed and complained of the shortage of food. Their camp isn't too bad. Three miles away, one can Lot's Tomb, with generally, they say, a Turkish patrol on it. Sheikh Saad is supposed, J.K. says, to be Sodom. If you took our troops away, another dose of brimstone would do it and its inhabitants a lot of good.

Then I saw Captain —— of the Indian Transport. He was miserable at the way that his men were treated. He said:

1. The drivers did not receive pay equal to *sepoys*, nor did they receive allowances, which mountain battery drivers and ammunition column drivers did receive. The work the transport drivers did was equally dangerous and more onerous.

2. There were no spare men. A transport driver went sick and the next man had to look after his animals.

3. They got no fresh clothes. Their clothes were in rags.

4. They had 21-lb. Tents for four men. In a hot or a cold climate this is unhealthy; very bad here. Also they have only one flap, so later on they'll be bound to get sunstroke.

5. They do not get milk, cigarettes, or tobacco.

6. They get no presents such as the other Indian regiments have received.

7. The treatment of transport officers is not equal to that of a *sepoy* officer. (*Vide* Subadar Rangbaz Khan, about thirty years' service.) Recommended with many others. No notice taken. Only two recommendations given, those for actual valour. This man, if he had been with his relations in the cavalry, would probably have done less good work, but would have been covered with medals.

I walked back through rain, with frogs everywhere, a plague. It's a pity we can't get our men to eat them. One can't even teach the officers to eat them. John said the Arabs sniped them most nights, but they were well and not too uncomfortable. Jack Amory was there, but I didn't see him. He was out shooting sand-grouse.

*Sunday, May 7th, 1916.* H.M.S. *Mantis.* Harris came up last night. He said all was quiet down the river. Subhi Bey, with a good many troops, had tried to cut us off at Kumait, but the floods were out. He said that last year Cowley prophesied that when the hot weather came the river would fall and that five-eights of our transport would be useless. Cowley was generally right. If he was wrong then, he will probably be right now. Harris had been fishing the other day, when two of the Devons suddenly appeared, naked, beside him. They had swum the river, being carried a mile and a half down, and intended to swim it again. It's very dangerous. They are wonderful fellows. I am on the *Waterfly* now.

Early this morning a telegram arrived to say the Corps Commander wanted me at once. I spoke on the telephone to H.C. Cassel said: "Our men have fired on the Turks and they have collared the *Sikhim.* You must come and get her out. . . . I transferred to the *Waterfly* and came up with Harris. I knew this would happen. What, apparently, happened was that the Turks fired four shots at the *Sikhim.* The Turkish officer was angry, and rigid orders had been issued to the Turks not to fire again. Then our men had opened fire. . . . But they don't all tell the same story. . . . I have now got five contradictory orders from H.Q.

*Tuesday, May 9th, 1916.* Felahiah. The last boatload of wounded is coming down and the truce will, I suppose, end. The *Silhim* had made her last journey. A telegram arrived from the admiral ordering me to go at once to Bushire. I am to get on board the *Lawrence,* sailing the

12th from Bushire, and join him at Bushire. . . . (Here indescribable things follow.) I went round and said goodbye to everybody.

There is a lot of cholera. General Rice died last night. There are many bodies floating down the river. It's tremendously hot. I have just seen Williams, the doctor of the *Sikhim*. He says the Turks have been good throughout. The Arabs have looted at the beginning, but this has been put an end to. It's not going well with the Arabs. . . . We must largely depend on them for supplies.

*Wednesday, May 10th, 1916.* H.M.S. *Mantis.* I was to have left on S.1, but when it was apparent that it would not start that night, I went off to the *Mantis.* Buxton telephoned from Sheikh Saad that he would take me to Amara, if I could get there by 4.30 a.m. I came down with Colonel James. Many bodies in the river and much cholera at Wadi. Our men lack every mortal thing. I should like to send a telegram like this home, but don't expect I should be allowed to:

> From my experience in this country, I see that, unless certain action is taken immediately, consequences that are disastrous to the health of the troops must follow. All realize here that the past economy of the government of India is responsible for our failure (*vide* Sir W. Meyer's Budget speech). Unless his is realized in England and supplies taken out of the hands of the government of India, altogether, or liberally supplemented from home and Egypt, the troops will suffer even more during this summer than last year. Condensed milk and oatmeal are essential to the troops. India cannot provide these under three months, by which time we shall have sustained great and unnecessary losses. Supplies of potatoes and onions will cease at the end of this month. If cold storage is found to be impossible, a substitute, e.g. dried figs, must be found. India cannot provide these substitutes in time. Sufficient ice-machines and soda-water machines are as essential to prevent heat-stroke in the trenches as to cure heat-stroke in the hospitals. India, unless ordered to commandeer these from clubs, private houses, etc., cannot provide them. Many Indian troops are in 21-lb. Tents, single flap, one tent to four men. Numbers of these will get sunstroke. If you mean to hold this country, you can't do it on the lines of Sir W. Meyer. A railway is essential. A fall in the river would render half our present transport useless, above Kurna. Many of the troops here

are young and not strong. If a disaster to their health, which, in its way, is as grave as the fall of Kut, and due to the same reason, lack of transport, is to be prevented, supplies must be taken in hand from England and Egypt.

*Thursday, May 11th, 1916.* H.M.S. *Mantis.* Amara. Yesterday was one of the most beautiful days imaginable. We came very fast down the river, with a delicious wind against us. On both banks there were great herds of sheep, cattle, and nice-looking horses. Every horse there is blanketed by the Arabs, only our horses not blanketed. The Arabs vary a lot in looks. One man, towing a *bellam*, glancing back over his shoulder, was the picture of a snarling hyena. A great many of them were handsome.

We came to Amara in the evening and found a lot of cholera. I went to the bazaar and bought what I could for J.K. and his mess, and cigarettes for the men, but couldn't get fishing-tackle. Amara looked beautiful in the evening—fine, picturesque Arab buildings, and palm groves and forests up and down both sides of the lighted river. At night we anchored to a palm and slept well, in spite of great gust of wind occasionally, which roared through the palm forests, and bursts of rifle fire on the banks by us, at Arabs, who were stealing or sniping us. Jackals cried in a chorus.

Today the river has been enchanted. Long processions of delicately built *mehailahs*, perfectly reflected in the water, drifted down, often commanded by our own officers. The river turned into a glowing, limpid lake, almost without a land horizon. We passed the *Marmariss*, which the Turks fought until she caught fire. The Arab villages were half afloat. There was a look of peace everywhere, and the flood is too high to allow an attack on us. There was a glorious, dangerous sunset. The sky was a bank of clouds that caught fire and glowed east and west over the glowing water. The palms looked like a forest raised by magic from the river. It was like the most magnificent Mecca stone on the most gigantic scale.

Pursefield, whose last night it is in Mesopotamia, asked me how much I wanted to get on. I said I couldn't see the people I wanted to that night, so it was the same to me if we got in after dawn next morning. We tied up in mid-stream, to avoid being sniped. No flies at all. Sherbrooke and I talked after dinner.

*Friday, May 12th, 1916.* H.M.S. *Lawrence.* The army commander and General Money were both away, and I only spent twenty minutes at Basra. I saw Bill Beach and Captain Nunn and wrote a line to Gertrude Bell and George Lloyd. I wish I could have seen them both. The *Sikhim* is there, in quarantine, her Red Cross looking like a huge tropical flower. I got on to the *Lawrence*. Cleanliness and comfort and good food. I wish the others could have it too.

LEONAUR

# ALSO FROM LEONAUR
**AVAILABLE IN SOFTCOVER OR HARDCOVER WITH DUST JACKET**

**AFGHANISTAN: THE BELEAGUERED BRIGADE** *by G. R. Gleig*—An Account of Sale's Brigade During the First Afghan War.

**IN THE RANKS OF THE C. I. V** *by Erskine Childers*—With the City Imperial Volunteer Battery (Honourable Artillery Company) in the Second Boer War.

**THE BENGAL NATIVE ARMY** *by F. G. Cardew*—An Invaluable Reference Resource.

**THE 7TH (QUEEN'S OWN) HUSSARS: Volume 4**—1688-1914 *by C. R. B. Barrett*—Uniforms, Equipment, Weapons, Traditions, the Services of Notable Officers and Men & the Appendices to All Volumes—Volume 4: 1688-1914.

**THE SWORD OF THE CROWN** *by Eric W. Sheppard*—A History of the British Army to 1914.

**THE 7TH (QUEEN'S OWN) HUSSARS: Volume 3**—1818-1914 *by C. R. B. Barrett*—On Campaign During the Canadian Rebellion, the Indian Mutiny, the Sudan, Matabeleland, Mashonaland and the Boer War Volume 3: 1818-1914.

**THE KHARTOUM CAMPAIGN** *by Bennet Burleigh*—A Special Correspondent's View of the Reconquest of the Sudan by British and Egyptian Forces under Kitchener—1898.

**EL PUCHERO** *by Richard McSherry*—The Letters of a Surgeon of Volunteers During Scott's Campaign of the American-Mexican War 1847-1848.

**RIFLEMAN SAHIB** *by E. Maude*—The Recollections of an Officer of the Bombay Rifles During the Southern Mahratta Campaign, Second Sikh War, Persian Campaign and Indian Mutiny.

**THE KING'S HUSSAR** *by Edwin Mole*—The Recollections of a 14th (King's) Hussar During the Victorian Era.

**JOHN COMPANY'S CAVALRYMAN** *by William Johnson*—The Experiences of a British Soldier in the Crimea, the Persian Campaign and the Indian Mutiny.

**COLENSO & DURNFORD'S ZULU WAR** *by Frances E. Colenso & Edward Durnford*—The first and possibly the most important history of the Zulu War.

**U. S. DRAGOON** *by Samuel E. Chamberlain*—Experiences in the Mexican War 1846-48 and on the South Western Frontier.

LEONAUR

# ALSO FROM LEONAUR
## AVAILABLE IN SOFTCOVER OR HARDCOVER WITH DUST JACKET

**THE 2ND MAORI WAR: 1860-1861** *by Robert Carey*—The Second Maori War, or First Taranaki War, one more bloody instalment of the conflicts between European settlers and the indigenous Maori people.

**A JOURNAL OF THE SECOND SIKH WAR** *by Daniel A. Sandford*—The Experiences of an Ensign of the 2nd Bengal European Regiment During the Campaign in the Punjab, India, 1848-49.

**THE LIGHT INFANTRY OFFICER** *by John H. Cooke*—The Experiences of an Officer of the 43rd Light Infantry in America During the War of 1812.

**BUSHVELDT CARBINEERS** *by George Witton*—The War Against the Boers in South Africa and the 'Breaker' Morant Incident.

**LAKE'S CAMPAIGNS IN INDIA** *by Hugh Pearse*—The Second Anglo Maratha War, 1803-1807.

**BRITAIN IN AFGHANISTAN 1: THE FIRST AFGHAN WAR 1839-42** *by Archibald Forbes*—From invasion to destruction-a British military disaster.

**BRITAIN IN AFGHANISTAN 2: THE SECOND AFGHAN WAR 1878-80** *by Archibald Forbes*—This is the history of the Second Afghan War-another episode of British military history typified by savagery, massacre, siege and battles.

**UP AMONG THE PANDIES** *by Vivian Dering Majendie*—Experiences of a British Officer on Campaign During the Indian Mutiny, 1857-1858.

**MUTINY: 1857** *by James Humphries*—Authentic Voices from the Indian Mutiny-First Hand Accounts of Battles, Sieges and Personal Hardships.

**BLOW THE BUGLE, DRAW THE SWORD** *by W. H. G. Kingston*—The Wars, Campaigns, Regiments and Soldiers of the British & Indian Armies During the Victorian Era, 1839-1898.

**WAR BEYOND THE DRAGON PAGODA** *by Major J. J. Snodgrass*—A Personal Narrative of the First Anglo-Burmese War 1824 - 1826.

**THE HERO OF ALIWAL** *by James Humphries*—The Campaigns of Sir Harry Smith in India, 1843-1846, During the Gwalior War & the First Sikh War.

**ALL FOR A SHILLING A DAY** *by Donald F. Featherstone*—The story of H.M. 16th, the Queen's Lancers During the first Sikh War 1845-1846.

LEONAUR

# ALSO FROM LEONAUR

## AVAILABLE IN SOFTCOVER OR HARDCOVER WITH DUST JACKET

**ZULU:1879** *by D.C.F. Moodie & the Leonaur Editors*—The Anglo-Zulu War of 1879 from contemporary sources: First Hand Accounts, Interviews, Dispatches, Official Documents & Newspaper Reports.

**THE RED DRAGOON** *by W.J. Adams*—With the 7th Dragoon Guards in the Cape of Good Hope against the Boers & the Kaffir tribes during the 'war of the axe' 1843-48'.

**THE RECOLLECTIONS OF SKINNER OF SKINNER'S HORSE** *by James Skinner*—James Skinner and his 'Yellow Boys' Irregular cavalry in the wars of India between the British, Mahratta, Rajput, Mogul, Sikh & Pindarree Forces.

**A CAVALRY OFFICER DURING THE SEPOY REVOLT** *by A. R. D. Mackenzie*—Experiences with the 3rd Bengal Light Cavalry, the Guides and Sikh Irregular Cavalry from the outbreak to Delhi and Lucknow.

**A NORFOLK SOLDIER IN THE FIRST SIKH WAR** *by J W Baldwin*—Experiences of a private of H.M. 9th Regiment of Foot in the battles for the Punjab, India 1845-6.

**TOMMY ATKINS' WAR STORIES: 14 FIRST HAND ACCOUNTS**—Fourteen first hand accounts from the ranks of the British Army during Queen Victoria's Empire.

**THE WATERLOO LETTERS** *by H. T. Siborne*—Accounts of the Battle by British Officers for its Foremost Historian.

**NEY: GENERAL OF CAVALRY VOLUME 1—1769-1799** *by Antoine Bulos*—The Early Career of a Marshal of the First Empire.

**NEY: MARSHAL OF FRANCE VOLUME 2—1799-1805** *by Antoine Bulos*—The Early Career of a Marshal of the First Empire.

**AIDE-DE-CAMP TO NAPOLEON** *by Philippe-Paul de Ségur*—For anyone interested in the Napoleonic Wars this book, written by one who was intimate with the strategies and machinations of the Emperor, will be essential reading.

**TWILIGHT OF EMPIRE** *by Sir Thomas Ussher & Sir George Cockburn*—Two accounts of Napoleon's Journeys in Exile to Elba and St. Helena: Narrative of Events by Sir Thomas Ussher & Napoleon's Last Voyage: Extract of a diary by Sir George Cockburn.

**PRIVATE WHEELER** *by William Wheeler*—The letters of a soldier of the 51st Light Infantry during the Peninsular War & at Waterloo.

LEONAUR

# ALSO FROM LEONAUR
## AVAILABLE IN SOFTCOVER OR HARDCOVER WITH DUST JACKET

LEONAUR

# ALSO FROM LEONAUR
## AVAILABLE IN SOFTCOVER OR HARDCOVER WITH DUST JACKET

**ADVENTURES OF A YOUNG RIFLEMAN** *by Johann Christian Maempel*—The Experiences of a Saxon in the French & British Armies During the Napoleonic Wars.

**THE HUSSAR** *by Norbert Landsheit & G. R. Gleig*—A German Cavalryman in British Service Throughout the Napoleonic Wars.

**RECOLLECTIONS OF THE PENINSULA** *by Moyle Sherer*—An Officer of the 34th Regiment of Foot—'The Cumberland Gentlemen'—on Campaign Against Napoleon's French Army in Spain.

**MARINE OF REVOLUTION & CONSULATE** *by Moreau de Jonnès*—The Recollections of a French Soldier of the Revolutionary Wars 1791-1804.

**GENTLEMEN IN RED** *by John Dobbs & Robert Knowles*—Two Accounts of British Infantry Officers During the Peninsular War Recollections of an Old 52nd Man by John Dobbs An Officer of Fusiliers by Robert Knowles.

**CORPORAL BROWN'S CAMPAIGNS IN THE LOW COUNTRIES** *by Robert Brown*—Recollections of a Coldstream Guard in the Early Campaigns Against Revolutionary France 1793-1795.

**THE 7TH (QUEENS OWN) HUSSARS: Volume 2—1793-1815** *by C. R. B. Barrett*—During the Campaigns in the Low Countries & the Peninsula and Waterloo Campaigns of the Napoleonic Wars. Volume 2: 1793-1815.

**THE MARENGO CAMPAIGN 1800** *by Herbert H. Sargent*—The Victory that Completed the Austrian Defeat in Italy.

**DONALDSON OF THE 94TH—SCOTS BRIGADE** *by Joseph Donaldson*—The Recollections of a Soldier During the Peninsula & South of France Campaigns of the Napoleonic Wars.

**A CONSCRIPT FOR EMPIRE** *by Philippe as told to Johann Christian Maempel*—The Experiences of a Young German Conscript During the Napoleonic Wars.

**JOURNAL OF THE CAMPAIGN OF 1815** *by Alexander Cavalié Mercer*—The Experiences of an Officer of the Royal Horse Artillery During the Waterloo Campaign.

**NAPOLEON'S CAMPAIGNS IN POLAND 1806-7** *by Robert Wilson*—The campaign in Poland from the Russian side of the conflict.

LEONAUR

# ALSO FROM LEONAUR
## AVAILABLE IN SOFTCOVER OR HARDCOVER WITH DUST JACKET

**OMPTEDA OF THE KING'S GERMAN LEGION** *by Christian von Ompteda*—A Hanoverian Officer on Campaign Against Napoleon.

**LIEUTENANT SIMMONS OF THE 95TH (RIFLES)** *by George Simmons*—Recollections of the Peninsula, South of France & Waterloo Campaigns of the Napoleonic Wars.

**A HORSEMAN FOR THE EMPEROR** *by Jean Baptiste Gazzola*—A Cavalryman of Napoleon's Army on Campaign Throughout the Napoleonic Wars.

**SERGEANT LAWRENCE** *by William Lawrence*—With the 40th Regt. of Foot in South America, the Peninsular War & at Waterloo.

**CAMPAIGNS WITH THE FIELD TRAIN** *by Richard D. Henegan*—Experiences of a British Officer During the Peninsula and Waterloo Campaigns of the Napoleonic Wars.

**CAVALRY SURGEON** *by S. D. Broughton*—On Campaign Against Napoleon in the Peninsula & South of France During the Napoleonic Wars 1812-1814.

**MEN OF THE RIFLES** *by Thomas Knight, Henry Curling & Jonathan Leach*—The Reminiscences of Thomas Knight of the 95th (Rifles) by Thomas Knight, Henry Curling's Anecdotes by Henry Curling & The Field Services of the Rifle Brigade from its Formation to Waterloo by Jonathan Leach.

**THE ULM CAMPAIGN 1805** *by F. N. Maude*—Napoleon and the Defeat of the Austrian Army During the 'War of the Third Coalition'.

**SOLDIERING WITH THE 'DIVISION'** *by Thomas Garrety*—The Military Experiences of an Infantryman of the 43rd Regiment During the Napoleonic Wars.

**SERGEANT MORRIS OF THE 73RD FOOT** *by Thomas Morris*—The Experiences of a British Infantryman During the Napoleonic Wars-Including Campaigns in Germany and at Waterloo.

**A VOICE FROM WATERLOO** *by Edward Cotton*—The Personal Experiences of a British Cavalryman Who Became a Battlefield Guide and Authority on the Campaign of 1815.

**NAPOLEON AND HIS MARSHALS** *by J. T. Headley*—The Men of the First Empire.

LEONAUR

# ALSO FROM LEONAUR
## AVAILABLE IN SOFTCOVER OR HARDCOVER WITH DUST JACKET

**COLBORNE: A SINGULAR TALENT FOR WAR** *by John Colborne*—The Napoleonic Wars Career of One of Wellington's Most Highly Valued Officers in Egypt, Holland, Italy, the Peninsula and at Waterloo.

**NAPOLEON'S RUSSIAN CAMPAIGN** *by Philippe Henri de Segur*—The Invasion, Battles and Retreat by an Aide-de-Camp on the Emperor's Staff.

**WITH THE LIGHT DIVISION** *by John H. Cooke*—The Experiences of an Officer of the 43rd Light Infantry in the Peninsula and South of France During the Napoleonic Wars.

**WELLINGTON AND THE PYRENEES CAMPAIGN VOLUME I: FROM VITORIA TO THE BIDASSOA** *by F. C. Beatson*—The final phase of the campaign in the Iberian Peninsula.

**WELLINGTON AND THE INVASION OF FRANCE VOLUME II: THE BIDASSOA TO THE BATTLE OF THE NIVELLE** *by F. C. Beatson*—The final phase of the campaign in the Iberian Peninsula.

**WELLINGTON AND THE FALL OF FRANCE VOLUME III: THE GAVES AND THE BATTLE OF ORTHEZ** *by F. C. Beatson*—The final phase of the campaign in the Iberian Peninsula.

**NAPOLEON'S IMPERIAL GUARD: FROM MARENGO TO WATERLOO** *by J. T. Headley*—The story of Napoleon's Imperial Guard and the men who commanded them.

**BATTLES & SIEGES OF THE PENINSULAR WAR** *by W. H. Fitchett*—Corunna, Busaco, Albuera, Ciudad Rodrigo, Badajos, Salamanca, San Sebastian & Others.

**SERGEANT GUILLEMARD: THE MAN WHO SHOT NELSON?** *by Robert Guillemard*—A Soldier of the Infantry of the French Army of Napoleon on Campaign Throughout Europe.

**WITH THE GUARDS ACROSS THE PYRENEES** *by Robert Batty*—The Experiences of a British Officer of Wellington's Army During the Battles for the Fall of Napoleonic France, 1813.

**A STAFF OFFICER IN THE PENINSULA** *by E. W. Buckham*—An Officer of the British Staff Corps Cavalry During the Peninsula Campaign of the Napoleonic Wars.

**THE LEIPZIG CAMPAIGN: 1813—NAPOLEON AND THE "BATTLE OF THE NATIONS"** *by F. N. Maude*—Colonel Maude's analysis of Napoleon's campaign of 1813 around Leipzig.

LEONAUR

# ALSO FROM LEONAUR
**AVAILABLE IN SOFTCOVER OR HARDCOVER WITH DUST JACKET**

**BUGEAUD: A PACK WITH A BATON** *by Thomas Robert Bugeaud*—The Early Campaigns of a Soldier of Napoleon's Army Who Would Become a Marshal of France.

**WATERLOO RECOLLECTIONS** *by Frederick Llewellyn*—Rare First Hand Accounts, Letters, Reports and Retellings from the Campaign of 1815.

**SERGEANT NICOL** *by Daniel Nicol*—The Experiences of a Gordon Highlander During the Napoleonic Wars in Egypt, the Peninsula and France.

**THE JENA CAMPAIGN: 1806** *by F. N. Maude*—The Twin Battles of Jena & Auerstadt Between Napoleon's French and the Prussian Army.

**PRIVATE O'NEIL** *by Charles O'Neil*—The recollections of an Irish Rogue of H. M. 28th Regt.—The Slashers—during the Peninsula & Waterloo campaigns of the Napoleonic war.

**ROYAL HIGHLANDER** *by James Anton*—A soldier of H.M 42nd (Royal) Highlanders during the Peninsular, South of France & Waterloo Campaigns of the Napoleonic Wars.

**CAPTAIN BLAZE** *by Elzéar Blaze*—Life in Napoleons Army.

**LEJEUNE VOLUME 1** *by Louis-François Lejeune*—The Napoleonic Wars through the Experiences of an Officer on Berthier's Staff.

**LEJEUNE VOLUME 2** *by Louis-François Lejeune*—The Napoleonic Wars through the Experiences of an Officer on Berthier's Staff.

**CAPTAIN COIGNET** *by Jean-Roch Coignet*—A Soldier of Napoleon's Imperial Guard from the Italian Campaign to Russia and Waterloo.

**FUSILIER COOPER** *by John S. Cooper*—Experiences in the 7th (Royal) Fusiliers During the Peninsular Campaign of the Napoleonic Wars and the American Campaign to New Orleans.

**FIGHTING NAPOLEON'S EMPIRE** *by Joseph Anderson*—The Campaigns of a British Infantryman in Italy, Egypt, the Peninsular & the West Indies During the Napoleonic Wars.

**CHASSEUR BARRES** *by Jean-Baptiste Barres*—The experiences of a French Infantryman of the Imperial Guard at Austerlitz, Jena, Eylau, Friedland, in the Peninsular, Lutzen, Bautzen, Zinnwald and Hanau during the Napoleonic Wars.

LEONAUR

# ALSO FROM LEONAUR
## AVAILABLE IN SOFTCOVER OR HARDCOVER WITH DUST JACKET

**CAPTAIN COIGNET** *by Jean-Roch Coignet*—A Soldier of Napoleon's Imperial Guard from the Italian Campaign to Russia and Waterloo.

**HUSSAR ROCCA** *by Albert Jean Michel de Rocca*—A French cavalry officer's experiences of the Napoleonic Wars and his views on the Peninsular Campaigns against the Spanish, British And Guerilla Armies.

**MARINES TO 95TH (RIFLES)** *by Thomas Fernyhough*—The military experiences of Robert Fernyhough during the Napoleonic Wars.

**LIGHT BOB** *by Robert Blakeney*—The experiences of a young officer in H.M 28th & 36th regiments of the British Infantry during the Peninsular Campaign of the Napoleonic Wars 1804 - 1814.

**WITH WELLINGTON'S LIGHT CAVALRY** *by William Tomkinson*—The Experiences of an officer of the 16th Light Dragoons in the Peninsular and Waterloo campaigns of the Napoleonic Wars.

**SERGEANT BOURGOGNE** *by Adrien Bourgogne*—With Napoleon's Imperial Guard in the Russian Campaign and on the Retreat from Moscow 1812 - 13.

**SURTEES OF THE 95TH (RIFLES)** *by William Surtees*—A Soldier of the 95th (Rifles) in the Peninsular campaign of the Napoleonic Wars.

**SWORDS OF HONOUR** *by Henry Newbolt & Stanley L. Wood*—The Careers of Six Outstanding Officers from the Napoleonic Wars, the Wars for India and the American Civil War.

**ENSIGN BELL IN THE PENINSULAR WAR** *by George Bell*—The Experiences of a young British Soldier of the 34th Regiment 'The Cumberland Gentlemen' in the Napoleonic wars.

**HUSSAR IN WINTER** *by Alexander Gordon*—A British Cavalry Officer during the retreat to Corunna in the Peninsular campaign of the Napoleonic Wars.

**THE COMPLEAT RIFLEMAN HARRIS** *by Benjamin Harris as told to and transcribed by Captain Henry Curling, 52nd Regt. of Foot*—The adventures of a soldier of the 95th (Rifles) during the Peninsular Campaign of the Napoleonic Wars.

**THE ADVENTURES OF A LIGHT DRAGOON** *by George Farmer & G.R. Gleig*—A cavalryman during the Peninsular & Waterloo Campaigns, in captivity & at the siege of Bhurtpore, India.

LEONAUR

# ALSO FROM LEONAUR

**AVAILABLE IN SOFTCOVER OR HARDCOVER WITH DUST JACKET**

**THE LIFE OF THE REAL BRIGADIER GERARD VOLUME 1—THE YOUNG HUSSAR 1782-1807** *by Jean-Baptiste De Marbot*—A French Cavalryman Of the Napoleonic Wars at Marengo, Austerlitz, Jena, Eylau & Friedland.

**THE LIFE OF THE REAL BRIGADIER GERARD VOLUME 2—IMPERIAL AIDE-DE-CAMP 1807-1811** *by Jean-Baptiste De Marbot*—A French Cavalryman of the Napoleonic Wars at Saragossa, Landshut, Eckmuhl, Ratisbon, Aspern-Essling, Wagram, Busaco & Torres Vedras.

**THE LIFE OF THE REAL BRIGADIER GERARD VOLUME 3—COLONEL OF CHASSEURS 1811-1815** *by Jean-Baptiste De Marbot*—A French Cavalryman in the retreat from Moscow, Lutzen, Bautzen, Katzbach, Leipzig, Hanau & Waterloo.

**THE INDIAN WAR OF 1864** *by Eugene Ware*—The Experiences of a Young Officer of the 7th Iowa Cavalry on the Western Frontier During the Civil War.

**THE MARCH OF DESTINY** *by Charles E. Young & V. Devinny*—Dangers of the Trail in 1865 by Charles E. Young & The Story of a Pioneer by V. Devinny, two Accounts of Early Emigrants to Colorado.

**CROSSING THE PLAINS** *by William Audley Maxwell*—A First Hand Narrative of the Early Pioneer Trail to California in 1857.

**CHIEF OF SCOUTS** *by William F. Drannan*—A Pilot to Emigrant and Government Trains, Across the Plains of the Western Frontier.

**THIRTY-ONE YEARS ON THE PLAINS AND IN THE MOUNTAINS** *by William F. Drannan*—William Drannan was born to be a pioneer, hunter, trapper and wagon train guide during the momentous days of the Great American West.

**THE INDIAN WARS VOLUNTEER** *by William Thompson*—Recollections of the Conflict Against the Snakes, Shoshone, Bannocks, Modocs and Other Native Tribes of the American North West.

**THE 4TH TENNESSEE CAVALRY** *by George B. Guild*—The Services of Smith's Regiment of Confederate Cavalry by One of its Officers.

**COLONEL WORTHINGTON'S SHILOH** *by T. Worthington*—The Tennessee Campaign, 1862, by an Officer of the Ohio Volunteers.

**FOUR YEARS IN THE SADDLE** *by W. L. Curry*—The History of the First Regiment Ohio Volunteer Cavalry in the American Civil War.

LEONAUR

# ALSO FROM LEONAUR
## AVAILABLE IN SOFTCOVER OR HARDCOVER WITH DUST JACKET

**LIFE IN THE ARMY OF NORTHERN VIRGINIA** *by Carlton McCarthy*—The Observations of a Confederate Artilleryman of Cutshaw's Battalion During the American Civil War 1861-1865.

**HISTORY OF THE CAVALRY OF THE ARMY OF THE POTOMAC** *by Charles D. Rhodes*—Including Pope's Army of Virginia and the Cavalry Operations in West Virginia During the American Civil War.

**CAMP-FIRE AND COTTON-FIELD** *by Thomas W. Knox*—A New York Herald Correspondent's View of the American Civil War.

**SERGEANT STILLWELL** *by Leander Stillwell* —The Experiences of a Union Army Soldier of the 61st Illinois Infantry During the American Civil War.

**STONEWALL'S CANNONEER** *by Edward A. Moore*—Experiences with the Rockbridge Artillery, Confederate Army of Northern Virginia, During the American Civil War.

**THE SIXTH CORPS** *by George Stevens*—The Army of the Potomac, Union Army, During the American Civil War.

**THE RAILROAD RAIDERS** *by William Pittenger*—An Ohio Volunteers Recollections of the Andrews Raid to Disrupt the Confederate Railroad in Georgia During the American Civil War.

**CITIZEN SOLDIER** *by John Beatty*—An Account of the American Civil War by a Union Infantry Officer of Ohio Volunteers Who Became a Brigadier General.

**COX: PERSONAL RECOLLECTIONS OF THE CIVIL WAR--VOLUME 1** *by Jacob Dolson Cox*—West Virginia, Kanawha Valley, Gauley Bridge, Cotton Mountain, South Mountain, Antietam, the Morgan Raid & the East Tennessee Campaign.

**COX: PERSONAL RECOLLECTIONS OF THE CIVIL WAR--VOLUME 2** *by Jacob Dolson Cox*—Siege of Knoxville, East Tennessee, Atlanta Campaign, the Nashville Campaign & the North Carolina Campaign.

**KERSHAW'S BRIGADE VOLUME 1** *by D. Augustus Dickert*—Manassas, Seven Pines, Sharpsburg (Antietam), Fredricksburg, Chancellorsville, Gettysburg, Chickamauga, Chattanooga, Fort Sanders & Bean Station.

**KERSHAW'S BRIGADE VOLUME 2** *by D. Augustus Dickert*—At the wilderness, Cold Harbour, Petersburg, The Shenandoah Valley and Cedar Creek..

LEONAUR

# ALSO FROM LEONAUR
## AVAILABLE IN SOFTCOVER OR HARDCOVER WITH DUST JACKET

**THE RELUCTANT REBEL** *by William G. Stevenson*—A young Kentuckian's experiences in the Confederate Infantry & Cavalry during the American Civil War..

**BOOTS AND SADDLES** *by Elizabeth B. Custer*—The experiences of General Custer's Wife on the Western Plains.

**FANNIE BEERS' CIVIL WAR** *by Fannie A. Beers*—A Confederate Lady's Experiences of Nursing During the Campaigns & Battles of the American Civil War.

**LADY SALE'S AFGHANISTAN** *by Florentia Sale*—An Indomitable Victorian Lady's Account of the Retreat from Kabul During the First Afghan War.

**THE TWO WARS OF MRS DUBERLY** *by Frances Isabella Duberly*—An Intrepid Victorian Lady's Experience of the Crimea and Indian Mutiny.

**THE REBELLIOUS DUCHESS** *by Paul F. S. Dermoncourt*—The Adventures of the Duchess of Berri and Her Attempt to Overthrow French Monarchy.

**LADIES OF WATERLOO** *by Charlotte A. Eaton, Magdalene de Lancey & Juana Smith*—The Experiences of Three Women During the Campaign of 1815: Waterloo Days by Charlotte A. Eaton, A Week at Waterloo by Magdalene de Lancey & Juana's Story by Juana Smith.

**TWO YEARS BEFORE THE MAST** *by Richard Henry Dana. Jr.*—The account of one young man's experiences serving on board a sailing brig—the Penelope—bound for California, between the years 1834-36.

**A SAILOR OF KING GEORGE** *by Frederick Hoffman*—From Midshipman to Captain—Recollections of War at Sea in the Napoleonic Age 1793-1815.

**LORDS OF THE SEA** *by A. T. Mahan*—Great Captains of the Royal Navy During the Age of Sail.

**COGGESHALL'S VOYAGES: VOLUME 1** *by George Coggeshall*—The Recollections of an American Schooner Captain.

**COGGESHALL'S VOYAGES: VOLUME 2** *by George Coggeshall*—The Recollections of an American Schooner Captain.

**TWILIGHT OF EMPIRE** *by Sir Thomas Ussher & Sir George Cockburn*—Two accounts of Napoleon's Journeys in Exile to Elba and St. Helena: Narrative of Events by Sir Thomas Ussher & Napoleon's Last Voyage: Extract of a diary by Sir George Cockburn.

LEONAUR

# ALSO FROM LEONAUR
## AVAILABLE IN SOFTCOVER OR HARDCOVER WITH DUST JACKET

**ESCAPE FROM THE FRENCH** *by Edward Boys*—A Young Royal Navy Midshipman's Adventures During the Napoleonic War.

**THE VOYAGE OF H.M.S. PANDORA** *by Edward Edwards R. N. & George Hamilton, edited by Basil Thomson*—In Pursuit of the Mutineers of the Bounty in the South Seas—1790-1791.

**MEDUSA** *by J. B. Henry Savigny and Alexander Correard and Charlotte-Adélaïde Dard* —Narrative of a Voyage to Senegal in 1816 & The Sufferings of the Picard Family After the Shipwreck of the Medusa.

**THE SEA WAR OF 1812 VOLUME 1** *by A. T. Mahan*—A History of the Maritime Conflict.

**THE SEA WAR OF 1812 VOLUME 2** *by A. T. Mahan*—A History of the Maritime Conflict.

**WETHERELL OF H. M. S. HUSSAR** *by John Wetherell*—The Recollections of an Ordinary Seaman of the Royal Navy During the Napoleonic Wars.

**THE NAVAL BRIGADE IN NATAL** *by C. R. N. Burne*—With the Guns of H. M. S. Terrible & H. M. S. Tartar during the Boer War 1899-1900.

**THE VOYAGE OF H. M. S. BOUNTY** *by William Bligh*—The True Story of an 18th Century Voyage of Exploration and Mutiny.

**SHIPWRECK!** *by William Gilly*—The Royal Navy's Disasters at Sea 1793-1849.

**KING'S CUTTERS AND SMUGGLERS: 1700-1855** *by E. Keble Chatterton*—A unique period of maritime history-from the beginning of the eighteenth to the middle of the nineteenth century when British seamen risked all to smuggle valuable goods from wool to tea and spirits from and to the Continent.

**CONFEDERATE BLOCKADE RUNNER** *by John Wilkinson*—The Personal Recollections of an Officer of the Confederate Navy.

**NAVAL BATTLES OF THE NAPOLEONIC WARS** *by W. H. Fitchett*—Cape St. Vincent, the Nile, Cadiz, Copenhagen, Trafalgar & Others.

**PRISONERS OF THE RED DESERT** *by R. S. Gwatkin-Williams*—The Adventures of the Crew of the Tara During the First World War.

**U-BOAT WAR 1914-1918** *by James B. Connolly/Karl von Schenk*—Two Contrasting Accounts from Both Sides of the Conflict at Sea D uring the Great War.

LEONAUR

# ALSO FROM LEONAUR
## AVAILABLE IN SOFTCOVER OR HARDCOVER WITH DUST JACKET

**IRON TIMES WITH THE GUARDS** *by An O. E. (G. P. A. Fildes)*—The Experiences of an Officer of the Coldstream Guards on the Western Front During the First World War.

**THE GREAT WAR IN THE MIDDLE EAST: 1** *by W. T. Massey*—The Desert Campaigns & How Jerusalem Was Won---two classic accounts in one volume.

**THE GREAT WAR IN THE MIDDLE EAST: 2** *by W. T. Massey*—Allenby's Final Triumph.

**SMITH-DORRIEN** *by Horace Smith-Dorrien*—Isandlwhana to the Great War.

**1914** *by Sir John French*—The Early Campaigns of the Great War by the British Commander.

**GRENADIER** *by E. R. M. Fryer*—The Recollections of an Officer of the Grenadier Guards throughout the Great War on the Western Front.

**BATTLE, CAPTURE & ESCAPE** *by George Pearson*—The Experiences of a Canadian Light Infantryman During the Great War.

**DIGGERS AT WAR** *by R. Hugh Knyvett & G. P. Cuttriss*—"Over There" With the Australians by R. Hugh Knyvett and Over the Top With the Third Australian Division by G. P. Cuttriss. Accounts of Australians During the Great War in the Middle East, at Gallipoli and on the Western Front.

**HEAVY FIGHTING BEFORE US** *by George Brenton Laurie*—The Letters of an Officer of the Royal Irish Rifles on the Western Front During the Great War.

**THE CAMELIERS** *by Oliver Hogue*—A Classic Account of the Australians of the Imperial Camel Corps During the First World War in the Middle East.

**RED DUST** *by Donald Black*—A Classic Account of Australian Light Horsemen in Palestine During the First World War.

**THE LEAN, BROWN MEN** *by Angus Buchanan*—Experiences in East Africa During the Great War with the 25th Royal Fusiliers—the Legion of Frontiersmen.

**THE NIGERIAN REGIMENT IN EAST AFRICA** *by W. D. Downes*—On Campaign During the Great War 1916-1918.

**THE 'DIE-HARDS' IN SIBERIA** *by John Ward*—With the Middlesex Regiment Against the Bolsheviks 1918-19.

LEONAUR

# ALSO FROM LEONAUR
## AVAILABLE IN SOFTCOVER OR HARDCOVER WITH DUST JACKET

**FARAWAY CAMPAIGN** *by F. James*—Experiences of an Indian Army Cavalry Officer in Persia & Russia During the Great War.

**REVOLT IN THE DESERT** *by T. E. Lawrence*—An account of the experiences of one remarkable British officer's war from his own perspective.

**MACHINE-GUN SQUADRON** *by A. M. G.*—The 20th Machine Gunners from British Yeomanry Regiments in the Middle East Campaign of the First World War.

**A GUNNER'S CRUSADE** *by Antony Bluett*—The Campaign in the Desert, Palestine & Syria as Experienced by the Honourable Artillery Company During the Great War .

**DESPATCH RIDER** *by W. H. L. Watson*—The Experiences of a British Army Motorcycle Despatch Rider During the Opening Battles of the Great War in Europe.

**TIGERS ALONG THE TIGRIS** *by E. J. Thompson*—The Leicestershire Regiment in Mesopotamia During the First World War.

**HEARTS & DRAGONS** *by Charles R. M. F. Crutwell*—The 4th Royal Berkshire Regiment in France and Italy During the Great War, 1914-1918.

**INFANTRY BRIGADE: 1914** *by John Ward*—The Diary of a Commander of the 15th Infantry Brigade, 5th Division, British Army, During the Retreat from Mons.

**DOING OUR 'BIT'** *by Ian Hay*—Two Classic Accounts of the Men of Kitchener's 'New Army' During the Great War including *The First 100,000 & All In It.*

**AN EYE IN THE STORM** *by Arthur Ruhl*—An American War Correspondent's Experiences of the First World War from the Western Front to Gallipoli-and Beyond.

**STAND & FALL** *by Joe Cassells*—With the Middlesex Regiment Against the Bolsheviks 1918-19.

**RIFLEMAN MACGILL'S WAR** *by Patrick MacGill*—A Soldier of the London Irish During the Great War in Europe including *The Amateur Army, The Red Horizon & The Great Push.*

**WITH THE GUNS** *by C. A. Rose & Hugh Dalton*—Two First Hand Accounts of British Gunners at War in Europe During World War 1- Three Years in France with the Guns and With the British Guns in Italy.

**THE BUSH WAR DOCTOR** *by Robert V. Dolbey*—The Experiences of a British Army Doctor During the East African Campaign of the First World War.

LEONAUR

# ALSO FROM LEONAUR
## AVAILABLE IN SOFTCOVER OR HARDCOVER WITH DUST JACKET

**THE 9TH—THE KING'S (LIVERPOOL REGIMENT) IN THE GREAT WAR 1914 - 1918** *by Enos H. G. Roberts*—Mersey to mud—war and Liverpool men.

**THE GAMBARDIER** *by Mark Severn*—The experiences of a battery of Heavy artillery on the Western Front during the First World War.

**FROM MESSINES TO THIRD YPRES** *by Thomas Floyd*—A personal account of the First World War on the Western front by a 2/5th Lancashire Fusilier.

**THE IRISH GUARDS IN THE GREAT WAR - VOLUME 1** *by Rudyard Kipling*—Edited and Compiled from Their Diaries and Papers—The First Battalion.

**THE IRISH GUARDS IN THE GREAT WAR - VOLUME 1** *by Rudyard Kipling*—Edited and Compiled from Their Diaries and Papers—The Second Battalion.

**ARMOURED CARS IN EDEN** *by K. Roosevelt*—An American President's son serving in Rolls Royce armoured cars with the British in Mesopatamia & with the American Artillery in France during the First World War.

**CHASSEUR OF 1914** *by Marcel Dupont*—Experiences of the twilight of the French Light Cavalry by a young officer during the early battles of the great war in Europe.

**TROOP HORSE & TRENCH** *by R.A. Lloyd*—The experiences of a British Lifeguardsman of the household cavalry fighting on the western front during the First World War 1914-18.

**THE EAST AFRICAN MOUNTED RIFLES** *by C.J. Wilson*—Experiences of the campaign in the East African bush during the First World War.

**THE LONG PATROL** *by George Berrie*—A Novel of Light Horsemen from Gallipoli to the Palestine campaign of the First World War.

**THE FIGHTING CAMELIERS** *by Frank Reid*—The exploits of the Imperial Camel Corps in the desert and Palestine campaigns of the First World War.

**STEEL CHARIOTS IN THE DESERT** *by S. C. Rolls*—The first world war experiences of a Rolls Royce armoured car driver with the Duke of Westminster in Libya and in Arabia with T.E. Lawrence.

**WITH THE IMPERIAL CAMEL CORPS IN THE GREAT WAR** *by Geoffrey Inchbald*—The story of a serving officer with the British 2nd battalion against the Senussi and during the Palestine campaign.

Lightning Source UK Ltd.
Milton Keynes UK
UKOW051810071111

181627UK00001B/77/P